MW01479761

SWINDLERS

$WIND

AL ROSEN & MARK ROSEN

# LER$

CONS & CHEATS
AND HOW TO PROTECT
YOUR INVESTMENTS FROM THEM

MADISON
COMMERCE

Text © 2010 Accountability Research Corporation
Editorial, Compilation, and Design © 2010 The Madison Press Limited

All rights reserved. No part of this book may be reproduced or transmitted in any form
or by any means, electronic or mechanical, including photocopying, recording,
or by any information storage and retrieval system, without written permission from
the copyright holders except for brief passages quoted by a reviewer.

ISBN: 978-1-897330-76-0

LIBRARY AND ARCHIVES CANADA CATALOGUING IN PUBLICATION
Available upon request to the publisher.

Madison Press Books
1000 Yonge Street, Suite 303
Toronto, Ontario, Canada
M4W 2K2
madisonpressbooks.com

This title may be ordered by mail or email directly from the publisher by cheque or credit card.
Please include cover price plus $3.50 for postage and handling. *But try your local bookseller first!*

Books are available at quantity discounts when used to promote products or services.
For information regarding corporate, premium, or special sales, please write to Premium and
Special Sales Department at Madison Press Books, or email us at orders@madisonpressbooks.com.

Front-cover photo: Jan Stromme/Getty Images
Back-cover photo: KC Armstrong

A Madison Lester Edition
Produced by Madison Press Books

| | |
|---:|:---|
| *Design* | Ingrid Paulson Design |
| *Editorial* | Lesley Fraser, Bruce McDougall, |
| | Cynthia Stasinski, Janice Zawerbny |
| *Index* | Jenny Govier |
| *Production* | Brendan Davis, Zane Kaneps |
| *Publisher at Large* | Malcolm Lester |

The publisher would also like to thank Ramik Akhund, Duncan Goodwin, John Lorinc, and Jonathan
Webb for their very valuable contributions at an early stage in the development of this work.

NOTICE
The scanning, uploading, and distribution of this book via the Internet or via any other
means without the permission of the publisher is illegal and punishable by law. Please purchase
only authorized electronic editions, and do not participate in or encourage electronic piracy of
copyrighted materials. Your support of the authors' rights is appreciated.

Printed in Canada by Transcontinental

14  13  12  11  10    1  2  3  4  5

*For Nicole and Darlene*

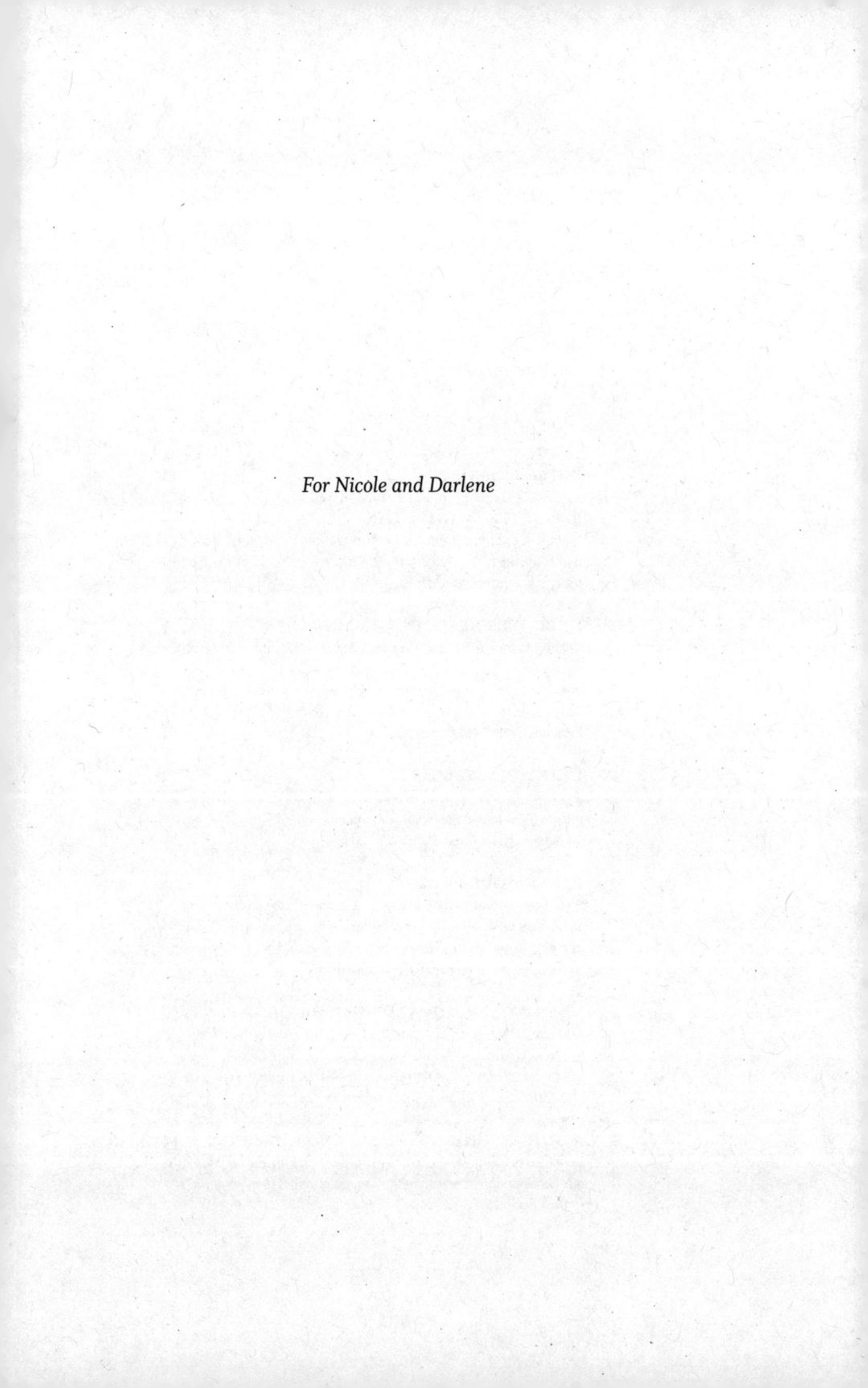

# CONTENTS

Introduction     XI

1 · BOGUS GOLD AND OTHER TALES OF WOE     1
It's not hard for a company's management to deceive investors when auditors accept their word at face value about the company's financial condition.

2 · HERCULES RESCUES THE AUDITORS     7
In making an informed investment decision, investors might feel reassured by an audited financial statement. That's a big mistake. Auditors say that investors cannot rely on annual audited financial statements to make investment decisions, and the Supreme Court of Canada agrees with them.

3 · LEAKY UMBRELLAS     13
Since they can't rely on an annual audited financial statement to inform them about a company's financial condition, investors have to do their own sleuthing. Here's what to look for.

4 · BLEAK HOUSE REVISITED     22
If investors decide to pursue a legal settlement from auditors who sign off on misleading financial statements, they can expect a long and expensive battle. One case began in 1992 and has turned into the longest-running trial in Canadian history.

5 · THE FOX STILL GUARDS THE HENHOUSE     28
Canada has an abysmal record of investigating and prosecuting white-collar swindlers. In large part, that's because Canada's securities and audit communities regulate themselves, and the regulations have little to do with protecting investors.

6 · A QUICK GUIDE TO SCAMS AND COVER-UPS     35
Deceitful executives have many recipes for cooking the books. With our lax regulatory environment, Canada provides them with the key to the kitchen.

7 · **THE NUTS AND BOLTS OF REVENUE SCAMS**  40
As revenues rise, so does a company's stock price. No wonder scam artists focus on manipulating revenue, and they do it in all sorts of ways.

8 · **PONZIS IN HIGH PLACES**  50
When Charles Ponzi used investors' money to provide a return on money raised from previous investors, he didn't realize that his name would be forever associated with the scam that will never die. Offering returns that are too good to be true, the same basic scheme continues to fool investors to this day. And most investors should know better.

9 · **THE WILTING CROCUS**  57
If investors need more proof that they can't rely on regulators and auditors to protect them, they can look at the multi-million-dollar collapse of Crocus Investment Fund in Manitoba. In this case, investors sued the auditors, the board of directors, and the Manitoba Securities Commission.

10 · **CANADA'S SECURITIES COMMISSIONS: ALL TALK, NO ACTION**  63
In 1999, Ontario's Securities Commission promised to clamp down on accounting shenanigans. As usual, the public-relations bark was worse than the regulatory bite—by far. The ensuing scams proved it.

11 · **SEE NO EVIL, HEAR NO EVIL, SPEAK NO EVIL**  70
While their investors wait patiently for a return on their money, executives of public companies play games that allow them to line their own pockets. With weak accounting rules in place, they have no trouble getting away with it.

12 · **YOU'LL NEVER GET RICH**  77
Retail investors cannot easily evaluate the assets of a newly listed junior resource, technology, or biotech company. So why do they invest in such companies, especially when con artists will likely ensure that they never see a return?

13 · **PRIVATE PLACEMENTS, PUBLIC DISGRACE**  81
Brokers and executives may prosper, but retail investors will seldom see a dime from an investment in a private placement. At the very least, you should ask a few questions before you invest.

14 · **INADEQUATE RESOURCES**  86
Con artists love Canada's resource sector. Assisted by vague accounting rules and weak stock exchange controls, they can fudge information that investors need to make decisions and make themselves look much more promising than they really are.

15 · **ONE-SIZE-FITS-ALL SHOE STORE** 93
*With accounting rules that apply in the same way to sporting goods retailers as they do to gold-mining companies, Canada leaves its investors in the dark about what's really happening inside a public company. Such inadequate financial reporting has led to some of the country's biggest corporate failures.*

16 · **COOKING THE BOOKS, FEATHERING THE NEST, AND OTHER LESSONS IN MANIPULATION** 100
*From capitalized expenses to excessive executive compensation, companies have as many ways of manipulating accounting rules as investors have ways of misinterpreting the results.*

17 · **CASH IS TRASH** 110
*Investors can be misled by a company's cash-flow statements. A deceptive executive can manipulate cash flows just as easily as accrual income, and investors will never know it.*

18 · **DEATH BY NORTEL** 117
*Once Canada's biggest company, Nortel used funny accounting, executive fraud, lax securities regulation, and compliant brokers to persuade investors to make bad decisions. No wonder it went bankrupt.*

19 · **LESSONS FROM THE 1920S TO THE PRESENT** 123
*When it comes to protecting investors, Canada has not progressed far since the 1920s. Instead of making life difficult for scammers, con artists, and Ponzi-scheme promoters, our lawmakers sit back and watch them go to work.*

20 · **JUNKYARD BLUES** 131
*From translating systems to 3-D TV to the film business, scam artists operate in a wide range of industries. The scrapyard business seems to hold a particular attraction for fraudsters, who thrive, while our auditors and lawmakers look the other way.*

21 · **WHAT HAPPENS IF YOU SUE?** 136
*Investors in Canada stand little chance of recovering their money in court after a financial scam. The process takes years, and it costs an arm and a leg, and that assumes you can even find a law firm to take the case.*

22 · **TIRED MUSSELS** 141
*When a company promised to cultivate pearls from captive clams, it raised $7 million from public investors. But the clams stayed shut, and much of the money disappeared to Panama. If investors had looked beyond the company's audited statements, they'd never have given the company a penny.*

23 · NO TRUST, NO INCOME  147
*If investors need an example of the way lax regulators, self-interested auditors, and incompetent lawmakers enable scam artists to thrive in Canada, they should look at business income trusts. This scam wasn't new, the scam artists were familiar, and nothing has been done to stop it from happening again.*

24 · INSURED CONFUSION  155
*If you think your insurance policy is impenetrable, try reading an insurance company's annual report. Under current accounting standards, even the worst-run insurance company can make itself look good to investors, who don't know what to look for.*

25 · BANKING ON APATHY  163
*Thanks to Canada's accounting environment, banks can use their audited financial statements to distort their financial condition. Investors have to know what to look for.*

26 · SWIMMING WITH SHARKS  168
*To avoid getting burned, investors have to make sure they deal with reputable advisors, brokers, and financial professionals. Word of mouth is not enough.*

27 · TOO GOOD TO BE TRUE  172
*From income trusts to leveraged exchange traded funds to Nortel, the same advice applies: if it looks too good to be true, it probably is.*

28 · VANISHING YACHTS  176
*Just like the rest of us, high rollers in Canada fall for scam artists with a good story, especially if the story involves a reduction in taxes.*

29 · STAIRWAY TO NOWHERE  180
*Canada's premature adoption of International Financial Reporting Standards will leave investors more vulnerable than ever to financial scams.*

30 · MOVING FORWARD  195
*Here are some suggestions for improving the regulatory and reporting environment in which investors make decisions in Canada. But if you expect them to be adopted, don't hold your breath.*

APPENDIX A · FIFTY CANADIAN FINANCIAL FIASCOS  203

APPENDIX B · FINANCIAL STATEMENT INTERPRETATION  206

APPENDIX C · SIGNIFICANT NUMBERS: THE EXAMPLE OF NATIONAL BUSINESS SYSTEMS  216

| | | |
|---|---|---|
| APPENDIX D · | CURRENT VS. NON-CURRENT ASSETS AND THE CASH-FLOW STATEMENT | 219 |
| APPENDIX E · | YIELD COMPUTATIONS FOR INCOME TRUSTS | 221 |
| APPENDIX F · | DISCOUNTED CASH FLOW UNDER IFRS | 223 |
| APPENDIX G · | REVERSE MORTGAGE COMPANIES | 225 |
| APPENDIX H · | IFRS: TREND LINES AND CASH FLOWS | 227 |
| APPENDIX I · | THE RISK OF FOREIGN-CURRENCY-DENOMINATED PREFERRED SHARES | 229 |
| APPENDIX J · | A LETTER TO THE ONTARIO SECURITIES COMMISSION | 231 |
| | *Acknowledgements* | 255 |
| | *Index* | 257 |

INTRODUCTION

> "On the whole, human beings want to be good, but not too good, and not quite all the time."
>
> GEORGE ORWELL

**JUDGING FROM** the stories that run in the newspaper, you probably think that Canada is a pretty safe place to invest your money. After all, we just survived one of the worst economic downturns since the Great Depression. Some of the biggest names in the world of banking and finance have disappeared, but not a single Canadian bank collapsed. Canada must be doing something right, right?

If you believe that, we have some bad news. The risks you take by investing in Canada have never been greater. And the so-called protection that Canadians think they receive from regulators, lawmakers, and auditors has never been weaker. In fact, investor protection in this country is a joke. It simply doesn't exist.

It's true that you seldom read about financial swindles in this country, but that's not because they don't happen. It's because no one in this country does anything about them. It seems that we depend on the US to do that work for us.

While Canada's regulators sit back and watch, US regulators have continually blown the whistle on Canadian Ponzi frauds. Regulators in the US, not Canada, prosecuted Conrad Black. They were the first to move on Livent and Nortel, and they did this while they prosecuted their own cases such as Enron and WorldCom. In fact, if they act at all, Canadian regulators step up only after the US has embarrassed them into action.

As you'll discover in this book, swindlers, scam artists, flim-flams, and Ponzi schemes are attracted to Canada because they know they can get away with their shenanigans. Even if they get caught, they know they'll receive only a slap on the wrist. And chances are good that they won't get caught at all.

There are several reasons why Canada has become such a soft touch for dishonest operators. First, unlike the US, Canada operates without a national securities regulator. Our provincial securities regulators try to balance the needs of investors with the desire of corporations to operate without restriction. Corporate lobbying power and the absence of an organized investor voice in Canada means that most regulatory actions favour corporate interests.

Second, our accountants and auditors regulate themselves. Canada is the only major country in the world that allows the same people who audit public companies to financially control the process that sets the auditing rules. This basic and fundamental conflict of interest means that auditors can set rules that cater to their paying corporate clients over the needs of investors.

Third, auditors have washed their hands of responsibility to individual investors in Canada, and the nation's highest court has supported them in doing it. By law, a public corporation must issue annual audited financial statements, but according to the auditors, individuals base their investment decisions on these statements at their peril. If the report is misleading or fraudulent, investors have no one to blame but themselves.

Obviously, if investors cannot rely on an audited statement to guide them in making basic investment decisions, why do companies obtain audits in the first place? The problem is that auditors cannot be held accountable for approving misleading financial statements, and without that consequence they have little incentive to perform a decent job for investors. They simply need to please the corporate executives who approve their audit bill.

Finally, investors themselves have to take some of the blame. As we've seen over and over again, investors continually fall for schemes that appeal to their greed, not their common sense. As we'll repeat throughout this book, if an investment looks too good to be true, it usually is. You just have to follow the money.

There's a lot of money involved in these financial cons. Based on our extensive experience with auditor negligence and executive dishonesty, we estimate that investors have lost hundreds of billions of dollars to scams in Canadian financial markets. Even if you haven't invested a penny in the stock market yourself, these losses affect you. Anyone who collects a pension, saves for his children's education, or simply pays her taxes like an honest citizen suffers from the disinterest of our regulators and lawmakers in prosecuting dishonest corporate executives, aided by acquiescent auditors.

And soon it will get even worse.

Thanks to our self-regulated auditors, Canada will soon adopt new accounting and auditing standards called International Financial Reporting Standards (IFRS). Under IFRS, corporate managers will have even more freedom to distort and manipulate their financial reports to make themselves look better than they really are.

Despite the devastating impact it will have on investors and the utility of financial statements in general, auditors succeeded in pushing through the change because of complete disinterest from lawmakers and a lack of recognition by investors that auditors have no interest in upholding their needs. Canadians simply assume that a self-regulatory body like the auditors would look after public interests, not just their self-interests.

The main reason that auditors pushed through the change was for money. They are in the process of raking in untold millions for switching all public companies over to the new accounting rules. And the auditors do not bother mincing words about it either. They plainly state that continuing to maintain Canadian accounting rules is "no longer cost effective" for them. After all, since they no longer have any incentive to act on behalf of investors, why take on the added cost to maintain and improve accounting standards at the annoyance of their paying corporate clients? In a move that's the envy of capitalists everywhere, the auditors turned what was previously a cost centre into a very lucrative profit centre. And they now have their sights set on converting non-public companies and private enterprises to IFRS. Auditors just continue printing money at the expense of investors and business owners for no discernable benefits in return.

As a result of uninterested and conflicted media and lawmakers, swindled Canadians have had great difficulty getting their voices heard, despite the gravity of the attacks on their savings. Too often, legislators and media alike seek the counsel of the people most responsible for investors being wronged: the self-interested agencies responsible for financial reporting and securities enforcement.

In the meantime, investors must pursue alternatives and take issues into their own hands. Investors need to understand how accounting can be manipulated and cash flows can be faked. More importantly, it's imperative for investors to understand how loose financial reporting and auditing rules are bad for them, even if company executives are honest, which is not always the case.

Claims that Canada is relatively free of securities crime are simply not supported by the facts. Investors must realize that they have been effectively abandoned. They now must become their own auditors, analysts, and securities police.

The key is to remember that, if an investment opportunity seems too good to be true, it usually is. But investors can always follow the money to discover the source of the scam. And, after reading this book, you'll know exactly how to do it.

CHAPTER ONE

# Bogus Gold and Other Tales of Woe

*"Those who stand for nothing fall for anything."*
                                              ALEXANDER HAMILTON

**ELIZABETH MONTGOMERY** and Frederick Burgess wanted more money, and they found an easy way to get it. As a refiner and manufacturer of gold, their company, International Nesmont Industrial, sold shares to investors on the Vancouver and NASDAQ exchanges. That in itself didn't attract much money, however. There were lots of gold-mining companies listed on both exchanges. Not all of them made a profit, though.

Profits affect the price of a company's shares. The higher a company's audited profits, the more money an investor will pay for the company's stock. For two years, Montgomery, Nesmont's CFO, and Burgess, its head assayer, made sure that their company reported a substantial profit and that the company's auditors confirmed it. All they needed were a few hunks of brass painted gold.

Over that two-year period, Nesmont reported combined earnings of almost $1 million. The company's auditors, Coopers & Lybrand (now PricewaterhouseCoopers), confirmed the reported earnings. Each year, a junior auditor opened the door of Nesmont's vault and gazed inside at stacks of golden bars. Satisfied that they existed, just as management had said they did, he signed off on the company's reported earnings. Supported by an audited record of earnings, the company's stock price rose to more than $9 a share. The company succeeded in selling 400,000 shares at that price. You might have even bought some of those shares yourself. Many people did. Most of them assumed they could rely on the company's audited reports to obtain a reasonable picture of Nesmont's financial health. They were wrong.

In fact, the company hadn't earned a profit at all. It hadn't even come close. Over the two-year period, Nesmont should have reported losses of $5.7 million.

After two years, warning signs started to appear. Concerned by "certain undisclosed issues," Nesmont's auditors said they would not sign the next year-end audit report. A month later, Nesmont commissioned another audit firm, Deloitte & Touche, to assist in the "resolution of the issues." The company then revealed "certain deficiencies" in its accounting systems. By the time new managers replaced Montgomery and Burgess and discovered the fraud, the stock had fallen to less than $2 a share. By then, Montgomery's mom had managed to unload her shares for almost US$300,000, while the company's remaining shareholders were left with almost nothing.

If Nesmont represented an isolated case of fraud and deception, we would not have written this book. But it doesn't. In our capacity as forensic accountants, we see similar cases every day. (We've listed fifty of them in Appendix A, but we could have listed far more.) Some of them involve deceptive practices so basic a five-year-old could understand them. Brass passed off as gold. Six inches of high-grade copper covering a barrel full of second-grade scrap. Other scams, as we'll see, require more ingenuity. Some scams last for only a year or two. Others can continue undetected for years, if not decades. The longest scam we have witnessed in our work was committed over a span of twenty-four years. But to be successful, all these scams were dependent on a combination of conflicted auditors, inadequate or nonexistent regulation, ill-informed directors, crooked managers, and gullible investors.

Investors need to learn that they can't distinguish the good from the bad simply by looking at the size of the dollars on a balance sheet. Based on the price of its outstanding shares, Nortel once had a value of $374 billion, thanks to misleading financial reporting and accounting misrepresentations. Today, Nortel shares are worthless. Business income trusts (BITs) were once valued at more than $70 billion, based on unwarranted market hype to investors, who believed it all. Today, BITs have lost half their value and all of their cachet. Non-bank asset-backed commercial paper attracted $32 billion from investors, who now wonder how Canada's regulators and lawmakers ever allowed the market to operate.

The total amount that investors have lost to fraud, accounting chicanery, crooked underwriters, dishonest stockbrokers, and financial trickery is incalculable. These losses affect all Canadians, whether they invest in the stock market, purchase units of a mutual fund, or save for retirement through their corporate pension plans.

Even banks get bamboozled. In Manitoba, a rapidly expanding distributor of fishing supplies borrowed money equivalent to about 50% of its audited inventory. The inventory consisted of hundreds of items, from fishing lures to hip waders, imported primarily from Asia. As the company expanded rapidly in sales and inventory, so did its bank loan.

The company had a particularly large customer in the US, to whom it shipped some of its inventory directly from the Asian manufacturers. This made it difficult for auditors to track the location of the inventory. The company, meanwhile, produced hundreds of pages of inventory printouts that carried as many as fifty items on a page. The auditors didn't look closely at the printouts, but did their best to count the inventory on a sample basis and attach costs to each sampled item.

As the company's inventory grew, the bank became very interested in its potential value and saleability. Rather than seeking opinions about the items from fishing specialists, the auditors asked the company's managers if they thought they'd stocked too many items, or if any of the products were obsolete. As the years passed, the auditors appeared to be doing their job, until a new auditor arrived on the scene.

Curious about the amount of inventory stored on site compared to the amounts recorded on the books, the new auditor performed a standard procedure that had not been conducted in the past two years. He added up the numbers. Then he compared the total to the amount reported in the company's financial statements. Simply by doing the arithmetic, he discovered that the company had overstated its inventory by 50%, and had done the same thing for the past two years. This was no honest mistake. The money borrowed from the bank, based on the company's inflated inventory, went into the owners' pockets, some of it through the US customer, who happened to be closely related to the owners. Once the scam was uncovered, the company went bankrupt, and the bank recovered only a portion of its money, all because the auditors had failed to perform some simple math.

If scams like this occurred only once or twice a year, none of us would worry much. Thousands of companies operate in Canada, borrow money, and sell shares to investors. There's bound to be one bad management apple in their midst. But in our experience, deception, treachery, and dishonesty occur far more often. We sometimes see three or four new examples every week.

They occur in all industries and involve companies of all sizes. They go undetected because auditors, regulators, lawmakers, and self-regulated professions in Canada have little incentive to uncover them until after they occur. Under pressure to meet budgets and deadlines, auditors place their trust in a company's management to provide them with reliable information. They often follow a standard, one-size-fits-all audit plan, applying the same routine procedures without changing or adapting to the business from one year to the next. Auditors tend to take the word of a company's managers, and they readily accept their guidance when they check selected samples of inventory, accounts payable, and accounts receivable. To accommodate management's suggestions, they can easily override the audit systems and procedures that are supposed to ensure the selection of random items for testing. Managers know that auditors won't take the time to distinguish gold bars from brass, or add up thousands of numbers on page after page of computer printouts. If they do, the auditors have to justify their increased fees to the company that pays them.

When embarrassing discrepancies appear between a company's audited figures and the true story, auditors quickly paint themselves as the victims. "We were the target of a well-orchestrated fraud," they say. And according to auditors in Canada, it's not their job to look for fraud anyway.

Perhaps that explains why auditors didn't look very hard at the numbers provided by a financial institution in Western Canada that lent more than $2 million to the owners of several properties about five kilometres from downtown Edmonton. When the owners failed to pay any interest on the loan, the institution added the unpaid amount to the loan itself, recorded as an asset on its balance sheet. By the time the financial institution failed, the value of the loan, plus several million in accumulated interest, amounted to more than 110% of the alleged fair-market value of the property.

The lender had approved the loan based on an allegedly independent appraisal of the properties commissioned by the borrower. Along with the dollar value of the properties, the appraiser had included a separate sheet of paper describing a major assumption made in the process of valuing the land. For several years, however, auditors had accepted the appraisal at face value without referring to the other page.

If they had looked at the other page provided by the appraiser, the auditors would have discovered that the value of the properties recorded on the institution's books, and used as collateral against the loan, depended on a fairly improbable event. Downtown Edmonton would have to shift 4.6 kilometres to the west of its current location. If all the buildings in downtown Edmonton had made that short journey, the value of the borrower's property would have increased enormously. But that didn't happen, and the lender eventually took a big hit as it adjusted its numbers. It also put the properties on the market, although potential buyers didn't exactly jump at the chance to acquire a piece of Edmonton's future downtown that was 4.6 kilometres from the one that was already in place. Why buy swampland in Edmonton when you can get it in Florida?

As we've discovered, Canadian investors are on their own when it comes to safeguarding their investments. If auditors seem disinterested in uncovering financial flim-flams, Canada's securities regulators, accountants, lawmakers, and self-regulatory organizations have contributed as well to the complete and utter breakdown of investor protections in Canada. In the never-ending tragedy of investor fleecings, individuals have had to fight one-handed against the misleading, and sometimes truly crooked, actions of corporate executives, brokers, money managers, underwriters, accountants, lawyers, and other financial salesmen.

In the coming years, investors can anticipate even more dubious practices as Canada embarks on an unwise deregulation of financial reporting that will present opportunities to companies to manipulate their profit numbers. Rule changes will allow management to write down inventory, for example, from its cost in one year, and then write it back up to its original cost the next year. Management can then fiddle with their bonuses simply by adopting an optimistic or pessimistic view of inventory costs and values. As companies adjust the value of their inventory as often as every quarter, time-short and experience-challenged junior auditors will have even more trouble catching the manipulations of management. More than ever, auditors will rely on the word of company executives, which will only mean bad news for investors.

The good news is that you can take steps to protect yourself. Just don't expect any help from the individuals and organizations who appear to have your interests at heart. They don't.

CHAPTER TWO

## Hercules Rescues the Auditors

*"The path of least resistance is what makes rivers run crooked."*
ELBERT HUBBARD

**ACCORDING TO** federal and provincial legislation, auditors owe their primary responsibility to investors. According to the handbook of the Canadian Institute of Chartered Accountants (CICA), financial statements are used primarily by investors and creditors. With this in mind, investors might be forgiven if they took some reassurance from these suggestions that their best interests were covered.

In the spring of 1997, however, the Supreme Court of Canada rendered a decision that left most shareholders out in the cold. The case involved an investment company called Hercules Managements and the accounting firm of Ernst & Young. Investors claimed that they'd lost money after making investment decisions based on audit reports that they said had been prepared negligently. To the dismay of shareholders across the country, the Supreme Court said that audited financial statements in an annual report are not produced to enable shareholders to make investment decisions. For the most part, the court said, auditors bear no duty of care toward investors. Among other things, the court's decision meant that investors stand little or no chance of success if they sue auditors who sign off on misleading annual financial statements.

Shareholders, who had for years regarded audited annual reports as financial road maps to guide them in their investment decisions, now discovered that the maps weren't necessarily reliable. If an audited annual report showed a direct route to Montreal, shareholders couldn't blame the auditors if they ended up in Moose Jaw instead.

Considering the contradictions between existing legislation, the CICA *Handbook,* and the court's decision, you would expect governments to amend their laws and make it clear that the Hercules decision was an anomaly. You would expect governments to make a clear statement to investors that they can rely on audited annual financial statements. You might even expect the CICA to emphasize this point. But since 1997, when the Supreme Court handed down its decision, none of this has happened. Whether they know it or not, investors rely on audited annual financial statements at their own peril.

So what is the purpose of a legislatively mandated audit, if not for the benefit of investors? Surely an audit report must be meant for something more than just lining the birdcage.

Here, with some minor ellipses, is what the Supreme Court said:

The directors of a corporation are required to place the auditors' report before the shareholders at the annual meeting in order to permit the shareholders, as a body, to make decisions as to the manner in which they want the corporation to be managed, to assess the performance of the directors and officers, and to decide whether or not they wish to retain the existing management or to have them replaced. On this basis, it may be said that the auditors' purpose in preparing the reports was, precisely, to assist the collectivity of shareholders of the audited companies in their task of overseeing management.

In other words, audited reports are prepared for the guidance of current shareholders, not for prospective shareholders, and not for creditors. They are to be used by shareholders collectively, not individually. The ruling also means audited reports are to be used to evaluate management performance, not to make a decision to sell, hold, or buy more shares. Considering the amount of money paid every year by thousands of companies to engage an auditor, the resulting financial statements seem to provide only questionable value to shareholders.

The court's decision seems to raise even more questions, and to lead to even more dubious consequences. If a company's management were honest, then why would investors need an audit in the first place? Knowing that the apparent purpose of an audit is to assess their performance, why shouldn't a company's management manipulate the accounts to suit their purposes? Why would management produce accounting results that could get them fired? The first purpose of an audit, in most cases, is to help management hold on to their jobs.

The court made one exception in the Hercules case. If auditors prepare a financial statement expressly for the purpose of helping shareholders to make investment decisions, then the auditors owe a duty of care to the shareholders. In other words, if investors want an audited statement to reassure them about their investment decisions, they have to commission it themselves. We wish you luck when you contact the CFO of your favourite public company to tell him that you've commissioned an independent audit of his books.

If investors had to drive on our public highways under the same conditions as they navigate through our public stock markets, they'd probably walk instead. All of us assume, for example, that we won't drive over a hill and tumble into a huge crevasse on the other side. After all, if our car disappeared into a pothole that had gone unattended on the highway for years, we could sue the province, or municipality, and receive compensation. Knowing that our governments would never take this kind of risk, we can go about our daily lives more efficiently and our society can function. Unfortunately, investors in Canada cannot make a similar assumption about the country's financial highways. In deciding on the direction they'll follow, the route they'll take, and the speed they'll travel, investors cannot trust a company's financial statements to guide them. If an investor relies on an audited statement to choose his course but tumbles into a financial crevasse the audited statement failed to acknowledge, he has no one to blame but himself.

The implications of the Hercules decision are extensive. Considering that they abandoned their role as the "shareholders' auditor," contrary to their own rules, auditors should immediately have been disallowed by governments from choosing the wording of accounting and auditing rules. Instead, auditors continue to make the rules and then apply them as they see fit. This has led to all sorts of problems, as we'll discuss later.

Despite the implications, few Canadians have raised any objections to the court's decision. Since the decision was made, auditors who have approved of materially misleading or bogus annual audited financial statements have simply referred to Hercules to defend themselves successfully against investor lawsuits.

Ironically, another case in 1997 supported investors who rely on audited financial statements, but only if the statements appear in a prospectus intended to sell shares or debentures. The decision by the British Columbia Court of Appeal involved a case called *Kripps v. Touche Ross,* in which investors had relied on audited financial statements in a prospectus in deciding to buy the debentures of a mortgage company.

At the time of issuing the prospectus, as much as one-quarter of the company's loan portfolio had been in default for more than 90 days. With the approval of the auditors, however, management excluded this information from the company's financial statements. The auditors argued in court that the self-imposed rules of the accounting profession did not require them to include it. The appeal judges said the statements might have complied with Generally Accepted Accounting Principles (GAAP), but they did not fairly present the financial condition of the company. The court said a profession cannot bind the public to standards that it sets for its members. If it could, then it could immunize its members against accusations of negligence. The financial statements might have been prepared in accordance with the accounting profession's rules, the court said, but the auditors should have known that they were misleading.

Unfortunately, this decision doesn't extend protection to many investors. The vast majority of public trading in Canada occurs in the secondary market between institutions or individuals, typically on a stock exchange or other trading platform. In the primary market, companies sell equity or debt directly to institutions or individuals. The Kripps case, and the investor protection it affords, refers only to the primary market and to investors who rely on misleading financial statements that are provided as part of a prospectus. Only about 1% of investors in Canada ever rely on financial statements provided as part of a prospectus. The rest of us, including retail and institutional investors and their advisors, are on our own. The Hercules decision confirms that fact. And few of us even know it.

Despite the court's decision in Hercules, a few pieces of legislation suggest that investors may have a glimmer of hope if they've been misled by audited financial statements. But the glimmer is faint, indeed. The Civil Code in Quebec, for example, allows for an easier attachment of liability to auditors. But most investor actions in Canada are launched in Ontario, because the country's major stock exchange, the Toronto Stock Exchange (TSX), is located there.

Legislation in Ontario attempted to add investor protection provisions in 2003 under a section of the Ontario Securities Act, but the legislation makes it difficult and costly to pursue a case, and very few investors have overcome the restrictions and qualifications involved. The cost of pursuing a case can well exceed any potential financial recovery, and the maximum penalties involved seem almost incidental. Many lawyers regard the legislation as nothing more than window dressing.

Ontario took the measures in response to alarming financial catastrophes in the US involving companies such as Enron and WorldCom. But just as Canada failed to put into place a national securities commission after the 1929 stock market crash, our lawmakers have dragged their feet more recently as well, presumably hoping that investors would forget about their perilous situation. For self-preservation or other reasons, lawmakers do not seem inclined to hold directors, officers, and auditors accountable when they display blatant negligence and self-serving and protectionist behaviour. Furthermore, extensive political lobbying by corporations and their auditors invariably stalls action for reform on behalf of investors.

Most non-Canadians regard the Hercules decision, and the feeble measures taken under the Ontario Securities Act, with astonishment. It sometimes seems as if Canada's lawmakers have wilfully forgotten the 1950s and 1960s, when many Canadians would not invest in equities because they didn't trust the market. To add insult to injury, auditors are now seeking further legal immunity. In theory, when an auditor could have called a halt to a scam, but chose not to do so, the auditor should incur total liability for his negligence. But the auditors feel otherwise.

So we're left with the Hercules decision, which rules out the use of audited annual financial statements by investors in making decisions to buy a company's shares or debt. If investors feel misled, they can sue a company's directors and officers, while the auditors remain almost fully protected from litigation. This leaves investors wondering if auditors really represent their interests at all, or whether they're just protecting themselves, and others.

Hercules was the beginning of the end for Canadian investors. Based on the Hercules decision, auditors were given a free pass to mess up annual audits, freeing themselves from lawsuits against them, and to set self-serving auditing and accounting rules that flattered management.

The fact that the Hercules case was not challenged by legislatures across Canada sent a clear message that lawmakers had abandoned investors. Yet few investors noticed. This decision opened the gates to many of the subsequent fiascos detailed throughout this book. The securities administrators took their lead from the lawmakers and caved in, leaving investors on their own to deal with the consequences.

CHAPTER THREE

# Leaky Umbrellas

*"Among the safe courses, the safest of all is to doubt."*
SPANISH PROVERB

**WITH THE** blessing of the courts, auditors in Canada have disavowed their duty of care to investors. Earning hundreds of millions of dollars in low-risk fees, they fulfill a legislative mandate by performing largely meaningless audits. Auditors now carry so little responsibility when they sign a company's financial statements that they can regard a major audit foul-up as just the simple cost of doing business. In the small number of cases that wind their way though the legal system, the cost of defending themselves pales in comparison to the fees they receive.

Few investors understand how little reassurance they can take from an auditor's signature on a financial statement. That's because auditors have done an excellent job of making an audit sound like a thorough verification of a financial statement's credibility. Perhaps investors confuse a financial-statement audit with detailed income tax auditing, in which their finances are scrutinized down to the penny. Or perhaps they just assume that something of value must result from the money that ends up in auditors' pockets.

The reality of an audit is quite different from what many investors have been led to believe. The auditing of financial statements seldom involves detailed scrutiny, so an audited statement should provide investors with no reassurance about a company's financial condition. Before they can make an informed decision, investors have to read audit reports carefully to determine the quality of audit checking involved. Does the auditor provide a form of audit warranty, for example? Under which country's laws was the audit conducted? Does the auditor specify that the financial statement is free of material misstatements?

If the auditor says a report is "free of material misstatements," the investor then has to determine the accounting standards that underlie that statement. An audited financial statement often does not describe in detail any of the self-dealing transactions between a public company and related companies owned by its executives. Nor does an audited financial statement have to record such related-party transactions at fair market values. Executives could sell products from their own companies to the public company for a much higher price than the market value, pocket the mark-up, and leave investors in the dark.

Not only can a company's managers receive such unfair benefits through self-dealing, but accountants and auditors have created their own rules that absolve them of responsibility for reporting these transactions in any detail. Instead, they pass along that responsibility to the public company's board of directors. Aided in these transactions by complicit accounting rules, the executives who sign the auditors' cheques can easily mislead their board.

Auditors themselves see their roles differently, depending on their disposition. Some auditors may feel professionally obligated to look more closely at potentially fraudulent transactions. Others may choose to remain wilfully blind. Still others may report their concerns to the corporate executives involved, who may then choose to do nothing.

In theory, at least, shareholders in Canada may still believe that auditors act on their behalf. The handbook of rules prepared by Canada's national accounting association still says that investors use financial statements prepared by its members. Provincial and federal legislation says auditors act on behalf of shareholders, checking management's figures and other representations in financial statements. But when dragged into court, auditors tell a different story. As we've seen in the Hercules case, auditors have testified before the Supreme Court of Canada that they do not produce annual audited financial statements as a guide for making investment decisions. And the court agreed.

Investors may indeed use audited financial statements, but when the chips are on the line, they shouldn't necessarily believe them. An audited annual financial statement affords about as much protection from management fraud and manipulation as a leaky umbrella from a thunderstorm.

Contradicting their own handbook of rules, and 150 years of British law, Canadian auditors have circumvented the country's securities legislation and resigned from their long-held role as a shareholder's ally in uncovering management's financial deceits.

Without the equivalent of a national securities regulator in Canada similar to the US Securities and Exchange Commission (SEC), no one has a voice in this country loud enough to alert Canadians to the danger. Lawmakers, who should have expressed outrage on behalf of individual investors, have ignored the mess and made it even worse by assigning responsibility for accounting and auditing standards to the very people who have disavowed their duty of care to investors. With little or no interest in shareholders, auditors are now free to put their own interests ahead of investors when companies issue misleading annual audited financial statements.

As an investor, you must remain vigilant. We strongly urge you to keep the following points in mind:

1. *Auditors apply different rules in different ways in Canada, the US, and other parts of the world.* As Canada adopts international auditing rules, you should be aware that these rules are loaded with unfortunate cop-outs. In particular, they enable auditors to blame corporate executives for most malfeasance, as they try to absolve themselves of legal liability.
2. *Auditors use sampling techniques and do not come anywhere close to checking the details of most corporate transactions, including transactions involving complex financial derivatives.* To detect errors or frauds,

they often rely on a company's internal control system. But some companies have better internal control systems than others, and auditors should look beyond these systems to verify transactions. Whether they do this or not often becomes subject to litigation.
3. *Auditors are supposed to gather evidence to substantiate management's numbers, generally from reliable external sources.* They should not rely primarily on management's unsupported assertions. Unfortunately, in a large number of court cases, auditors have signed their audit reports based largely on management and executive fabrications alone.
4. *In North America, audited financial statements are supposed to be "fairly presented in accordance with Generally Accepted Accounting Principles."* Such a statement should provide reasonable assurance that it does not contain materially misleading information. The adoption of International Financial Reporting Standards will only provide less assurance to investors. IFRS has not been tested before courts in Canada, or very extensively in other countries. Until this happens, no one can say whether judges will support the low quality of international auditing.

Quite obviously, Canada has to rethink the obligations of auditors. Why invest in Canadian companies, protected only by inadequate Canadian laws and the auditing community's self-imposed regulations, if the safety net for investors is so flimsy?

In the past, investors could at least catch a glimpse of some of the flaws. Until the late 1980s, Canada conducted judicial inquiries into more serious corporate financial collapses. One of the last published inquiry reports addressed the collapse of Northland Bank and the Canadian Commercial Bank. Both banks were based in Alberta, and both collapsed over the Labour Day weekend in 1985.

The author of the report, a former Supreme Court of Canada justice named Willard Estey, said management of both banks had responded to a grave situation by shoring up their banks' income statements and protecting their balance sheets. But he questioned management's techniques for trying to keep their banks afloat. Management used some questionable strategies, which would have been clearly apparent to trained auditors.

Yet the auditors still unconditionally approved the banks' financial statements. Noting the unfortunate "closeness" of the auditors to the opinions of management, Estey said the auditors had approved management strategies that the banks' own internal auditors would have questioned.

Similar audit failures have occurred in Canada every year since Estey issued his report. Despite some improvements in Canada's auditing environment, auditors in general continue to rely inordinately on management in approving financial statements. Far from learning a lesson from these bank failures and taking a more independent position on behalf of shareholders, auditors simply disavowed their responsibilities to shareholders altogether.

The country's lawmakers have done nothing to help remedy the situation. Instead, they continue to permit auditors to set their own rules. Such unchecked freedom has allowed auditors to systematically curtail their responsibilities for examining a company's information over the years. The current rules do not inspire auditors to look behind the numbers that they receive from management. Instead, they limit the responsibilities of auditors and absolve them of blame if management bamboozles them, even if they should have known better.

To maintain confidentiality and competitive advantage, companies may place limits on reporting activities, such as product research or legal strategy in a court case. But surely companies should have to disclose more than a series of boilerplate platitudes. Investors want to know as much as possible about the companies they own. They want to know about cash flows, profits, developments, trends, and their financial implications so that they can make better-informed decisions.

If investors receive little of value from the windy bromides of management, they don't receive much more from auditors. Operating under the vague and evasive rules that they devise for themselves, an annual audit may allow a company to comply with the Canadian Companies Act and Canadian Securities Act, but it's practically worthless for investors. In fact, legislated audits may do more harm than good by encouraging investors to rely on misleading information.

This situation promises to become even worse, once Canada adopts IFRS. Inadequate auditing rules under IFRS will allow auditors to dump almost all responsibility for financial statement figures onto corporate management. Management can therefore report whatever it wants, while the role of the auditor diminishes or, in certain cases, vanishes altogether.

As Canada prepares to adopt these international standards, few of the country's lawmakers appreciate the dire implications for investors. Despite very limited consultations with investors and lawmakers, auditors in Canada unilaterally decided to adopt IFRS. In the process, they forfeited much of the work that has been done in Canada over the years to strengthen accounting rules and close loopholes. Perhaps our auditors simply couldn't resist the revenue windfall from switching their clients to IFRS.

As IFRS perpetuates toothless financial reporting and costly, but valueless, auditing in Canada, investors will have to verify every number and phrase that a company reports. Basically, investors will have to become their own forensic accountants.

As an alternative, Canadian investors may choose to limit their investment activities to Canadian companies that follow US accounting and auditing guidelines. While Generally Accepted Accounting Principles (GAAP) and Generally Accepted Auditing Standards (GAAS) are not perfect, they at least offer more assurance to investors that the numbers reported in an annual financial statement are reasonable.

Unfortunately, only a few Canadian companies adhere to US guidelines. With the exception of audited financial statements that form part of a prospectus to offer shares or debt to the public, investors in most Canadian companies cannot feel certain that an audit has addressed a company's financial reporting weaknesses. They cannot assume that auditors have corrected management's financial manipulations before a company publishes its audited annual financial statements.

In some cases, investors can argue in court that auditors relied on an inadequate sample or a sample that did not reasonably represent a company's activities in reaching their conclusions. They can also argue that auditors should have followed up on discrepancies that would have revealed management manipulation. In these cases, a judge decides whether the auditors acted negligently.

This will change under IFRS. It will take at least five years before judgments emerge from the courts regarding management manipulation under IFRS. By then, investors could very well have lost billions of dollars to financial misbehaviour.

And it wouldn't be the first time investors have lost their money. Again and again, auditors have remained silent as managements swindled investors out of billions of dollars. It happened with Nortel, and it happened with business income trusts (BITs).

BITs fooled investors by downplaying income and emphasizing an ill-defined concept called distributable cash. Management sometimes regarded anything that moved as distributable cash. Profit could be $1 million, but distributable cash could amount to twice as much. Naturally, management and trustees hyped the higher figure to investors.

In the case of Nortel, management used something called a pro-forma adjustment to convert audited net losses into operating profits. The net losses had actually been poorly audited and had to be corrected and republished many times. As if by magic, however, management used the profits, which once were losses, to calculate their executive bonuses. And again, the auditors remained silent.

By not speaking out to regulators, demanding changes from lawmakers, or educating investors promptly about problems that they well understood, auditors led investors into a financial reporting trap. Investors took the auditors' silence as approval. And when investors lost money, the auditors said once again that they owed no duty of care to investors. According to their own rules, they were under no obligation to warn investors about potential chicanery, especially if such a warning would upset their paying clients, the corporations and BITs that employed them. The plump fees paid by these organizations buy the allegiance of their auditors, and investors don't stand a chance.

Weak or inadequate auditing can occur at any time, in any industry, but we encounter problems most frequently in the following circumstances:

1. *When accounting rules are weak.* Unfortunately, as we'll discuss in more detail, they'll likely become much weaker under IFRS.
2. *In non-manufacturing, non-retail businesses, and especially finance companies, credit unions, banks, loan enterprises, real estate, and resource*

sectors. These are troublesome because inadequate monitoring of cash inflows and outflows often cause corporate failures.
3. *In construction-type enterprises that have to be scrutinized for cash-flow problems, faked revenue, and transfers of cash into private businesses owned by executives.*
4. *When dealing with non-arm's-length transactions, which are usually poorly handled by auditors, especially in smaller public companies.*
5. *In identifying frauds, which tend to be handled at least as poorly as non-arm's-length dealings.* When such cases go to trial, it is not unusual to identify several warning signs or red flags that auditors missed.
6. *When dealing with receivables, inventory, and revenue.* These almost inevitably raise sore spots in audits. Companies typically play dirty tricks on their loan officers and bankers, for example, by refreshing the age of receivables through credit notes. They reschedule due dates and terms of loans or manipulate aged lists of receivables. The most common cookie jar for manipulating income is an estimated liability, such as a provision for product warranties. When a company wants to record more income, it reduces its estimated liability for future warranty costs. The difference boosts reported income.
7. *When corporate restructuring charges exist.* Accountants tightened reporting rules a few years ago, but excessive write-downs can creep back into regular income by various means. Executives can build cookie jar reserves by overestimating the expected cost of a restructuring or acquisition. At the time of the reported expense, investors perceive them as one-time charges and might be inclined to ignore them, but since they are phony, they can be reversed in future quarters and used to make operating income look better than it otherwise would.
8. *When capitalized expenses are present on the balance sheet.* Auditors frequently pay less attention to this area than they should. Self-constructed assets (assets that the company builds for its own use) tend to open the door to regular expenses being dumped into asset accounts, producing inappropriate profit one year and then a decline the next year. When a company essentially determines the cost of its own assets by building them itself, it can divert regular operating expenses away from income. The charges are added to the asset's

reported value on the balance sheet, which may or may not be expensed in future periods, distorting reported income.

In later chapters, we'll point out further problems with auditing. They occur, for example, when one company acquires another and has to integrate the new company's accounts into its own assets and liabilities. They also occur when companies account for financial instruments such as derivatives, hedges, and cash equivalents.

CHAPTER FOUR

# Bleak House Revisited

*"Justice too long delayed is justice denied."*

MARTIN LUTHER KING, JR.

**IN 1853,** in a book called *Bleak House*, Charles Dickens described a court case that was "no nearer to its termination now than when it was begun." The case had involved thirty to forty counsels appearing at one time. "Costs have been incurred to the amount of seventy thousand pounds." This friendly lawsuit, Dickens said, had continued for twenty years.

More than 150 years later, you might roll your eyes and chuckle at the Dickensian legal environment in which a case could continue for twenty years. But then again, you may not have heard of a case in Canada called *The estate of the late Peter N. Widdrington v. Elliot C. Wightman et al.* Better known as the Castor Holdings case, it began in 1992 with the filing of seventy-five lawsuits. The actual trial began in 1998, focusing on just one of them. Some plaintiffs expected the trial to last about eight months. But after twelve years, it has become the longest-running trial in the nation's history, and at the time of writing, the outcome was still unknown.

Typical of most white-collar crime cases heard in Canada, the Castor case has involved an endless barrage of challenges, motions, and examinations for discovery. It began in Montreal on a cold winter morning in February 1992, when the creditors and shareholders of Castor Holdings learned that the company had suddenly filed for bankruptcy, the largest in Canadian history at the time, involving losses before interest of roughly $1 billion.

The news came as an immense shock, because audited annual financial statements from 1977 to December 31, 1990, showed that Castor was hugely successful. Profits had increased every year, attracting significant investments from numerous sources, including the Chrysler Canada pension plan, several Canadian insurance companies, and European banks. The reported assets of Castor exceeded $1.5 billion, and the audited financial statements showed annual profits in the range of 15% to 20% of assets. To many onlookers, Castor was a money-making success.

The plaintiff in the action, the late Peter Widdrington, was the former CEO of John Labatt in the 1980s. He oversaw the company's expansion into dozens of non-brewing ventures, including the founding of sports channel TSN. Widdrington was chairman of the Toronto Blue Jays when they won back-to-back World Series championships in 1992 and 1993. He was also the chairman of Laidlaw International when it settled a class action lawsuit for misrepresenting its financial condition to investors, and also when it collapsed into bankruptcy following an acquisition spree in the transportation sector.

The first named defendant, Elliot C. Wightman, was a senior partner at Coopers & Lybrand (now part of PricewaterhouseCoopers), which handled Castor's audit. The audit firm itself was also named, and its reputation and fortunes arguably hang in the balance.

Widdrington lost $2.7 million when Castor collapsed. The members of the Chrysler Canada pension fund lost more than $200 million. Members of a Saskatchewan credit union and the Alberta Teachers' Retirement Fund, along with dozens of individual investors, also lost hundreds of millions. In dozens of separate lawsuits, they have sought more than $800 million from Coopers & Lybrand. With so much at stake, the accounting firm has spared no expense in defending itself, especially since the protection afforded to auditors by the Hercules decision did not likely apply in Quebec.

Castor Holdings was founded in Montreal in the late 1970s by German businessmen Wolfgang Stolzenberg and Karsten von Wersebe. Both were highly charismatic, claiming aristocratic origins and adopting a haughty and high-handed attitude toward anyone who questioned Castor's apparent success in too much detail. Shortly after co-founding Castor, von Wersebe started another company, York-Hannover Developments, which held mortgages in numerous real estate projects. York-Hannover was involved in several Canadian projects, including the Montreal Eaton Centre, Maple Leaf Village in Niagara Falls, Hazelton Lanes in Toronto, and the Skyline Hotels in Ottawa, Toronto, and Calgary. The company received so much of its funding from Castor that the fates of the two companies were inextricably linked, much like those of Stolzenberg and von Wersebe. Together they set up a global financial web that extended through Canada, Ireland, Cyprus, Switzerland, Germany, Lichtenstein, and the Dutch Antilles, to name but a few. The network of financial subsidiaries was so complex that investigators untangled it only with great difficulty.

Under the terms of the loans to York-Hannover and related companies, Castor required monthly interest payments in cash. Castor recorded the payments as interest revenue and reported a profit in its audited annual financial statements based on the assumption that Castor had received the cash. Unfortunately, that assumption seems to have been mistaken. According to court testimony, York-Hannover owed overdue interest and principal on a large portion of the loans from Castor and did not make cash payments to Castor on a monthly or even an annual basis.

Nevertheless, Castor's annual audited financial statements showed millions of dollars of interest revenue. The company's balance sheet also showed investments and loans receivable worth many millions more. Among these assets was interest due on Castor's loans that had not been paid for several years. To an investor reading Castor's balance sheets, however, it was not clear that these unpaid interest payments had been included among other assets.

Year after year, Castor kept adding to the amounts on its balance sheet, on the unlikely assumption that it would eventually collect the cash, perhaps by selling its loans or gaining legal title to the property pledged as collateral. For investors and auditors, the probable sale price of such property became critical. But Castor had made the loans in the form of second and third mortgages, which meant that after the company went bankrupt, the claims of other creditors took precedence over Castor's. By the time their turn came, there was little or nothing left.

No one would have anticipated this dismal turn of events from looking at the audited financial statements published by Castor over the ten years before its bankruptcy. These statements showed a steady increase in profits and cash flow. Based on such glowing reports, investors poured millions of dollars into Castor with the stated purpose of lending it again to selected real-estate ventures.

The Quebec court will have to decide whether the audited annual financial statements misled investors in a material way. In the process, other questions will need to be addressed. Do Canada's accounting rules permit the reporting of management hopes and dreams about the value of seized land and buildings as opposed to the price that outside parties will likely pay? Would investors have lent money to Castor if they had known that the company had not received regular cash interest payments to service the millions of dollars of loans on its books? In other words, were the assets on Castor's balance sheet worth the amounts indicated, or did Castor simply report huge losses as assets?

The plot thickened when allegations arose about investments made jointly by Stolzenberg and the wife of the partner in charge of Castor's audit for more than twelve years. The court will have to decide whether this relationship might have compromised the independence of Castor's auditors.

Castor also allegedly reported income from the sale of a $100 million debenture that, in fact, the company sold to itself through its consolidated companies, generating no new cash. To what extent did auditors try to trace movements of cash underlying the supposed sale of the debenture? Did the auditors verify the receipt of $100 million in cash? If they did, where did it come from? Was the transaction conducted at arm's-length and verified as such?

On another occasion, Castor made nine loans worth $40 million just prior to the company's 1990 fiscal year-end. The timing of these transactions was suspicious, to say the least. Again, the court will have to decide whether auditors took sufficient measures to investigate the nature of these transactions, and whether these measures were reflected in the financial statements.

Regardless of the guidelines that auditors have set for themselves, the court in the Castor case may decide that Canada's accounting and auditing rules fall short of the standards of equity and fairness to which Canadian investors are entitled. If the court decides that the rules are too loose, it might require a new minimum reporting standard. Should Castor's audited annual financial statements have disclosed, for example, that Castor had received only a fraction of the cash due in principal on its mortgage loans? If Castor's balance sheets showed investments that grossly exceeded their cash-equivalent values, when and how should creditors and shareholders have been informed?

None of this offers much reassurance to investors. Despite the anticipation of a welcome decision from the court in the Castor case, investors cannot assume that courts will intervene on their behalf. They must learn to protect themselves. Auditors have repeatedly stated in court that they owe no obligations to investors for identifying major errors in annual audited financial statements. Given that they have no duty of care toward investors, why should auditors be allowed to determine the rules and control the definition of adequate financial reporting to investors? A completely independent body, free from the influence, intimidation, and financial control of practising auditors, should set financial reporting and accounting rules. Until that happens, Canadian investors should exercise extreme caution.

As the Castor case demonstrates, white-collar court cases in Canada can drag out for many years. For example, after the ousting of company founders Garth Drabinsky and Myron Gottlieb from Livent, it took more than ten years before the two were convicted in 2009 for accounting fraud. In civil cases, the side with the most money to pay the lawyers has a distinct advantage. Individual investors simply do not possess the wherewithal or financial means to take on companies, or well-paid executives, or auditors. If an individual investor can reach a financial settlement, it often amounts to less than the legal fees already incurred.

Institutional investors could exercise their clout, but few of them seem willing to pursue white-collar fraud. Either they don't want to expose their investing missteps to greater public scrutiny, or they don't want to ruffle the feathers of their corporate cohorts in the tightly knit community of Canadian public companies.

In contrast, the US tends to deal swiftly with white-collar securities scams. It took just 200 days after the exposure of Bernie Madoff's Ponzi scheme for the court to sentence Madoff in 2009. The resolution of the Livent case took nineteen times as long. The Castor case has dragged on thirty-four times as long, and it's still running as we write. Madoff received 150 years in jail, while Canadian courts have only recently handed out a white-collar fraud sentence that exceeds ten years.

Castor is not an isolated case in Canada. Other major financial entities have gone bankrupt without warning as well, including Canadian Commercial Bank and Northland Bank in Alberta, along with dozens of trusts and credit unions. Investors should keep in mind that a company that reports steadily increasing profits, year after year, may be engaging in accounting chicanery. If an investment looks too good to be true, and if investors cannot get answers to allay their suspicions, the investment should be avoided, no matter what the audited financial statements say.

Cases like Castor cannot be ignored. Investors and legislators must pay attention to them so they can counteract the obfuscation created by auditors in defending their very cozy and lucrative status quo. In the best possible outcome for investors, the court will decide that the auditors were negligent in their duties. Even then, and ignoring probable appeals, investors will have spent nearly two decades and millions of dollars to recover some of their losses. The alternative, though, raises a nightmare scenario for Canadian investors. It would mean that companies could go bankrupt overnight, with no warning in their financial statements, and ultimately no recourse for investors to recover their losses.

Given that Castor remains before the courts, it would not be appropriate to comment on the application of liability and damages. However, one simple fact cannot be avoided: Castor went bankrupt and investors and creditors lost more than $1 billion. Yet in every year before the company declared bankruptcy, Castor had clean audit reports.

CHAPTER FIVE

## The Fox Still Guards the Henhouse

*"When money speaks, the truth keeps silent."*
RUSSIAN PROVERB

**WHENEVER ANOTHER** high-profile securities scandal emerges in Canada, lawmakers point to token changes made to improve investor protection. But regulators and lawmakers have missed the point completely when it comes to securities regulation in this country. While they might address the issue of minimum prison sentences for certain types of white-collar crime, for example, they do nothing to raise the number of cases that get investigated in the first place. Nor do they bother to analyze why a large proportion of white-collar cases that make it to court end up failing. Changing the minimum sentencing requirement has no meaningful impact on reducing the number of investors swindled in Canada every year. Of far more concern is Canada's poor record of investigating and prosecuting these cases in the first place.

To excuse their inactivity, Canadian lawmakers often use examples of fraud in the US. If American investor protections do not work perfectly, they say, why should Canada adopt a similar system? Such specious reasoning merely diverts attention from more important facts. Many scams that succeed in Canada never get off the ground in the US. As we'll discuss in detail, Canada, not the US, allowed the creation of business income trusts. And Canada, not the US, provided a welcome environment for flawed non-bank asset-backed commercial paper to flourish. Despite names like Enron and WorldCom that we associate with scandal and deceit, no case in the US rivals the extent of Nortel's treachery on a proportionate basis. Despite the frequency and severity of these investment disasters, Canada has launched no legislative investigations into their causes, and the country's lawmakers have made few concrete changes in the way this country protects investors.

BITs, for example, emerged under the noses of the very people charged with protecting investors from such boondoggles. Initially, a few BITs made sense, but as underwriters became bolder, they slapped together an increasing number of these trusts without much regard for their practicality as investments. As the quality of these trusts deteriorated over several years, who stood on the sidelines while investors were misled? None other than the financial statement auditors, provincial securities regulators, and lawmakers who constitute, in theory, Canada's investor safety net. When many poor-quality business trusts collapsed, the blame focused on a change in tax policy. Political interest never extended to the misleading sales practices employed by peddlers of BITs. Regulators and auditors expressed no serious concerns because they remain as fundamentally conflicted as ever, serving the companies they regulate and audit, and who pay their fees, while supposedly keeping in mind the interests of investors, who don't.

Canada continues to present itself as a safe place to invest, despite mounting evidence to the contrary. In fact, the securities industry in Canada frequently feeds the investing public with nonsense. To give the impression that they want to improve investor protection, corporate governance, and related issues, the industry trumpets the establishment of committees, panels, advisory groups, and stakeholder councils to represent investor interests. But in many cases, these bodies have a much different agenda, aimed at placating individual investors, while discouraging government interference in the affairs of the investment industry.

The first decade of the new century was an appalling period for investors, not just because of poor investment returns, but because of

Canada's deteriorating investor safety net. The power to make decisions that might protect investors continues to devolve to the very self-regulated organizations that disavow any responsibility to investors at all. Our lawmakers allow this to happen, either out of ignorance or, worse, out of complicity in the deceit.

Caving in to lobbyists from the securities, auditing, and investment communities, lawmakers have allowed pro-business law firms, which often represent defendants in investor lawsuits, to edit proposed legislation meant to protect investors. Meanwhile, law firms that usually represent investors in such cases receive no similar opportunity, leaving investors with deliberately watered-down protections.

If this leaves you feeling vulnerable, you have two choices: either you can look beyond Canada for investment opportunities and enjoy greater protection, or you can learn how to navigate through the treacherous waters of Canadian investments with only the flawed, inadequate, and often self-imposed regulations of Canada's auditing and securities communities to protect you.

Our proclivity in Canada for such self-regulation has become our fatal flaw. When investment scandals occur in Canada, our legislators and regulators too often seek guidance from the professional bodies whose members have caused the problem in the first place. Lawmakers too often look for the easy answer, and the self-regulatory organizations (SROs) make sure that the politicians have one ready whenever a scandal erupts.

Some SROs work, but many fall short in their performance and tend to ride on the coattails of the more successful bodies. These SROs are supposed to serve the public interest as well as their members. But when the public interest conflicts with the interests of their members, the SROs usually put their members first. Their responsibility to the public gets downplayed or eliminated, with no safeguards in place to prevent this from happening.

Responding to public concerns, several SROs in the 1990s formed oversight committees to ensure their organizations behaved responsibly. As members of these oversight boards, they appointed old acquaintances or individuals whose work depended on the SROs' support. With such oversight boards simply rubber-stamping important decisions without debate, supposed oversight became yet another exercise in smoke and mirrors.

The exercise seemed to fool Canada's lawmakers. Time after time we've corresponded with them about SROs that fall well below international standards in terms of controlling their own oversight structure, but we seldom elicit much interest.

Canada allows an SRO to control the process of developing accounting and auditing rules, for example, including the auditing of financial statements. Unlike most of the industrialized world, Canada allows this SRO to manhandle its own oversight boards. Without effective oversight, auditors can set vague and weak accounting and auditing rules that do not offend their paying clients, the corporations whose accounts they audit. If investors need tighter rules and clear prohibitions that increase the quality of financial reporting, they don't get them from the SRO that's supposed to represent their interests.

Questioned about their self-interested practices, SROs argue that they must maintain a balance between the needs of investors and the priorities of corporate executives. They also emphasize the added costs of increased regulation. Considering the landslide of securities scams in Canada, however, the word "balance" invoked by self-interested SROs becomes jawdropping in its audacity. By our estimation, in conflicts between corporate interests and investor needs, corporations win more than 90% of the time.

Curiously, a rough balance once existed between corporate management and investors when it came to auditing. It ended during the economic recession in 1981 and 1982. As their interest in shareholders receded, auditors became marketers of various accounting consulting services, including how to pretty-up a company and its books during tough economic times.

Since then, Canada's lawmakers still have not realized that auditors have no interest in looking after investors' needs. Even when auditors' representatives argued before the Supreme Court of Canada, as they did in the Hercules case, that investors should not rely on audited annual financial statements to make investment decisions, Canadian lawmakers hardly batted a collective eye. While investors were left to their own devices to evaluate a company's worth, the need for an audit went up in smoke.

Having kissed goodbye their traditional responsibilities to shareholders, auditors continued to regulate themselves. Without the public interest to distract them, these alleged professionals have systematically weakened Canada's auditing and accounting rules, with the full approval of our courts and lawmakers.

Despite a growing epidemic of missing financial chickens, the fox now guards the investment henhouse in Canada. The very people who have stated to Canada's highest court that investors should not use annual audited financial statements for investment decisions now control the writing and amending of Canada's accounting and auditing rules. Corporations, in turn, have clear interests in minimizing scrutiny of their finances and restricting the scope of accounting and auditing rules. Corporations prefer rules that can be interpreted as loosely as possible, and auditors are happy to oblige. If some beleaguered investor calls for stronger accounting and auditing rules in Canada, the auditors can refer him to an inadequately staffed and overworked oversight committee for help.

Of all countries of significance in the world, only Canada allows such a blatant conflict of interest to continue. Canadian lawmakers seem unaware of standard operating procedures applied in other countries to oversee auditors. Meanwhile, Canadian auditors claim to have established a unique solution to the situation by establishing a lame-duck oversight board, which, in truth, represents no solution at all.

Since 1998, Canadian auditors, through their umbrella organization, the Canadian Institute of Chartered Accountants, have lobbied extensively to keep their cozy empire in place. With their encouragement, the implications of the Hercules decision remain unaddressed. The legal precedent established by the case has forced investors to abandon countless cases of alleged auditor negligence.

Auditors have directed other lobbying efforts at the Canadian Senate, which investigated Canada's regulatory and oversight environment after the Enron debacle and the collapse of accounting firm Arthur Andersen. Despite considerable evidence to support major changes to the auditing landscape in Canada, the Senate Banking Committee lifted a phrase directly from the auditors' testimony and lobbying materials and issued a report entitled "The Perfect Storm." The report made little mention of the serious problems that needed immediate correction. Nor did it draw much attention to the fundamental differences between Canadian and US auditing. Clearly, the lobbying efforts of the auditors had succeeded again.

National print journalists in Canada have also swooned under auditors' lobbying and public relations efforts. In fact, it would be interesting to see the auditors' budget for public relations compared to their budget for improving accounting and auditing standards to accommodate investor interests. Auditors must regard PR as a necessary expense in maintaining the status quo, while the budget for improving standards represents an annoying cost that should be minimized as much as possible. In any case, some journalists in Canada favour minimal securities regulation and audit oversight initiatives, apparently taking the auditors' PR materials at face value. These journalists seem not to recognize that the absence of effective regulation leaves investors vulnerable to repeated swindles under our current Canadian system.

In the US, auditors apply more rigorous standards to achieve more transparent reporting. Rather than following the US model more closely, Canada's auditors appear to have rejected it outright. According to their arguments, US reporting requirements failed to prevent the Enron fiasco and similar scandals. They also argue that improved financial reporting and greater regulatory oversight would cost too much.

The first criticism is simply absurd. No system catches every violation. Indeed, most systems need to be maintained and improved regularly to keep up with inevitable changes. The US actively pursues most criminal activity, but the same can hardly be said for Canada. In fact, a disturbingly large proportion of Canadian-based scams operating under the noses of our own provincial securities regulators come to light only after US authorities detect them. Rather than feeling smug about our inviolable securities environment, Canadians should feel acutely embarrassed by this. More importantly, we should understand the implications for the safety of our Canadian investments.

For most corporations, compliance with US rules certainly costs more than meeting Canadian requirements. But the US is far more successful than Canada in safeguarding investments. Since the US Securities and Exchange Commission was formed in the 1930s, the US has accommodated concerns about fairness to investors. In contrast, Canada has limped along with SROs, which develop and apply rules in their own best interest, with little or no concern for investors. Since the early 1980s, this inadequate system has failed dismally.

Unlike Canada's self-regulated auditing community, US rule makers at least attempt to provide transparency for investors. US reporting rules and concepts also prevent many types of financial games that occur regularly in Canada. US rule makers seem well aware that financial swindlers and con artists can easily circumvent mere principles or ideals. They seem to understand better than Canadian authorities that investor protection requires prescriptive prohibitions, which are continually updated to keep pace with changing times.

In other areas of Canada's regulatory landscape, we recognize the need for carefully enacted and tightly worded rules to discourage swindlers and con artists. Our income tax legislation, for example, seems airtight compared to the inadequate rules applied to accounting and financial reporting. Why do our lawmakers assume that Canada has no securities shysters, while assuming that all of us will cheat on our taxes? Anyone who has been the subject of a tax audit would beg for the treatment afforded to crooked corporate executives in Canada. Canada has special legislation, courts, and hardened field investigators to enforce the voluminous prohibitions needed to rein in tax games, and imposes jail sentences when they're appropriate. When it comes to corporate financial reporting, we have none of that. The assumption is that all executives are innocent, with no attempt made to prove otherwise.

Living next door to the US, but choosing to adopt vastly inferior International Financial Reporting Standards, Canada's accountants and auditors have raised some serious questions. Among other things, IFRS assumes a naive trust in corporate executives that blatantly contradicts Canada's history of securities scandals, and the failure of this country to investigate and prosecute such transgressions.

Under IFRS, corporate executives can report figures that make them appear most competent, because it functions under the assumption that management knows its company best. This may be true, but management also knows how to choose numbers that make it look good. In maintaining the so-called balance between corporate and investor interests, will the so-called shareholders' auditors step in to overrule management greed? The answer is no. And why should they? Inactive lawmakers, compliant securities regulators, and the Supreme Court of Canada have all said they don't have to.

CHAPTER SIX

# A Quick Guide to Scams and Cover-Ups

*"Corporation: an ingenious device for obtaining individual profit without individual responsibility."*

AMBROSE BIERCE

**CANADIAN SECURITIES** regulators claim frequently that Canadian investors do not have to worry about executives cooking the books. Their proof? They have seldom convicted anyone of the offence in recent memory. It's amazing what you don't see when you don't bother looking.

If you look more closely, as we do every day, you'll find some astonishing opportunities for manipulation of financial reports. The looser the accounting rules, the more easily a company's management can alter the reported numbers, audited or not. Management usually wants the manipulated figures to fall within a category or range that will not raise an alarm with investors. If management can keep investors in the dark, it will inject capital into ugly situations with remote prospects of future profitability. Nortel, Livent, and many business income trusts attracted investors in this way. So did Northland Bank, Canadian Commercial Bank, Confederation Life, and Confederation Trust.

These cases, and many others, occurred in the context of principles-based accounting and auditing rules, an unfortunate situation that will only get worse under IFRS. Instead of applying clear, concrete, well-defined rules, accountants and auditors interpret principles in a way that seems fair. Investors might ask, "Fair to whom?"

A principles-based approach to financial reporting becomes particularly unsuitable when the principles are vague and unenforceable, boards of directors are not familiar with the so-called principles, and a country's legal system makes it difficult to prosecute even the most blatant cases of manipulation of corporate financial statements. Such an approach simply encourages financial swindlers, who quickly notice the absence of prosecutions and convictions for engaging in accounting scams.

We're not the first ones to observe that principles-based reporting does not make sense if the people in charge of preparing and checking the financial statements have no principles. Since you cannot accept without question a company's financial numbers, investors need to dig deeper. Instead of basing decisions on the numbers that management has reported, investors have to determine if a company has manipulated its figures through aggressive methods, assumptions, or estimates. After that, investors have to ask: By how much? For how long? And for what apparent reasons?

Under principles-based rules, and with our lax regulatory and auditing oversight, the temptation for management to fiddle with the accounting figures sometimes proves too hard to resist. Management can turn the principles to their favour to inflate their company's financial results, along with their own egos. The inflated results can be used, for example, to buy more time for an operational turnaround. Whether or not the turnaround ever succeeds, investors in an active market for the company's shares will be trading constantly on false information.

Management can also use the cover-up game to avoid violations of banking restrictions or financial covenants. Management might have made unfortunate decisions that have caused cost overruns, declining cash flows, operating losses, and much more. Instead of acknowledging the financial consequences, management can manipulate the numbers, especially if they think that bankers and investors will believe their company's so-called audited financial statements without question.

Most disturbing of all for investors are the many situations that arise from management's bad decisions, or possibly bad luck, that require a financial restructuring of the corporation. In offering shares or debt as part of the restructuring, management may cook the books to make the business look more successful than it is. As for the company's board of directors, management can usually bamboozle the board's audit committee. Few board members have the expertise to challenge specific accounting and auditing choices, especially if they have to confront management and auditors in the process.

Cooking the books to make a company appear more successful than it really is constitutes a crime. With sufficient proof, a court may determine that management has committed fraud. But prosecutions are rarely pursued in Canada for such criminal offences, so investors have to protect themselves by looking behind the numbers. This isn't easy unless you know the precise nature and extent of the problems that management is trying to hide. Otherwise, management can pull off a successful cover-up without much difficulty, sometimes for a number of years, and always to the detriment of investors. Sometimes managers simply want larger bonuses, and they want to obtain them in some other way than simply working hard. If managers' bonuses are based on income or profits before tax, they'll focus on playing with revenue recognition and inappropriately reducing operating expenses.

Management may have other reasons, as well, for reporting higher income before tax for a year or two, despite underlying fundamental problems at the company. These reasons may include:

1. *Violations or potential violations of lending covenants that stipulate profitability ratios, such as those involving net income, income before tax, operating profit, earnings before interest, taxes, depreciation, and amortization (EBITDA), or even cash flows.* To avoid close scrutiny from bankers, management may fiddle with the company's financial ratios, with little risk that the bank will look closely at the calculations.
2. *Pressure from underwriters to get the company's profits higher before the sale of more shares to the public.* Fraud can be difficult to prove in such situations.

3. *Attempts to con bankers into lending more money, based on contrived figures to distort the reported growth or stability of the company.* In these cases, the company has serious undisclosed cash-flow problems and needs more cash fast. Revenue may suddenly appear as a result of accounting tricks. Inexperienced bankers are frequently conned by phony figures that show an improving growth trend at a potential borrower's company.
4. *An attempt to sell a subsidiary, or a division of the company, by reporting inflated profits.* The parent company might have cash-flow troubles, prompting it to sell operating assets to survive. A buyer of the subsidiary might end up paying too much for the company, based on its actual earning potential, if management has played accounting games.
5. *Attempts to keep the stock price up, even during economic recessions.* Why admit that a company is deteriorating when management can create the appearance that it is holding steady?
6. *Attempts to keep the value of stock options higher than they ought to be, in order to hold up company morale.* This might also be part of a greater plan to offer more share-based compensation and less cash-based salary and bonuses to key middle management.

These examples show how management can manipulate accounts to enhance profits and cover up problems at a company. As we'll discuss later, management may use other tactics, such as overstating assets and understating liabilities, to disguise more serious corporate difficulties.

Sometimes, management's reasons for playing accounting and financial reporting games do not become apparent even to forensic accountants until many quarters have passed. In such cases, investigators must scrutinize every press release and financial statement issued by the company, and compare financial statements over many months or years. Inexplicable figures often indicate problems with the company's operations or a flawed management motivation scheme.

As a company experiences serious financial problems, the number of accounting games increases year by year. A trick used in one year to cover up a $50-million overstatement of revenue often has to be covered up the next year by falsifying $100 million. That requires $50 million just to cover up the previous year's overstatement. If management wants to show continuing growth in a third year, it needs to find another $50 million in revenue enhancement. Investors should watch for escalations of financial trickery as the years go by. Eventually the cover-up will become unsustainable. Investors who pay attention to the early warning signs can head for the exits before the house of cards crashes down.

Investors must carefully read the notes to the financial statements, especially those that describe the circumstances under which revenue can be recognized on the company's income statement. Investors should be particularly aware of multi-year contracts, or projects that allow revenue to be reported this year instead of in subsequent years. For example, companies involved in long-term construction projects may, without much difficulty, overstate their progress toward completion, enabling them to record revenues prematurely. In other cases, management may reduce expenses inappropriately by adding them as assets to the balance sheet. Investors need to watch for interest expense and overheads. Usually these items are expensed, reducing a company's income accordingly. But sometimes management will add them to the cost of a long-lived asset on the balance sheet, so that they don't have an immediate impact on income.

Not all companies inflate their revenues. Some do just the opposite. As we'll see in the next chapter, majority owners sometimes try to demoralize minority shareholders by manipulating a company's earnings downward. They can do this in several ways, including expensing assets, such as inventory, to reduce income. With artificially depressed profits, the majority owners can then offer a low buy-out price for the minority's shares. When the majority owners buy a sufficient number of shares, they can stop their deceptions and allow profits to return to normal, raising the price of their shares. Such tactics tend to disrupt a company's financial trend lines and ratios established over a period of years. Investors who see such a disruption should proceed with caution.

In all cases, investors should carefully study any changes in the way a company accounts for a particular type of transaction, such as a warranty expense, from year to year. You can gain useful insights into executive priorities and ethics by observing the timing of the change, any explanations provided, and the dollar impact in current and future periods.

CHAPTER SEVEN

# The Nuts and Bolts of Revenue Scams

*"History is a better guide than good intentions."*
JEANE KIRKPATRICK

**IN THE** tech market mania of the early 2000s, companies that could not report a profit under conventional accounting principles turned to new and illogical valuation techniques. One of the most puzzling focused solely on expected revenue estimates. Manipulative management teams simply inflated their companies' revenue. They wasted no effort on other accounting games. Goosing revenue was all it took.

In the manic market of the time, investors accepted revenue numbers at face value in audited financial statements without allowing for even the most elementary of financial tricks. Many of these companies did not show positive cash flow or profit, so investors relied instead on valuations based on a multiple of revenue. (For an introduction to financial statements, see Appendix B.) Under IFRS, exaggerating or faking revenue becomes even easier. Unprincipled management can triple a company's sales revenue by using a variety of age-old accounting games.

Many of these revenue-bloating techniques have been in use for decades. Shares in a company called National Business Systems (NBS), for example, traded on the Toronto Stock Exchange until the late 1980s. As NBS's annual revenue increased, according to fully audited financial statements, the price of its stock rose, as well, at least until March 31, 1988. On that day, a revised auditors' report withdrew NBS's audited statements for the previous two years. Instead of recording an income, the auditors said NBS had actually suffered a loss. (For more details on the NBS scam, please see Appendix C.)

NBS had originally reported to shareholders an income of $13,696,000 for 1987. According to the revised audited financial statement, NBS had lost $26,277,000 in fiscal 1987. As a result, the company had no retained earnings, but rather a deficit of $25,288,000. This is quite a difference to a shareholder trying to decide whether or not he's made a good decision in buying the stock of NBS. Of the $39,973,000 difference between the income originally reported by NBS and the $25,288,000 loss, the auditors attributed more than 80% to "fictitious sales" and "billings to customers for product not shipped until after year end."

NBS had shipped more than $2 million in inventory to cover these fictitious sales. These shipments were then returned and placed back in inventory after the company's year-end, as if nothing had ever happened. NBS also overstated the value of assets by more than $5 million and executed other accounting manoeuvres that boosted the company's income by another $15 million. These are not minor distortions, and NBS is not the only company to try to get away with such blatant falsehoods. In recent years, Nortel Networks, Philip Services, and dozens of other Canadian financial failures have issued similar misstatements. To add insult to injury, NBS issued only one major revision of its audited financial statements. Nortel revised its audited financial statements four times.

The temptation to manipulate a company's figures remains powerful, especially when the company hits hard times. As management well knows, some of these manipulations of financial statements remain undetected for years. And when they do finally come to light, the punishment is mild, at best. Investors may not even realize that they have been the victims of such blatant manipulations, because many are invested in the problem companies through their pension plans or mutual funds. Even when these companies collapse, investors may not realize how much they've lost.

Companies don't always inflate their revenue, however. Sometimes they use loose accounting rules to deliberately understate income, usually when the majority owners want to depress a company's stock price. They often do this to persuade a minority shareholder group to sell their stock at low prices.

In private companies, owners might delay or avoid the recording of revenue to keep income taxes down. Such a tactic can backfire, though, and lead to criminal charges if tax auditors get wind of the deception. Tax auditors might notice, for example, that a restaurant owner has purchased far more food than the reported sales would justify. Or they might notice that a business owner injured in a car accident has reported a low income for tax purposes, but a much higher potential income on his insurance claim.

In fact, financial reports can easily be designed for a particular audience. For the purposes of paying income tax or spousal support, a business owner might report a low income. But for collecting on an insurance policy, the same owner might report a much higher income with healthy profits. As an investor, you have to make sure that you know why a company prepared its financial statements, who prepared them, and when they did it. Otherwise, you can't always make an intelligent interpretation of the numbers.

Investors have to apply the same degree of skepticism to public and private companies alike. All companies may issue audited financial statements that convey a distorted attitude of optimism or pessimism. Investors have to determine for themselves the attitudes and motivations of a company's management. Unless they understand the objectives of management, investors can make major mistakes in interpreting a company's financial results. A good place to start is a company's revenue-recording policies.

At the moment, most revenue-inflation techniques fall into three main categories:

1. Fake sales, sales to non-existent customers, and sales to customers with unacceptable credit rating.

2. Premature recording of revenue, possibly years in advance of the logical time for recording it.
3. Overstated dollar amounts of revenue, through swaps or related-party shenanigans.

Investors may not spot fake sales just by looking at a company's financial statements, but they may get a clue if they notice a large percentage of a company's sales revenue over a previous period remains uncollected. A company whose quarter-end accounts receivable represent 80% of the quarter's sales, for example, should raise a red flag with investors. A company should receive cash payment, at least in part, on sales made two months before quarter end. If it hasn't received payment, then perhaps it has concocted the sales in the last few days or weeks before the quarter end. Companies sometimes do this out of desperation to con their creditors. Bankers may feel more comfortable about their loans, for example, if a borrower presents a high balance of accounts receivable.

We have seen companies report accounts receivable that exceed 100% of sales in their most recent quarter. We have seen audited financial statements in which auditors contacted fictitious new customers to confirm that they truly intended to pay their debts to a company, without realizing that all the customers had sequential post-box addresses at the same postal station. Not surprisingly, each fake customer dutifully reported to the auditors that the payment would be made.

Instead of creating fictitious customers, some companies rely on customers with atrocious credit ratings and little means, or hope, of paying the receivable anytime soon. The company records the sale, knowing they'll never receive payment. To detect such customers, an auditor has to conduct a credit check and perform other audit procedures, which as we've seen is not a common practice.

Such deficient accounting and auditing practices happen all the time in Canada, but seldom come to light until a company collapses. As an investor, you must look yourself for the early warning signs of approaching trouble. Auditors won't do it for you. If the additional time and effort seem excessive, investors need to remind themselves of the number of companies that have collapsed in recent years because of flawed or faked financial reporting.

In conducting your investigation of a company's numbers, you should look for build-ups of receivables, compare receivables to revenue, and look for transfers out of receivables to non-current assets, which happen when a company accepts payment for outstanding receivables in shares of a customer's company instead of cash. Bankers can usually catch this type of scheme more readily than investors, because bankers usually have access to receivables listings as part of their lending agreements. But as an ordinary investor, you can still find this information on a company's balance sheet and cash-flow statements, although you may need to examine financial statements over several quarters to notice that receivables are out of line with revenue and cash collections.

Sales to a few companies with bad credit ratings usually require collusion between a company's credit manager, salesperson, and vice-president of finance to maintain the cover-up. Often, the salesperson shares the commission on the worthless sale with the credit manager and vice-president of finance. When the customer does not pay the invoice, the company may have to issue a credit note to prolong the fake revenue. A sequence of invoice, credit note, reinvoice, and new credit note sometimes occurs. Eventually, the company may turn the uncollectible receivable into an investment in the deadbeat customer. Otherwise, it would have to record the bad debt as an expense. The investment, in turn, may sit on the company's balance sheet for a few years, before the company writes it off. By then, many of the players will have switched positions, left the company or, unfortunately, been promoted.

Companies can also record fake sales by renting warehouses and shipping to the supposed wholesalers who operate them. These wholesalers are usually friends of the corporate executives who contract the fake sales.

None of these scams will end after Canada adopts IFRS. In fact, international accounting standards pay far too little attention to inappropriate recording of revenue when the payment is not assured. If auditors ignore such blatant scams, investors have to protect themselves.

It sometimes seems as if shady management has a limitless variety of tricks available to distort revenue figures. Some companies record revenue on their books long before they can realistically expect to receive the money. They can do this by:

1. *Recording revenue when they receive an order instead of much later, when they ship the goods or provide the service to the customer.* Since they don't receive the cash until well after the shipment date, these companies experience a long and potentially crippling delay between recording of the revenue and the receipt of cash required to operate the business.
2. *Immediately recording 100% of eventual revenue that might be received on a long-term contract.* A contract might call for shipments every 60 days, for example, over the next fifteen to eighteen months. The company may manufacture the goods over the next 60 days, but then store and insure them for the customer until shipment. By varying deposits on account, and manipulating the timing of shipments, companies can circumvent IFRS accounting rules.
3. *Offering discounts to boost sales for 30 or 60 days in order to meet a year-end sales quota or to pump up sales revenue before selling a company.* This is called filling the pipeline or stuffing the channel.

   A manufacturer may offer a 20% discount to dealers if they buy extra volume in November and December, rather than January to March of the following year when they usually make such purchases. By recording the sales in the current year, the executives get their bonus for meeting sales targets, or the company attracts a higher price from a purchaser.

   Unfortunately for investors, the company's sales next year will likely drop, when the dealers get overstocked and reduce subsequent purchases. Profits drop, possibly along with the company's stock price. IFRS does little or nothing to discourage these age-old scams of discounts and incentive schemes.
4. *Recording inventories at net realizable or cash value (NRV).* NRV represents the selling price minus the cost of the sale, such as delivery charges and commissions paid to sales personnel. By adopting NRV for inventories, companies recognize revenue immediately when the product becomes available, even though the sale may not occur for months, and the company may not receive payment for 60 days after delivery. The discrepancy between the recording of profit and the actual receipt of cash can create problems.

5. *Recording securities at market value.* As market values fluctuate, a company has to record gains and losses. Investors have to pin down these gains and losses in a company's financial reports, along with revenue from disposing of securities. Otherwise, investors may confuse actual revenue with changes reported in market value.
6. *Boosting sales revenue by including unusual transactions, such as the disposal of excess equipment or parts that were not intended for sale.* Revenues recorded from the sale of airplanes by an airline are different than revenues recorded from the sale of tickets to customers. But investors might confuse such a one-time event with an increase in sales. Companies may play this trick in other ways, by recording income from the cancellation of a currency hedge or other financial instrument, for example, generating income that is only remotely related to operating revenue.

Junior auditors tend to be unfamiliar with the difference between goods for resale, which constitutes a company's inventory, and spare parts for equipment repairs, which are long-term assets. Not only could a company record both items as inventory for resale, but it could also report sales of parts, or even transfers to a sister company, as sales revenue.

By faking sales revenue, a company may also distort its gross profit, calculated by subtracting the cost of goods sold from sales revenue. Investors should watch for changes in gross profit percentages and find out why they might vary from period to period.

The tricks don't end there. Some additional revenue games include:

1. *Sellers offering rebates for volume purchases over a one-year span.* Companies should estimate probable cash or other rebates that they will have to make each quarter and adjust their revenues accordingly. Yet some companies don't. Instead, they may wait to reduce revenue until a customer meets a specified volume target, even though the same customer has exceeded the target every year for a decade or more.
2. *Overcharging on shipments to a selected customer, then paying rebates directly to specified employees of the customer in the form of paid vacations, sports trips, or fancy dinners.* The company records the overstated

sales as revenue, but buries the rebates elsewhere on the income statement, which inflates the company's gross profit.

The situation gets trickier when a portion of the rebate is kicked back to an executive of the selling company. However, investors are unlikely to learn about such kickbacks until it is too late.

3. *Recording interest revenue that the company will likely never collect from a borrower who is close to bankruptcy.* This is a frequent problem in finance companies and banks.

4. *Loading essentially uncollectible fees for renegotiating loans.* This is a common problem among financial institutions. Lenders may extend the terms of loans, reduce monthly payments, lower interest rates, and so forth, but the lender will likely never receive the principal or interest. The added-on fees are neither revenue nor receivables, but cover-ups. Profits are being faked.

5. *Percentage-of-completion accounting.* At best, this is a can of worms. Under percentage-of-completion rules, a company can record percentages of revenue and costs each month based on the percentage that it has completed to date of a longer-term project.

Companies can manipulate and distort their calculations of the percentage-of-completion. If a company anticipates a loss on a contract, for example, logic requires that it would record 100% of the loss as soon as it becomes apparent. But companies often use percentage-of-completion accounting to postpone that inevitability.

Ideally, accounting rules would prevent early revenue recognition and overstatement of revenue using percentage-of-completion accounting. But IFRS encourages such manipulation through the elimination of what is known as completed contract accounting, whereby all revenue and costs are known, including whether a profit or loss was realized. Investors must read financial statement notes carefully to see how a company has used percentage-of-completion.

6. *Recording dividends on shares in another company as revenue.* This often causes two problems. First, if the company is not an investment firm, the dividend should be categorized as other income. Second, the dividend might be getting recorded prematurely, which should be done only when the company has a legal right to receive the dividend, not before. But some companies record a dividend in

one year, even though it is not approved by the paying company's board until the next year. The receiving company enhances its revenue in the current year, but the paying company makes no equivalent subtraction of equity until the next year. Such mismatches over company year-ends can be troublesome when related companies are involved.

Some companies use several tricks at the same time, combining revenue manipulations with understating the cost of earning that revenue.

A forest products company may be involved in logging, producing lumber, making forms of wallboard, cutting up wood for pulp chips, and similar activities. Because it owns the land, the company may harvest trees that have little or no cost because they were already on the property, grew naturally, or were planted decades earlier at negligible cost.

Under such circumstances, a company may fiddle with profits by assigning low costs to the products it sells. Basically, high revenue minus reduced cost equals enhanced profit. When the company has to account later for the higher costs for logging and processing, it can attach these costs to lower-quality products that remain in inventory over the company's year-end. After all, how can anyone apportion the total cost of a log between different lengths, widths, and quality of lumber?

In other instances, an expanding company may produce specialized machinery for internal and external sale on a cost-plus basis. That means the customer pays all costs incurred by the manufacturer in developing the machinery along with the manufacturer's mark-up. Not surprisingly, the manufacturer assumes little cost for making machinery for its new plant while passing along most of the costs to the external customer. Even if such a scam blows up when the external customer discovers the deception, investors might already have been fooled by the manufacturer's inflated profits.

A number of these revenue and related-cost manipulations have occurred over the years in Canada. Often, they remain undiscovered until some other scam comes to light.

In our experience as forensic accountants, revenue enhancement games often tell us much about the ethics of corporate management. We are not saying that other common tricks, such as non-arm's-length transactions or acquisitions of other companies, can be ignored, but deception often starts with revenue recognition. Knowing the different sources of revenue in a company in which you have invested, you can spot trends and determine the revenue sources that are profitable and the ones that are not. You may find it helpful to look at financial statement notes dealing with segmented profits.

Unscrupulous management teams try to cover up their previous bad decisions. They may try to make an unprofitable product line look better, for example, by shifting more revenue and less cost to the losing line. In some instances, they may sell packages of products to cover up the inferiority of one of them. A tour packager may sell a holiday package that includes airfare, parking at the airport, ground transportation, hotel accommodation, airport transfers at your destination, tickets for side-trips, and entertainment. Profitability and revenue recognition then becomes exceedingly difficult to unravel. You may find clues by reading the notes to the financial statements. Even skimpy revenue notes can enable you to assess management integrity and its commitment to transparency.

Analyzing sales revenue by quarter is also a useful exercise. You should look for seasonality in a business by examining trends over five to eight quarters within accounts receivable, inventory, accounts payable, sales revenues, and operating expenses. If dollar amounts or percentage increases in one category seem out of line with the others, you should proceed with caution. You should also compare period-end accounts receivable with the latest quarter's sales and look for increases and decreases in accounts payable and current liabilities.

While investors concentrate on these exercises, they will receive little or no help from a company's accountants or auditors. The organizations throughout the world that set the rules for accounting all acknowledge that they need to reduce the susceptibility of revenue figures to manipulation. They might move forward over the next few years, but we doubt they will plug many of the holes in the current rules, especially those that have been reopened under IFRS.

Once again, investors are on their own.

CHAPTER EIGHT

# Ponzis in High Places

*"Finance is the art of passing money from hand to hand until it finally disappears."*

ROBERT SARNOFF

**IN DECEMBER** 2007, the attorney-general for Iowa issued a warning to Canadian and US investors regarding a potential Ponzi scheme operating from Waterloo, Ontario. A Canadian Ponzi scheme was nothing unique, nor was the fact that a US law enforcement agency had lifted the veil on an alleged Canadian scam. But this particular Ponzi scheme came with a twist. It had nothing to do with investments in debt or equity markets. This one involved birds.

Through Pigeon King International, investors bought breeding pairs of pigeons. Once the pigeons mated and started to breed, Pigeon King said it would buy back all the offspring.

The founder of Pigeon King, Arlan Galbraith, claimed that bird flu had the potential to "destroy the chicken industry." Pigeons, he said, were practically immune from the disease. As the avian Armageddon decimated North America's supply of chickens, squab would replace them on the dinner plates of the continent.

The company sold pigeons for as much as $500 a pair and bought back their offspring for as much as $50 apiece. Figuring a bird in the hand was worth nine dead chickens in the ground, more than 1,000 farmers in twelve states and four provinces invested in the scheme. Three Hutterite colonies in Alberta invested more than $1 million apiece. Others invested as much as $100,000. Some farmers bought 900 pairs of pigeons, figuring they'd earn back their investment in three or four years.

The State of Iowa was the first jurisdiction to issue a warning and halt sales by Pigeon King. South Dakota, Maryland, and Washington issued similar warnings. Rather than selling the birds into the food market, they said Pigeon King was merely selling the offspring to new investors as breeding pairs. Pigeon King, according to these authorities, was allegedly operating a Ponzi scheme, paying a return to investors not from revenues generated by the operation, but from the proceeds from capital raised from new investors. Canadian authorities, in the meantime, did nothing. They maintained to the end that Pigeon King was doing nothing wrong.

Even if Canadian authorities don't recognize a Ponzi scheme when it flies by their window, they're not hard to spot. Named for Charles Ponzi, an Italian who immigrated to Boston in 1903, a Ponzi scheme basically involves paying a return to investors with money raised from new investors. A bank may offer a high rate of interest on deposits, for example, then make the interest payments with funds taken from new deposits rather than money earned on the initial deposits. Ponzi himself offered to double the money in 90 days of people who invested in a scheme to convert international reply coupons into more expensive US postage stamps, funding the investors' payments with the difference. He paid off a few initial investors, but when he couldn't exchange more coupons into US postage, he started paying the initial investors with new investors' money.

Living in the US, Ponzi was charged and imprisoned for his crimes. If he'd lived in Canada, who knows what might have happened? Most likely, nothing. After all, Canadians lost money on several business income trusts during the 2000s, and few of them realize how closely they mirrored a Ponzi scheme.

Lawmakers, securities regulators, auditors, and the news media all remained silent about the pyramid-like nature, precarious foundations, and unavoidable collapse of many BITs. No government or regulatory agency ever investigated the seriously misleading sales practices that prompted investors to buy into numerous low-quality BITs. Most observers and media accounts blamed their eventual collapse solely on a change in tax policy. As a result, no one learned any lessons from the fiasco, and investors remain vulnerable to future Ponzi-like investment schemes.

Ponzi schemes work because they lull investors into thinking they're getting more for their money than they could get anywhere else. For a few years, they receive a payment that seems too good to be true. It's not hard for a good swindler to do this. Saying that he'll give you a 15% return on your money, he'll ask for $10,000, but he won't steal the $10,000 as soon as you give it to him. Rather, he'll do exactly as he says: he'll send you a cheque for $1,500, every year. You think you're getting a 15% return on your investment, year after year, when in fact the swindler is simply sending you a portion of your initial investment. He can do this for six years and still send you only $9,000 of your initial $10,000 investment. In the meantime, though, you've told a few of your friends about the apparent 15% annual return, and the Ponzi trickster builds his empire. Fools do indeed rush in.

Swindlers use all sorts of stories to explain how an investment can generate such a high return. One scam artist said his company bought excess inventory for scrap value, then shipped it across the country for sale at higher regular prices. Another said that patents protected a company from competition, allowing it to generate huge profits.

What investors seldom ask is: Why me? Why has this seemingly unique, foolproof, and abundantly lucrative investment opportunity fallen into my lap? Most opportunities for outsized profits last for only a short time. If a scheme generates high returns for years, investors should ask questions. Why haven't millions of other people discovered it and bought in? What has prevented its duplication? How can profits remain so high, year after year?

To combat such skepticism, some swindlers set up waiting lists, delaying investors from putting money into their schemes for six months or more. Chomping at the bit, investors can hardly wait to toss their money away in case the opportunity passes them by. Once they make the investment, they feel reluctant to take their money out, because they were so lucky to be included in the first place. When the cheques start coming, as promised, they feel as if they've died and gone to heaven. And, of course, they start telling their friends—but only their good ones. Satisfied customers become non-paid sales personnel for the Ponzi scheme, unaware that they are guiding their associates down the path to financial disaster.

Ponzi artists often target people who share some common affiliation: executives of seniors' clubs, participants in religious groups, organizers of cooking classes, members of high-priced golf clubs. Many low-quality BITs were promoted by brokers hyping fake cash-yield figures. Often, it was difficult to tell which brokers knew that they were deliberately misleading their clients and which were just plain gullible.

Rogue money managers aren't the only ones in Canada promoting Ponzi frauds. Several Canadian corporations, when analyzed carefully, reveal themselves as little more than pyramid schemes, at least in part. They usually emerge when economic conditions start to deteriorate. New cash ends up chasing bad businesses, or paying out unsustainable dividends or distributions. All the while, executives take unwarranted salaries and bonuses. They report phony profits, equivalent to the fake returns of a classic Ponzi scheme, through manipulations in accounting. Sometimes they achieve their inflated returns by reporting a performance metric that falls beyond Generally Accepted Accounting Principles, such as cash operating earnings. These terms mean next to nothing, but they sound convincing to potential investors.

Investors concerned about Ponzis within corporations should first determine what happens with funds newly borrowed or raised by the firm. If the company uses new cash to pay interest expenses, executive compensation, dividends, or liabilities arising from daily corporate operations, you should proceed with caution. Circled cash, whereby a company uses the proceeds from a debt or equity issue to fund unsuccessful daily operations, also raises concern. As we've mentioned before, you should compare a company's previous quarterly and annual results to identify key trends. The company may be a losing proposition that has to keep borrowing to keep itself afloat. When it has pledged all worthwhile assets as collateral to creditors, bankruptcy could be next. Following the money is critical.

Unfortunately, most companies leave their options open these days when raising funds by stating in the prospectus that they may use the cash for "general corporate purposes." However, some may tell investors that they intend to apply the funds specifically to an expansion or acquisition, or to buy back debt. If the company is expanding by adding new products that generate cash, then investors can feel more assured. But when companies use newly received cash to pay for non-cash-generating product lines, investors need to look further. You have to weigh promises of "investing for the future" against the possibility that executives are simply trying to justify their existence or build a mini-empire. But feeding an unsuccessful business is foolhardy. Companies need additional profits to prevent themselves from falling backward.

In particular, you have to scrutinize a company's cash-flow statement. Typically it will be organized under three categories: financing, investing, and operations. An unscrupulous company may cook the figures, but for the moment, let's suppose they're legitimate.

The operations section of a cash-flow statement is crucial. If overall operations consume rather than generate cash, then daily cash operating expenses will likely exceed daily cash sales. A company has to offset negative cash from operations by using excess cash, borrowing funds, or selling equity. These will appear in the cash-flow statement under financing activities. Alternatively, the company may sell land, buildings, equipment, or other assets. These transactions will appear in the cash-flow statement under investing activities. Regardless of whether they appear as financing or investment activities in the cash-flow statement, you should regard such transactions as indicators of a potentially sinking ship.

During harsh economic times, companies may experience negative cash flow from operations for a year or two. But even over a shorter period, you should still watch the company's cash results carefully, quarter by quarter. The company could easily squander newly acquired cash on executive bonuses or bad operational choices, while using sneaky accounting to cover up the fact.

Such cover-ups represent a form of Ponzi scheme. The company is using false profits to entice creditors and investors into providing more cash. The tip-off for investors appears on the cash-flow statement, where a company has to reveal how it reconciles a declared profit with negative cash flow from operations. For example, the profit could have arisen from the sale of land and buildings. The profit, audited or otherwise, comes not from the company's regular sales or service operations, but rather from the liquidation of a portion of the business. To continue operations, the company has to rent land and buildings, which cannot be sold a second time to generate a fake profit next year.

Some corporate Ponzis can remain in place for several years, assisted by lax accounting and auditing rules. Not only has Canada failed to adopt accounting and auditing rules that reflect the increasing complexity of its businesses, but new accounting rules under IFRS will allow even more leeway for Ponzi fraudsters to con investors and devise cover-ups for their scams.

A potential Ponzi scheme exists, for example, whenever a company can inflate its income, even temporarily. A company may employ flimsy reporting rules that suppress pension expenses and lower its offsetting pension liability. The artificially reduced expense effectively increases the company's profit before income tax. In turn, executives may receive an increased bonus based on a percentage of the artificially reduced pension expense. The bonuses get paid in cash, which means that the cash is not available to earn future income and cash. The net increase in reported profits can con investors into unfairly bidding up the company's stock. Now the company issues more stock at its inflated price. With the added cash from the stock sale, the company continues its Ponzi scheme, distributing dividends to shareholders based on fake profits.

Strong accounting hampers the use of corporate Ponzi scams. Under tough rules for measuring and reporting income, bogus inflated profits get revealed, and Ponzi tricksters cannot so easily cover up their cash thefts from a company.

In Canada, weak accounting, auditing, and financial reporting rules contribute to the success of corporate Ponzi schemes. So do passive provincial securities commissions and silent auditors. Indeed, lawmakers might want to ask securities regulators and auditors to explain their role in society, just in case they have totally forgotten. In the meantime, Canada desperately needs revisions to companies and securities legislation.

Until we get them, investors have to search for Ponzis themselves, especially the ones that lurk within corporations and that occurred with several business income trusts. Following the cash is key.

Ponzis will not go away. They are far too lucrative for financial swindlers, and they will inevitably resurface again. For the perpetrators, Ponzis are perpetual theft machines. Swindlers can carry out their schemes many times over, on successive generations of Canadians. And who can blame them? Apart from a clear conscience and a sense of honour, they have nothing to lose under Canada's negligible enforcement of laughable rules against such scams.

CHAPTER NINE

# The Wilting Crocus

*"How could I have been so mistaken as to have trusted the experts?"*

JOHN F. KENNEDY

CROCUS INVESTMENT Fund had been set up in Manitoba in 1992 as a labour-sponsored venture capital fund. Like similar funds sponsored by labour unions in Canada, Crocus attracted money by providing shareholders with generous federal and provincial government tax breaks. By sheltering their investment in a registered retirement account, investors could supposedly balance the risk involved with the benefit of a tax-based discount. As part of the deal, Crocus shareholders had to hold their units for a mandatory period of seven or eight years.

On December 10, 2004, the apparent value of a share in Crocus was $10.45. That represented an increase of less than 5% in total over the first twelve years of the fund's existence. Without the tax breaks, investors didn't gain much by putting their money into the fund. Nevertheless, almost 34,000 Manitobans eventually invested in the fund, which had a reported net asset value of $154 million. Then they heard the bad news: trading in Crocus shares was halted so that the board could conduct a "comprehensive assessment of the value of its portfolio, precipitated by underperformance of the Fund and in light of new developments with key holdings in the portfolio." No one suspected what would happen next.

Like all labour-sponsored funds, Crocus focused on investing in small or medium-sized businesses that needed investment capital to grow. Among the investments in its portfolio, Crocus had extended money to more than fifty companies, including Wellington West Capital, a brokerage that would eventually be sued by Crocus shareholders for promoting the fund to its clients as an investment.

According to Crocus managers, shareholders could depend on them to do their homework before investing shareholders' money. Almost two years before Crocus shares stopped trading, a manager named Kelvin Maloney said, "We meet the company's auditors, we meet with their bankers, and we talk to their customers as well as their suppliers. We certainly do some due diligence in terms of the people we're going to be partnered with in terms of their background and the things they've done leading up to our investment. They'll often offer clues if something's not on the up and up."

About six weeks after the trading halt, investors learned that 88% of Crocus's portfolio had been revalued by outside parties and that overall asset value would decline by "a material amount." But with everything apparently still "on the up and up," the company assured investors that their shares would resume trading once the valuation was complete. Another ten weeks after that, the board announced that Crocus shares had fallen to less than $7. They'd lost one-third of their value since the last reported price. Two months after that, investors learned that Crocus shares would never resume trading. Instead, the fund's assets would have to be liquidated.

In 2009, almost five years after the fund's collapse, shareholders began to receive a small amount of their money back from the liquidation. The "up and up" had become a complete and utter downer.

It could have been worse. Compared to many other Canadian investment horror stories, Crocus ended more fairly than usual for investors. Shortly after Crocus was taken over by trustees, Manitoba legislators used their considerable power to seek answers to what happened. (In the US, this happens regularly. In Canada, it doesn't.) In May 2005, Manitoba's auditor general, Jon W. Singleton, issued a stinging 245-page report. Crocus, he said, "did not have in place the necessary leadership, the necessary structure, the necessary culture, and the necessary processes to handle the planning, growth, and monitoring of the investment portfolio."

Of the many lessons learned from Crocus, one of the most noteworthy is the way in which the fund's managers reported the value of its shares to unit holders. Essentially, shareholders received several pages of audited nonsense each year. Finally, aware of how they'd been bamboozled, unit holders initiated a class-action lawsuit. They sued all parties allegedly responsible for their losses: directors of Crocus, its officers, its auditors, the brokerages that promoted Crocus, the Manitoba Securities Commission, and the Manitoba government itself. Despite their objections, the Manitoba court allowed the trial to proceed. The lawsuit was eventually settled out of court. Although terms were not fully disclosed, several of the defendants contributed to the settlement fund.

Crocus had been designed as an open-ended mutual fund. Unlike shares in a public company that trade through a stock exchange between an individual buyer and an individual seller, units in Crocus were traded between the individual investor and the fund itself. Selling shares directly, at questionable unit prices, Crocus should have set off alarm bells with regulators and lawmakers.

There was more cause for alarm. A typical open-ended mutual fund invests primarily in securities with daily quoted market values, such as shares and bonds of other companies. Crocus invested heavily in illiquid, private companies. Such shares are difficult to sell, and are more than difficult to value. As well, the timing of possible sales of these private-company shares is often uncertain. Holding illiquid assets with a value that no one could guess, and without proper oversight, Crocus was a disaster waiting to happen.

For twelve years, Manitobans had remained oblivious to the danger. They bought and redeemed Crocus units based not on a market value established by individual buyers and sellers, but on prices chosen arbitrarily by Crocus management. Management, in turn, picked the private companies in which Crocus would invest unit holders' money. If management made investment mistakes, they had an easy time covering them up. They just placed a high value on a losing company, whether or not the value was justified. No one seemed to notice. The results fooled most of the people, most of the time.

Eventually, Crocus management placed valuations on private company investments that covered up all kinds of losses. How they determined those values was a mystery. How, for example, could management value a private company that was just starting up, and that might go bankrupt just as easily as it could succeed? How did management measure such a company's success? Did it have to make annual profits and distribute dividends? Did it have to be sold so that unit holders could get some cash back? Did the private company have to go public? Crocus needed a clear plan for each of its investments. Without such a plan, each investment could simply stagnate.

After several years, only a series of huge investment successes would have allowed Crocus to survive. When those didn't occur, the fund faced liquidity problems and cash shortages. Unable to sell the private-company investments, it sputtered to a halt.

Regulators, auditors, and promoters should have seen it coming. Management of Crocus not only chose the companies in which the fund invested, they also placed a value on these investments. Nothing is wrong with such an arrangement if all investors put their money into the fund when it commences and draw it out only when the fund winds up ten or twelve years later. But Crocus was set up differently; it was traded actively.

Investors in Crocus had to hold their shares for seven or eight years. After that, trading in Crocus units occurred monthly, and then weekly, as original investors sold and new investors bought units at prices determined by management's pie-in-the-sky estimates of their value. How the provincial securities commission ever approved this arrangement is still a mystery.

The values placed by management on the fund's investments not only affected the price at which investors bought units, it also affected the price at which unit holders redeemed their shares after the compulsory holding period. In some cases, a high price set by management delivered an unwarranted windfall to a redeeming unit holder. Excessive payments to redeeming unit holders sucked money out of the fund and reduced its ultimate liquidation value for investors who chose not to sell their units. If those investors had known that management's valuations were not being double- or triple-checked, they would (or should) have run for the exits.

Crocus did not even demand regular financial updates from the many private companies in which it held positions. By their nature, private companies have more urgent priorities than preparing frequent financial reports, and Crocus allowed them to go for a year or more before requesting reliable financial information. Even after management received such information, it could make only educated guesses in valuing its investments.

Despite the obvious red flags, the Manitoba Securities Commission, the auditors, the business valuators, the promoters, the managers, and the directors of Crocus did nothing. The agencies and individuals charged with helping investors to avoid needless losses allowed Crocus unit holders to remain seriously exposed.

To make matters worse, Crocus appeared to have attracted a $10-million injection of equity financing. The fund issued a press release in December 2002 that said, "Crocus attracts $10 million institutional investment." Sherman Kreiner, the president and CEO of Crocus said, "This is a strong endorsement of the Crocus management team and the Crocus Fund's investment portfolio." The fund's audited financial statements confirmed that Crocus had sold new shares, injecting more long-term equity into the business. In fact, the fund had simply borrowed $10 million, repayable at a high rate of interest within a few years.

Crocus management also failed to diversify the fund's investments. Instead, the fund made multiple investments in the same groups of people. Rather than placing a restriction on the number of highly speculative investments made by the fund, it kept pouring money into them. Instead of requiring frequent board-level reviews of portfolio risk to safeguard investors, the Crocus board let it happen.

In the last few years of Crocus's existence, it made practically no new investments at all. Management used funds received from selling new shares to cover operating expenses, pay out unit holders who redeemed their units, and provide more money to keep older, weak investments alive. Regulators should have noticed the stagnation of investments. Crocus's auditors and board of directors should have paid attention. Beyond the allegations of extensive negligence raised in the unit holders' lawsuit, no one knows exactly what happened, and without a court trial or judicial inquiry, we will never know.

We do know that shareholders should never have relied on Crocus's audited financial statements to make investment decisions. Without mentioning overvalued investments, inadequate write-downs, possible related-party transactions, and confusion over the exact nature of the $10-million injection of equity (or debt, or whatever it was), the audited statements weren't worth the paper they were written on, at least to the people who invested in the fund. Without a trial or inquiry, we can't say what evidence the auditors saw, did not see, or should have seen before they signed Crocus's audit reports and consent letters for the Manitoba Securities Commission. Nor do we know what the auditors told Crocus's board of directors. But at the very least, auditors and the board should have known the up-to-date resale values of each of Crocus's investments.

Equally troubling was the role of the unions and government employees in the sale of Crocus units each year, and especially during RRSP season in January and February. According to allegations by some investors, Crocus appeared to operate with the full support of the provincial government, and shareholders stated that they bought their units because they believed them to be safe.

One thing is clear, confined to a specific region of the country, Crocus operated in an all-too-cozy environment. Too little research was conducted into the operations of the fund, and too much reliance was placed on gossip or recommendations from friends. Dissenters were generally accused of being non-believers instead of receiving the attention they deserved.

Sadly, we can offer other observations to guide shareholders in Canada. First, you cannot place your faith in securities commissions or auditors to protect your savings. Audited financial statements too often can be meaningless or misleading. Crocus is but one example. Second, too many boards of directors do not provide necessary oversight, and they do not act promptly to correct growing problems. Under Canadian law, boards can usually walk away from many liability cases. Finally, little has happened in Canada to prevent another Crocus from happening. Information that is crucial for investment decisions is still not being provided to Canadian investors. Under the influence of corporate and auditor lobby groups, investors' rights in Canada are being eroded instead of strengthened. And more than seventy-five years after the US took action, Canada still does not have a national securities overseer similar to the SEC.

In short, investors have to protect themselves. You have no other choice.

CHAPTER TEN

# Canada's Securities Commissions: All Talk, No Action

*"There is no greater fraud than a promise not kept."*
                                                    GAELIC PROVERB

**FOR INVESTORS** who wanted to see Canadian securities regulators finally clamp down on rampant accounting fraud, 1999 seemed like a year full of promise. The recently installed chair of the Ontario Securities Commission (OSC), David Brown, was stumping around the country, making promises aplenty.

In June he gave a hopeful speech to the Institute of Chartered Accountants of Ontario, noting that companies and their auditors "stretch the interpretation of accounting standards beyond all reasonable limits. In many cases, the reasoning to support positions is weak or nonexistent. In other cases, it is clear that conclusions are based on narrow interpretations of a few words in a standard without regard to their broader context. Too often, we see an approach that treats standards like narrowly written rules rather than broad principles requiring the exercise of sound professional judgment in their application."

Having seemingly fired a shot over the auditors' bow, he followed up by warning investors in a September speech to the Investment Counsel Association of Canada that "too frequently, it seems that Generally Accepted Accounting Principles have become very elastic."

At the time, it seemed as if the OSC was finally formulating a sensible and determined response to white-collar crime, largely in reaction to two very high-profile scandals the previous year. Livent, the live theatre company run by Garth Drabinsky and Myron Gottlieb, had collapsed under the spectre of accounting fraud in 1998. The co-founders were indicted in New York on charges of conspiracy and securities fraud. However, after the pair failed to appear in court and were placed under fugitive arrest warrants, they continued to roam free in Canada, not having been charged in this country with anything.

Likewise, in 1998, US law enforcement agencies raided the Pennsylvania headquarters of a TSX-listed company called YBM Magnex International, which turned out to be a front for Russian mafia activity headed by Semion Mogilevich. The shares of YBM were worth more than $500 million before they collapsed in value virtually overnight. The scam eventually landed Mogilevich a spot on the FBI's Ten Most Wanted list.

Thanks to scams, such as Livent and YBM, being pursued and prosecuted by US regulators, Canada's stock markets were fast becoming an international embarrassment. The markets welcomed Brown's promises of change with relief.

Those changes never came, however. In the end it was all just public-relations bunk. Viewed in retrospect, Brown's comments were all couched in a way that seemed dedicated to maintaining the status quo of securities enforcement apathy. For instance, Brown promised that the OSC would "identify creative accounting techniques that don't comply with GAAP and use our enforcement powers to have them rectified." With his reference to GAAP as the appropriate standard, however, he left the door wide open to inaction. That's because GAAP seems to accommodate several misleading financial reporting practices, especially when guidance in interpreting the loose rules comes from the large audit firms.

Likewise, Brown noted that "we are prepared to use the muscle of the commission to bring about change where change is necessary." Once again, he left the door open to taking action or not.

Despite claims that a task force had been set up to get tough on creative accounting, very few companies were ever formally brought under investigation. Likening some companies to steroid users, Brown said that the commission would have to develop "more effective screening procedures to detect sophisticated uses of performance enhancers in the form of creative accounting treatments." If this was done, it certainly was not evident in the commission's enforcement record. Since Brown made his promises of big change, you can count on one hand the number of cases that the OSC heard on the grounds of allegedly inappropriate accounting or financial reporting. Brown himself had said in 1999 that the OSC had "some fairly strong powers to override sections of the accounting principles and accounting practices. They're not instruments we've resorted to at the present time, and we're hoping we don't have to." Apparently, Brown got what he hoped for. If the OSC found that accounting rules under GAAP had fallen short of serving investors' needs, it certainly didn't do anything about it.

In the US, the Securities and Exchange Commission occasionally overrides the US Financial Accounting Standards Board (FASB). Too bad the OSC didn't do the same thing in this country. Instead, the OSC apparently relied on the advice of conflicted auditors, who have no responsibility to protect investors and have every interest in setting weak standards that protect their corporate clients.

Brown assumed the role of OSC chair at a time when Livent and YBM had clearly irked Canadian investors. He responded by making big promises that temporarily mollified the market but were ultimately never kept. Investors were probably not surprised when those assurances fell through, though. They've long become accustomed to desultory securities regulation in Canada.

Under the watch of the British Columbia Securities Commission (BCSC), the Vancouver Stock Exchange (VSE) ran roughshod over investors for decades. Dubbed by *The New York Times* as "the wild west of stock exchanges," the VSE nurtured a steady stream of stock swindles. "Canada," said *The Times*, "produces more stock fraud, at least per capita, than do other countries." *Forbes* magazine said Vancouver was simply "the scam capital of the world."

With such a dubious track record, the BCSC made an unlikely training ground for regulators. Yet early in 1999, about a year after Brown's arrival as chair, the OSC hired Michael Watson as its head of enforcement. Before he got the job, Watson had been head of enforcement at the BCSC. It was hardly an appointment to inspire confidence in investors. Watson oversaw a dismal time for enforcement in the Canadian markets. The vast majority of high-profile enforcement initiatives led nowhere or resulted in minimal fines that fell far short of a deterrent to further shady practices.

US regulators and law enforcement agencies continually showed up the OSC. Not only did they act first in prosecuting the executives behind the YBM and Livent cases, they also took the lead in seeking justice in the scams involving Hollinger and Nortel. In proportion to its jurisdiction, the SEC was no larger than the OSC, but unlike the OSC, the US organization managed to keep its own house in order, in addition to cleaning up several embarrassing Canadian messes.

As the OSC's head of enforcement, Watson seemed to think that Canada did not have a systemic problem. The country was just experiencing a temporary surge of cases that would soon pass. "You have to be careful about bulking up on staff to meet an anomaly in work," he said, "because then you're going to wind up with staff not necessarily fully utilized."

Unmotivated to pursue Canadian scam artists, the OSC proceeded to bury its head deeper into the sand. Asked why Canada lags behind the US in high-profile enforcement cases, the commission said that less enforcement was needed in Canada because we do such a superior job of prevention in the first place. "What is unseen," said Lawrence Ritchie, an OSC vice-chair, "are the cases that have been prevented. Cases where it's not necessary to proceed with enforcement proceedings, because the decision is made that public markets have been adequately protected."

A more reasonable explanation for Canada's sterling record of securities offences is that the commission can't prosecute offenders if it never bothers to look for them. The OSC seemed content to sit back and see "if something big falls out of the sky," to use the words of enforcement chief Watson.

With Brown and Watson in control, the commission's poor enforcement record expanded. It failed almost completely to investigate accounting chicanery and met with a string of high-profile failures in prosecuting cases of insider trading.

One of the highest-profile cases involved a former investment banker with RBC Dominion Securities named Andrew Rankin. Rankin was found guilty in July 2005 of providing stock tips to his friend, Daniel Duic, using insider information and was sentenced to six months in jail. To obtain the conviction, the OSC allowed Duic to keep more than half of his ill-gotten gains in return for his testimony against Rankin. The OSC had hardly started to gloat in triumph before the courts overturned Rankin's conviction and criticized the OSC's tactics in the case. Eventually, the commission settled the case with its tail between its legs, prying from Rankin merely the costs of the investigation and a ten-year ban on trading in Ontario. The penalty didn't amount to much, since, by then, Rankin had left the industry and moved to California.

In the same year as the Rankin fiasco began its arduous path through the legal system, the OSC's own commissioners dismissed insider-trading charges against the former chairman of ATI Technologies, K.Y. Ho, and his wife. The OSC had pursued the case for five years, but the commissioners did not think it had a sufficient case to make the charges stick.

The OSC had also pursued a case against another well-known Canadian executive, Michael Cowpland, founder of Corel. The commission settled with Cowpland after six years, and he ended up paying little more than what the OSC claimed he'd made on insider trades in the first place.

After such embarrassments as these, the OSC now seems to prefer silence to launching public investigations. If it enforces the rules at all, it calls closed-door meetings with offending companies and requests politely that they correct the problem. If there are lessons to be learned from these exercises, the public never hears about them. Meanwhile, such kid-glove treatment practically guarantees that companies will continue to push the regulatory envelope.

Without public prosecutions to alert the market to clean up its act, the OSC remains wholly unprepared and unable to react to broad-based market problems. When many companies at once step over the bounds of acceptable market behaviour, the OSC could correct the problem by making an example of the few, knowing that the rest of the market will take notice. When it fails to act, the commission merely encourages unacceptable behaviour from other companies. As we'll discuss later, the pro-forma financial reporting of Nortel, and the reporting of distributable cash by business income trusts, would never have become such acute problems if the OSC had acted promptly and publicly. If the OSC had made an example of a few companies at the outset, it would have saved investors from a world of hurt.

Time and again, the OSC stands back while authorities in other jurisdictions expose the questionable behaviour of Canadian companies. It happened again in 2006, when US authorities investigated more than 130 companies, including Apple and Dell, for the backdating of stock options awarded to their executives. By backdating the options, directors ensured that executives could purchase shares in their companies at a lower price than the current market value. If the practice of backdating wasn't illegal, it certainly lacked integrity. Not only did it confer on executives an immediate paper gain, it also enabled the companies involved to boost their income for accounting purposes by reducing the total cost of the options.

In the US, the crackdown resulted in the dismissal of more than fifty executives and directors. In Canada, the OSC found good evidence that at least thirty-five other Canadian companies had likely engaged in the practice. But the commission charged only one company, Research In Motion (RIM), and you can bet it acted only because RIM had a dual stock listing on the TSX and the NASDAQ, prompting the involvement of the SEC.

Even when the OSC does issue a public fine, it usually amounts to a slap on the wrist for the company involved. In the US, the SEC fined Nortel $35 million as punishment for restating its financial statements four times. In Canada, the OSC imposed no fine against Nortel at all. It merely made the company contribute to the costs of its investigation. Instead of seeking jail terms for white-collar criminals, authorities in Canada impose inadequate fines that most companies regard as a cost of doing business. "The attitude in Canada," explained Michael Watson, "is that there is a lot more room for compassion and understanding and rehabilitation."

And a lot more room for fraud, as well.

The OSC's lack of interest in accounting issues, its unwillingness to make examples out of companies in order to correct broad market misbehaviour, and its refusal to get tough on white-collar crime, will place investors in even greater jeopardy when Canada adopts IFRS. While a national securities regulator in the US imposes heavy fines against companies that defy the rules, Canada relies on provincial securities commissions to enforce the rules. Unfortunately, securities officials in other provinces act with no more determination or effectiveness than the OSC.

The US formed its national securities regulator in 1934. For the rest of the century, and well into this one, Canada has continued to dither, while provincial regulators allow companies to get away with financial murder. Even as plans proceed to form a national securities regulator, the initiative will likely fall seriously short of the country's needs, especially in comparison to the SEC and its counterparts in other countries.

As if we wanted to shoot ourselves in the collective foot, Canada handed the mandate to form a national securities regulator to the man, Doug Hyndman, who had headed the BCSC for two decades. When Hyndman was in charge of securities regulation in the province, the VSE became notorious throughout the world for swindles, frauds, and penny-stock shenanigans. To make matters worse, Hyndman had argued for years against a national regulator in Canada. "Contrary to the claims of many single-regulator proponents," he said, mere months before he took up his new post, "we have a good system of securities regulation in Canada."

With Hyndman in charge, Canada will likely end up with a national securities regulator that focuses not so much on enforcement as on reducing the filing and registration costs associated with maintaining a publicly listed company. Regulation, like accounting under IFRS, will depend on the honesty of companies and their executives to abide by a set of loosely interpreted principles. In the UK, a similar principles-based regulatory environment failed, so there is no reason to think that it will succeed in this country.

Virtually no enforcement action has been taken on the financial reporting front in Canada for well over a decade, even as the situation has grown progressively worse for investors. It will not likely become any better under a national securities regulator either. As far as investors are concerned, the fox remains firmly in charge of the henhouse. (Read Appendix J for more.)

CHAPTER ELEVEN

# See No Evil, Hear No Evil, Speak No Evil

*"It is rascally to steal a purse, daring to steal a million, and a proof of greatness to steal a crown. The blame diminishes as the guilt increases."*
                                    JOHANN FRIEDRICH VON SCHILLER

**THE INADEQUATE** disclosure of executive compensation is one glaring example, among many, in which shareholders have been served badly by securities regulators in Canada. Executives can drain cash out of a public company year after year, sometimes without even drawing attention from the company's board. Companies may report annually to shareholders on executive salaries, bonuses, stock options, and similar share-based compensation, but executives can fill their pockets in other ways, as well, and investors never hear about it. Needless to say, a company's auditors completely disavow any responsibility for monitoring executive greed.

In addition to collecting excessive salaries and bonuses, executives may obtain compensation from their companies in the form of interest-free loans, often for spurious reasons: generous expense accounts; payments to family members in return for doing little of benefit to the company; paid vacations disguised as business trips;

free accommodation for family members; company-paid weddings, clothing, and car allowances; paid memberships to clubs that are fundamentally for personal use; and access to company-owned aircraft for personal trips.

In one of the most popular and lucrative schemes for sucking money out of a public company, executives set up their own companies that operate in parallel to the public operation. These parallel companies deal in the same products and services as the public company. Executives sell these goods and services to the public company at prices inflated well above fair market value. Then the executives report to the public company's directors that the goods are being transferred at cost, leading the board to believe that the executive company does not profit on the deal. The board is also led to believe that the deal is one of the best possible. The problem is that the executive's company determines the cost of the goods, and it can include all kinds of phony add-ons, such as overhead salaries for relatives, or for executives themselves.

Accounting rules, as set by the auditors, do not require the reporting of such transactions at fair market value, so shareholders in the public company never know they are being taken advantage of. Instead, the auditors claim that directors should catch these scams, and they typically refer to such accounting loopholes as "governance issues." Unfortunately, directors are often unaware that executives, adhering to auditor-chosen accounting rules, can manipulate the interpretation of a concept as apparently simple as the word "cost." To rub salt in the wound, the auditors take no responsibility for tightening the rules; instead they blame the boards of directors for allowing the misinterpretation.

Canada is far from the only country where such misinterpretations occur. Auditing and accounting rules in all countries contain cavernous loopholes in financial reporting. Once Canada adopts International Financial Reporting Standards, loopholes will only increase, as IFRS allows significant leeway in related-party deals, because it calls for disclosure only of certain limited transactions. In general, investors should regard most of the amounts reported in financial statements for related-party transactions with suspicion.

It should be noted that auditors are required to probe into suspicious transactions if they happen to stumble upon them. However, to limit their responsibility as much as possible, auditors have developed the following tactics:

1. *Auditors consider their obligations to have ended when they report their suspicions to a board of directors or trustees.* If the directors choose to do nothing, the shareholders or unit holders remain in the dark, and the scam lives on. Auditors may choose to perform other procedures, but they usually convey little benefit to investors.
2. *Auditors may design audit procedures that appear to address the possible problem, but fall far short of accomplishing anything worthwhile.* Auditors may require management to sign a letter, for example, declaring that they are honest, upstanding citizens. By obtaining such a meaningless letter from the people in a position to do the most harm to investors, many auditors believe that they have fulfilled their obligation to society.
3. *Auditors select samples for transactions that stand only a minimal chance, at best, of arousing suspicion.* In court, auditors frequently say, "It wasn't part of my audit sample." To this feeble excuse, we can only ask: "You mean in more than ten years of auditing, your sampling did not uncover any peculiar transactions? Did you review your sampling techniques to ensure that you were auditing a sufficient cross-section of transactions? How did you obtain adequate comfort to be able to sign your audit report?"

It is difficult to decide which is worse: the auditing or the financial reporting of related-party transactions. Financial reporting varies among countries, but none require companies to report that they carried out their deals with executives at fair market values determined through independent, third-party valuations. Although related-party transactions continually harm investors, auditors have washed their hands of responsibility for monitoring such transactions closely, offering lame excuses to support their inaction.

It's not as if auditors have no access to the required expertise for determining fair market value. In some cases, their own companies run a lucrative division that earns handsome fees for evaluating much more complex non-tangible assets, such as intellectual property or brand names. Yet the auditors claim that it is not their business to comment on the fair value of related-party transactions. Even under IFRS—which auditors sold to the world because it encouraged companies to fairly value all their assets and liabilities—auditors will continue to evade responsibility. That's because auditors seem to have excluded related-party transactions from the fair-valuing rules.

Unbeknownst to investors, unfair related-party transactions can continue for years. Occasionally, when an executive knowingly approves an obvious fraud of overcharging, authorities may lay charges, but, as happens so often in Canada, these occasional cases seem to settle with only minor slaps on the wrist.

If an auditor asks an executive to justify a price charged to a public company by an executive-owned company, the executive can resort to loose accounting rules. For example, an executive-owned company can buy a product for $10 per unit, and then turn around and charge the public company $50 for the same unit. In doing this, the executive-owned company appears to have made a profit per unit of $40.

The executive-owned company, however, needs somehow to cover up this excessive profit. To do this, it can add a pile of so-called costs to the $10 per unit. These phony add-on costs may include paying a salary to the executive and members of his family; adding bonuses and sales commissions for relatives; locating the executive-owned company's head office in a room in the executive's home and charging rent; and paying for vacations, cars, and other personal expenses through the executive-owned company.

The $50 per unit paid by the public company could also include a fake warranty charge, consulting fees, special return privileges, insurance coverage for the most unlikely events, hotline advice, and similar nonsense. Such unnecessary add-ons make it much harder to determine the unit's real market value. A reasonable estimate, though, might value the add-ons at perhaps 10¢ to 20¢ per unit, which is nowhere near the $40 profit made.

Investors almost never examine such related-party con games, because they think, mistakenly, that such transactions are priced at fair market value, consisting of the price that the executive company paid for the tangible inputs, plus some fairly valued overheads.

There are some protective steps investors can take to reduce their losses from dubious related-party dealings. Only governments, however, can take the major steps necessary to prevent corporations and their auditors from conducting such transactions. As long as auditors and their client corporations control the writing of accounting and financial reporting rules, they'll remain ineffective and deceptive. Nothing short of a completely independent body can write fair rules; otherwise, investors remain at the mercy of executives and others, who will continue to stuff their pockets with shareholders' money.

If investors want to examine a company's related-party transactions, they should start by reading the notes to its financial statements. Under "related party transactions," the investor can check to see if the company has engaged in transactions with companies owned by executives or corporate directors. The amounts involved will indicate whether the public company is too intimate with the related parties.

Investors should also dig in further, and follow up, if they notice any of the following:

1. *Any phrase within the related-party note that suggests the list of related-party transactions is not complete.* For example, a note might say, "Except as detailed elsewhere in the financial statements, the company's related party transactions include...." Such wording may warn you that the company has buried details about the other part of an unfair transaction in another note to the financial statements. You should consider all the related-party transactions and disclosures in order to get a clear idea of the amounts involved.
2. *Names of companies that are referred to as related parties yet have very similar names to the public company.* For financial reporting purposes, valid subsidiary companies are consolidated with the parent company. A 100%-owned subsidiary should not raise concern. But dubious executives sometimes incorporate their executive-owned companies under names very similar to the public company, trying to con investors into thinking that the executive-owned company is part of the public company. You should regard such practices with extreme

suspicion. Sometimes executives use this tactic to divert funds intended for one company directly into another.

3. *Subsidiary companies that are only partially owned by the public company.* Who owns the rest of the subsidiary? Quite possibly, executives do, and they're selling to the public company for amounts in excess of fair market value. Sometimes friends of the executives own the remaining portion of the company and they provide kickbacks to the executives on related-party transactions.

4. *Large transactions with related parties that include the purchase or sale of land, buildings, or even entire companies.* You should ask questions if a company reports the purchase and sale of large assets involving the same buyers and sellers in consecutive annual financial statements. Possibly, the transactions are legitimate, but you should never simply assume that they are.

5. *Rental payments by the public company to directors or executives of the public company, usually through their management-owned companies.* Under such cozy rental agreements between related parties, the public company often pays for repairs and upgrades that the executive-owned company should have absorbed, and the executive-owned company ends up with a risk-free guaranteed cash return on its investment in the land and building. Meanwhile, the public company gets charged for everything from a new security system to upgrades in mechanical equipment. Then, when the executive-owned building reaches its optimal value, the public company moves out and the new tenant signs a new lease at a higher rate for the sole benefit of the landlord, which is the executive-owned company.

Companies may describe in detail numerous related-party transactions in three or four separate areas of the financial statements. We often have to analyze statements over three and four years, and sometimes as far back as twelve years, to assemble the pertinent clues. Sometimes the same tricks involve several different executive-owned companies. As executives become greedier and more confident in their own duplicity, the situation may get worse.

Some related-party transactions do not even get recorded in the notes to the financial statements because auditors rely on management to identify the related-party transactions that they've conducted with the public company. Unscrupulous management may choose to withhold such information. In these cases, what you don't know will hurt you.

Securities commissions have largely ignored related-party transactions. In addition, auditors have set the financial reporting rules in a way that removes any incentive for them to pursue suspicious related-party dealings.

Under IFRS, matters will only get worse for investors. Auditors will be able to spout misleading claims about supposedly fair-valued financial statements, and investors will assume an even greater sense of false security.

CHAPTER TWELVE

# You'll Never Get Rich

*"It was not by gold or by silver, but by labour, that all the wealth of the world was originally purchased."*

ADAM SMITH

**MANY COMPANIES** stand little chance of surviving their first year. But some companies with good ideas and sound intellectual property manage to skate through the first few years with start-up funding from founders, friends, banks, and venture capitalists. Some companies even make it far enough to obtain a listing on a junior stock exchange, at which point they begin to target retail investors to raise new capital. It's unlikely, however, that a retail shareholder will make a profit on the investment.

In the resource sector, and especially in the technology and biotechnology sectors, retail investors seldom have a very good appreciation of the assets, intellectual property, or management talent behind a company. Quite often a venture fund with a major stake in the company wields significant influence and possesses insider-like information. This makes it unlikely that a retail investor will ever reap a reward. To avoid becoming a casualty yourself, you need to understand the many ways in which a company might milk its retail investors in order to fund operating losses for several years.

In one scheme, retail investors buy shares in a start-up technology company through a private placement or an exchange listing. At a crucial point when operating funds are low, the company obtains a loan from a finance company, secured by a promising technology that can be sold or salvaged. Along with a high interest rate on the loan, the finance company specifies a period of 120 days or 180 days, for example, during which the company must pay interest on the loan in full. If interest isn't paid within this period, the financing company assumes majority ownership of the technology company.

Not surprisingly, within a year or so, the tech company falls behind in its interest payments and the finance company takes control of the borrower company. This premeditated financing arrangement was planned so that the financing company could acquire majority control more cheaply, simply by waiting one or two years for the default in interest payments.

Next, the finance company gets rid of the minority shareholders by deliberately driving down the value of the stock. It does this by terminating any investor-relations initiatives, providing retail investors with little or no information, and by using loose accounting rules to create heavy losses. Finance companies can create losses in a number of ways: by lowering the dollar value of receivables and inventory; increasing accrued liabilities and warranties; writing down equipment and intangible assets; and restructuring in order to expense as much as possible. Faced with huge losses, most minority shareholders have no choice but to sell their shares into the market. The ones who stick with the company for another year or so will be offered only pennies for their shares. Of the few highly knowledgeable shareholders who may remain, the finance company can resort to legal mechanisms to squeeze them out.

Now in compete control, the finance company might shop the patents, patents pending, and in-process research to larger companies to turn a quick profit on the venture. The finance company may have even already begun informal talks prior to a full takeover. Alternatively, the finance company might consider taking the company public again by taking advantage of all the expenses recorded over previous periods to report a profit. The company may also start disclosing more information to investors, while engaging with potential underwriters and their analysts.

Once it has decided to take the company public again, the finance company can pull more tricks from its corporate sleeve. It can engage so-called specialists to value the technology and patents and can then lock in the aggressively high value of the assets by resorting to a sham back-and-forth sale with another entity controlled by the finance company. With the phony high prices placed on the technology assets of the firm, supported by a report or two from a consulting or auditing firm and the help of underwriters, the finance company can then sell shares to the public at a higher offering price, enabling them to recoup their initial investment plus a very handsome profit.

The finance company might also retain a significant stake, not just for appearances, but to start milking new investors, so they can start the whole scheme all over again. The cycle begins again when the finance company sticks the tech company with the substantial costs of underwriting rather than paying for those costs itself. The tech company, and its new retail shareholders, will also pay the costs of any secondary offerings if the finance company decides to sell more of its shares in order to make more money on the deal.

In the meantime, as owners of the tech company, the finance company can find other ways to exploit it. It can appoint management and board members, and continue to engage in questionable accounting, while reaping a continuing payoff with generous share-based compensation and bonus schemes. The finance company may also arrange additional financings with generous terms and warrants. At no point in this process does the retail investor ever benefit.

We have seen all these tactics, in various combinations, put into practice in the Canadian market with the same lack of response from lawmakers, regulators, auditors, and others from whom investors should expect support. Regulators have come to regard such schemes as just part of the market. Many auditors, underwriters, and other parties, who are aware of the inner workings of these scams, and even benefit from them, remain silent, if not content.

The Canadian media does not serve investors well when they pretend that such devious scams are a rarity. The media seldom expose these scams in detail, and they never illuminate the scope of the problem. With only minimal reporting of such flim-flams, investors remain unaware of what to look out for, seldom recognizing the early warning signs of a duplicitous investment scheme.

Swindlers may apply similar tactics to resource companies whose assets are just as difficult to value as technology or biotech. Take, for example, a company that owns three gold mines in Africa. More than half of its shareholders live primarily in Europe, and the company's head office and management team operate from Europe, as well. One set of company lawyers operates out of Montreal, while another set is based in Europe. Given that the assets, management, head office, and majority of shareholders are foreign, why is the company listed for trading on the Toronto Stock Exchange?

Many people will tell you that the TSX is the centre for mining listings in the world, but the question is why? Part of the reason is that we have a lot of resource companies in Canada, and underwriters and investors in this country are familiar with such companies. Another reason is that the TSX actively promotes itself throughout the world to attract resource listings. But is that the whole story?

Could Canada's lax enforcement, regulation, auditing, accounting, and media have something to do with it? We know for a fact that lax enforcement has encouraged many white-collar con artists to target Canada with their schemes because they know that prosecutions are rare, convictions even rarer, and fines and sentences, if any, are minimal.

Canada's reputation as a haven for resource investments presents an opportunity; unfortunately, it's only for the swindlers.

CHAPTER THIRTEEN
# Private Placements, Public Disgrace

*"The believer is happy; the doubter is wise."*
HUNGARIAN PROVERB

**HUNDREDS OF** pitches are made to investors every day for shoddy private placements. If you've never been on the receiving end of a private placement pitch, consider yourself lucky. The pitch goes something like this:

"Yes, the guys who operate Slag Heap Mines in northern Manitoba are planning on reopening the mine. I think that I'll be able to get private-placement shares for you at 25¢ apiece. They'll probably allocate 100,000 shares for you. I might take 200,000 shares myself. Do you want me to ask for 200,000 shares for you, as well?"

These pitches tend to come in a cold call from a brokerage house on the edge of respectability, but not always. There's a fine line between shady salesmen and slightly more respectable brokers working for firms with recognizable names. Even the investment advisor with whom you have done business before might pitch this "new type of investment." No matter who makes the pitch, you have to weigh any new investment vehicle on its merits, not on the assumed reputation of the firm behind it. Even the top firms pitch garbage, more often than you'd care to think.

So what are the merits of this latest private placement? You will not be able to sell the shares for four to five months, maybe longer because of the paperwork, but you'll be told that you should keep them for a few years anyway to reap the benefits. You might be told, as well, that rising metal prices will boost the value of the stock once Slag Heap Mines starts operating again. That, too, may not happen for a year, or maybe even longer. You'll hear that Slag Heap intends to apply to list the stock again on the Venture Exchange. When that happens, your shares will easily double or triple in value on that basis alone. The salesman might claim that he made a ton of money on Slag Heap ten years ago. It's a wonder it ever shut down, he'll say. Finally, you might be told that this share offering will raise all the money that Slag Heap needs to start operating again. After this, the company will not need to raise any more funds. You will be in on the ground floor, the salesman will say. Unfortunately, you're standing over a mine shaft, and there's no telling which way the elevator will go.

As a prospective shareholder, you'll likely receive few documents about the background of a company that tries to raise cash through a private placement. These companies usually try to raise money quickly through established contacts with brokers and others with access to accredited investors, the official term for wealthy investors.

Under Canadian securities law, wealthy investors who meet a designated threshold for net worth and/or income thresholds are presumed to be sophisticated enough in the world of finance to make their own decisions, without the help of legal and regulatory protection extended to their poor cousins, the more conventional investors. The threshold varies by province, but the general idea is the same. Presumably, legislators assume that, as a result of possessing a certain amount of money, investors do not require the full protection of securities laws and regulations, as weak in substance and application as they may be. The basis of this curious assumption is not really clear. Can we assume that money comes only to people who have brains? What happens when someone simply inherits considerable wealth from a parent or wife? What about all of those very intelligent people who continue to fall victim to these kinds of schemes? Do they seek consolation by reminding themselves that they can afford to lose more than others?

Whatever the rationale, accredited investors are more than likely to receive an offer to participate in a private placement. If you're one of them, you should know what you're in for. Buying shares at the commencement of a venture exposes you to greater risk, because the venture may quickly fail. Though it's difficult to quantify the odds, some people give a new venture only one chance in twenty of succeeding. At that rate, it'd be better to invest in twenty different schemes and hope that one of them increases in value more than twentyfold.

Prior to buying such shares, investors must do their homework. By asking even a few basic questions you can eliminate many investment pitches. For instance, how many shares in Slag Heap are already outstanding, and how much did the company receive in return? You may be paying 25¢ per share, but many others may recently have paid just 5¢. Furthermore, how many share warrants have been granted, to whom, and at what price? Insiders may be able to buy many more shares in Slag Heap through options or warrants, at, say, 8¢ a share, at any time over the next two or three years. If so, the value of your shares, purchased at 25¢ a share, will become seriously diluted.

In the case of Slag Heap, it is possible that millions of shares may still be outstanding from when it previously traded, some ten years ago. These old shares might have the same rights as the new ones. Buying into the private placement at 25¢, you stand at the end of a long line of shareholders, assuming the company ever gets off the ground.

If you remain convinced that that deal offers better odds of success than the local racetrack, then it is time to investigate the last ten deals the brokerage put together before it started pitching Slag Heap. Does it have a decent track record, or do most of its deals turn out to be duds?

Obviously, some companies succeed, and some well-known names among public companies today began yesterday as private placements. So investors shouldn't dismiss all such possibilities out of hand. But the fact remains that the majority of start-ups fail within a few years. In particular, a reopened mine raises concerns, because the best-quality ore might already have been extracted, leaving only the leftovers behind.

Given the extensive number of new resource ventures that get started or financed in Canada, it is crucial to ask some key questions before parting with your hard-earned savings:

1. Why are the private placement shares being offered to you in particular? Are you so important in the world that people would turn to you first when they needed start-up financing? Or have your previous donations to such new enterprises enshrined your name on a go-to list for brokers pitching private placements? If you rank low on your broker's status list, he may not even keep you up to date on the company's dealings once you have turned over your money. And being the last person to know about important events loses you money every time.
2. Who else owns shares in the private placement?
3. How many more rounds of financing will the company need before it becomes economically viable?
4. Who are the backers and managers of the investment, and what is their track record? Do they have a history of making subsequent private placements at lower prices because they can't effectively sell the attributes of the company? Do insiders seem to receive more favourable investment terms? Will your investment simply enable them to unload part of their initial investment in the company?
5. Do the promoters of the deal prosper at the expense of the company they're pitching? Many start-up companies can provide a comfortable life for the promoters. Salaries, bonuses, expense accounts, interest-free loans, services provided by friends at unfair prices, and much more can deplete the company's cash. Investors need to investigate and monitor all of these possibilities in the promoters' previous deals.
6. Does the rising price of the stock reflect actual revenue and growth, or has the price risen as a result of the promoters hyping the shares? If you get the feeling that the shares are being driven by hype, always take your money off the table. It can be a signal that the promoters and insiders are preparing to unload significant positions. Conversely, price increases that are not accompanied by fundamental improvements or tangible prospects for the company might also indicate good news ahead and that insider buying is moving the stock. But you'll likely be

the last to know, and such a gamble will not likely pay off. As a general rule, when you can't determine why the stock price is rising, sell your shares; otherwise, once the hype and price manipulation evaporates, the price of the stock may plummet.
7. Are cost overruns a serious problem? When cash is tight, the company may have to sell more shares. In such circumstances, the company can not likely borrow money because it has insufficient collateral security, and little or no cash flow to pay interest.
8. Has the company experienced delays and uncertainties caused by weather, regulatory obstructions, other excuses, or simply bad management? Such delays tend to eat up cash quickly. Sometimes it pays to sell your shares at a loss at the first sign of trouble rather than waiting for improvements that never come, and losing more.

Politicians talk endlessly about job creation and promoting the country from within through start-up enterprises. And we'd be the last to deny that job creation is vital to any economy. Unfortunately, our lawmakers do not protect investors from promoters who use the platform of job creation as a way of swindling them; instead, their apathy affords protection to inactive securities regulators and auditors. With the investment playing field so tipped against them, investors almost always lose.

For investors, the overriding consideration in private placement start-ups is that a group of insiders have all the operating details of the company and know exactly how much optimism is baked into the stock. Canada's largely inactive securities commissions rarely pursue these kinds of investment schemes. Accordingly, your chances are remote of buying in to a private placement at fair, low prices and selling at comfortable, high prices. Usually, the opposite occurs.

CHAPTER FOURTEEN

# Inadequate Resources

*"Do not hold as gold all that shines as gold."*
ALAIN DE LILLE

**WHETHER IT** comes from Slag Heap Mines or a better-known company, most financial reports from small and medium-sized resource companies in Canada contain little of benefit to investors. That's because auditors have created financial reporting rules that require their comment only on the most anodyne aspects of a resource operation, regardless of their relevance to investment decision-making. Auditors do not have to evaluate non-arm's-length transactions, for instance, which are commonplace in the mining industry. And, under IFRS, asset valuations will become even more opaque. No wonder con artists love Canada's resource sector.

Because it's so easy to cook the books, you should not underestimate the risks of investing in a Canadian resource company. Canada's securities commissions may have tightened the rules over the years with respect to reporting ore quality, quantity, and oil and gas reserves, but you still cannot expect much information from a resource company's financial reports, nor can you expect much protection from securities commissions and auditors. As usual, you have to follow the cash, but even that's not so easy in a resource company.

Some resource companies have only limited assets, perhaps just a single mine, or a few wells. These entities are known as declining resource companies. They will pull whatever they can of value out of the ground until the resource is depleted. At that point, the company might be wound-down. To calculate a so-called yield from an investment in a depleting resource company, you cannot compare dividends or distributions to your original investment. Whatever you receive in cash represents a combination of income plus a return of your original capital investment.

As with a Ponzi scheme, the return of your capital is not a yield. Only the portion of the dividend earned on the company's income really counts. Eventually, declining resource companies will stop earning an income because their underground reserves are limited. Unless the company is well diversified, its life ends when the reserves have been exploited. Most investors know that the dividend on such an investment includes a portion of their own money. But if you don't understand depleting-resource reporting, you can be conned by the composite dividend into thinking that your investment is more profitable than it actually is.

Resource companies come in all shapes and sizes, anywhere between a single mine operation to a well-diversified multinational. Many resources companies in Canada fall in between, which makes their depleting nature difficult to pin down and more prone to misinterpretation by investors. Forthright reporting by the company to investors who understand the nature of their investment can minimize that risk. Unfortunately, as they deplete their reserves, resource companies run the risk of resembling a Ponzi scheme.

As we'll discuss in more detail in the next chapter, resource companies use the same one-size-fits-all accounting as companies in other sectors. This makes their financial reporting potentially misleading. Here are some examples:

1. A timber company has owned land and harvesting rights in British Columbia for 100 years. For purposes of reporting on the company's balance sheet, the value of the trees is zero, because they grew on their own and did not cost the company anything. In contrast, a lumberyard

would show on its balance sheet whatever it paid a sawmill for the lumber. Even though the timber company and lumberyard have similar assets, the recorded values are vastly different.

2. A company in Alberta discovers oil or natural gas with minimal effort. On the balance sheet, the company records little or no cost for discovering the oil or gas, but it still represents a substantial asset. Another company may have spent considerably more to discover a similar amount of oil and gas and would therefore record those reserves at a much higher amount on the balance sheet. Though equal in value, the two companies would have very different looking balance sheets.

3. A mining company in Saskatchewan stumbles upon monstrous potash resources while conducting other activities. Again, the principal assets are underground and cost peanuts to discover. The balance sheet therefore ignores the essence of the company, namely, the valuable potash resources, until they are brought to the surface and sold.

Under comparable circumstances, a retail company could not record an asset on its balance sheet without incurring a cost. Yet resource companies follow the same cost-based accounting rules as retailers, with absurd results: trees that cost nothing, or oil and gas that costs peanuts. It makes little sense to compare apparently wealthy resource companies that report zero or near zero asset values to retail or manufacturing companies with ascertainable costs. Lawmakers should have dismissed the auditors' one-size-fits-all approach out of hand. Obviously, one size does not fit all. Instead, lawmakers in Canada succumbed to the blandishments of the auditing fraternity. Not only did our governments turn a blind eye to the one-size-fits-all approach, they tried to adopt the same accounting rules for themselves in government financial statements. Even though governments do not operate to make a profit, they adopted profit-based accounting methods much the same as retailers, manufacturers, and mining companies.

Once again, with respect to resource companies, investors are on their own. Investors must interpret the financial reporting of a resource company with care and pay close attention to cash flows, particularly the sources of cash. Beyond the information included in a financial report to shareholders, investors will need additional information, such as:

1. Reported reserves and resources: What areas have and have not been explored? What grades and quantities of resources has the company discovered, proven, or not? What inferred quantities and quality does it anticipate? When does it expect to extract the deposits?
2. How much will it cost to use different mining methods for different components of the ore body, at various times, over the next several years?
3. What major techniques will the company use in extraction, including prospective cost ranges and timetables?
4. What other cash costs per ton will the company incur to reach the refined metal stage?
5. What additional financing needs does it face, how much will it need, and when?
6. Does the company propose or have a hedging program in place? How much has it hedged, at what prices, and for what periods?
7. What non-arm's-length arrangements has the company undertaken with management and related companies? How did the board determine fair values and exchange values?
8. What financing arrangements has the company made? How many shares are outstanding, including warrants, options, control, or influence blocks?
9. What liquid resources does the company have? What are its offsetting cash obligations and contingencies?
10. Does the company have major contracts in place? For how long? For what amounts? With what key parties?
11. What obligations does the company face under labour contracts, environmental commitments, and similar responsibilities?
12. Is there any litigation under way? Has the government imposed regulatory sanctions on the company?
13. Does the company face income tax liabilities? How will they affect the company? What potential changes or temporary measures will the company face?
14. Who are the company's lawyers, technical advisers, and specialists? What are their backgrounds and qualifications?
15. What other potential material cash outlays or receipts might the company encounter?

Investors need information that enables them to project ranges of potential cash profits so they can properly estimate the value of a company. This list covers the basics, but you will likely have your own questions. We have emphasized cash receipts and disbursements, including extraction and refining costs, ore quality and quantity, and estimated dates, obligations, commitments, and contracts. Answers to these questions will help you to establish a cash budget for the company similar to the budget prepared for a real estate project in which longer-term leases are commonplace. Investors must keep in mind that very little crucial information will be found in the audited financial statements. Most will be in the company's Management Discussion and Analysis (MD&A) and various other disclosures, such as investor presentations and annual information forms.

Investors need to dig for this information. In many cases, resource companies will not present it on a silver platter. Instead, they may mislead investors by feeding them irrelevancies, while withholding important information.

Despite the critical importance of our resource industries, and the critical need for investment in these industries, financial reporting remains inadequate at best, and will only get worse under IFRS with the delegation of crucial valuation estimates to company management.

When securities commissions and auditors cling to a one-size-fits-all mentality, it opens up some serious gaps in the financial reporting of resource companies, including:

1. The reliability and adequacy of published data on the resource bodies, which is critical to investment decision-making.
2. The reporting of related-party transactions at fair market or inflated values.
3. The mixing of cash and non-cash numbers in financial statements, making the determination of extraction and refining costs virtually impossible in the majority of situations.

More discrepancies and deficiencies exist, but these alone present a major impediment to informed investment decisions. They also make Canada's resource industry a prime target for financial swindlers.

Investors can make disastrous decisions if they invest in resource industries using one-size-fits-all financial reporting statements developed for retailers and manufacturers. Such companies may not be reporting their main assets adequately on the balance sheet. Under IFRS, companies can record the same assets in several ways, including: virtually no cost at all; costs specific to the mine or well; a proportion of total company costs; a reasonable fair-value estimate; or a pie-in-the-sky management estimate. Auditors will be obliged to accept any of these choices and disavow any duty to investors to clamp down on unreasonable or inconsistent practices. Most troubling is that management can, somewhat arbitrarily, reverse asset write-downs taken in prior periods in order to boost income.

In Canada, securities legislation has essentially enshrined the auditors' own rules, even as the increasing complexity of financial arrangements has pushed the country even further out of date. Few in government have kept up with the changes, and the effects of neglect on investors have intensified. The past decade alone has been devastating for investors and their rights.

Today, Canadian lawmakers have backed themselves into a corner. They have nowhere to turn to receive an independent viewpoint. No independent national body devoted to investor protection exists to provide analysis and guidance to legislators on financial reporting matters.

The country requires capital investment to create jobs and maintain our standard of living, but lawmakers have chosen not to bother with the torrent of financial collapses arising from inadequate financial reporting and accounting. Even though investors provide essential capital, lawmakers have ignored their needs. As Canada's self-regulatory organizations follow a path that serves their own interests, aging boomers are withdrawing from equity markets that resource companies need to survive.

As a global centre of mining and resource investment, we suffer from weak financial reporting standards and weak stock exchange controls. Investors should consider the real reasons that so many foreign mining companies choose to list in Canada as opposed to anywhere else in the world. Instead of a one-size-fits-all approach, we need a more appropriate accounting and financial reporting system that pays attention to such matters as:

1. The extensive volume of cash transactions requiring a focus on liquidity and solvency in corporations, as well as conventional measures of income or profitability.
2. The magnitude of resource-based expenditures and financings, and whether transaction prices coincide with fair market values as opposed to unfair prices that only benefit insiders and promoters.
3. The extensive number of non-arm's-length transactions, and whether they are being fully and plainly reported, including any and all discrepancies from fair market values.
4. The magnitude of complex hedging and mark-to-market (MTM) transactions.

With IFRS, Canada will move even further away from such a system. Instead, IFRS will give even more reporting power and choice to management.

Canadian investors can always boycott companies that take advantage of IFRS to cover up bad management and negative operating results. US-listed stocks, for instance, are more closely regulated. But if Canada wants a robust economy in which investors provide much-needed capital to resource- and cash-based industries, lawmakers need to improve financial reporting rules to provide investors with a greater degree of fairness. Governments could start by asking investors themselves what they need so that they can continue to invest with a sense of safety in this country.

Canada has a wide variety of industries, with vastly different operating risks and accounting idiosyncrasies. A one-size-fits-all approach to financial reporting that treats resource companies like retail stores is grossly inadequate for investment decision-making.

CHAPTER FIFTEEN

## One-Size-Fits-All Shoe Store

*"The truth is rarely pure and never simple."*
OSCAR WILDE

**WOULD YOU** invest in a store that sells one-size-fits-all shoes? Probably not. An idea that works for toques and scarves doesn't work for footwear. So why invest in companies that practise one-size-fits-all accounting on the assumption that what works for one industry must work for them all? Unfortunately, investors have no choice. In Canada, any entity, from a retail store to an insurance company to an oil and gas exploration firm, reports its finances using the same flawed basic framework.

Accounting was originally designed to report the financial results of simple operations in manufacturing and retailing. These were cash-based industries with high inventory turnover and few, if any, complicating factors. Since then, these industries have outgrown this simple accounting framework in complexity. Retail establishments now engage in receivables securitization, significant real estate investments, and currency hedging. They offer credit cards, insurance, mortgages, and investment products, and accounting in Canada has not kept up. The US has special accounting rules for specific industries, while Canada, generally, does not.

Instead, the overly simplistic retail and manufacturing accounting model has been imposed on complex companies, conglomerates, and new industries, such as technology and biotech. Enabled by this model to withhold information from their competitors, the companies themselves do not particularly care about their increasingly incoherent financial statements. Nor, apparently, do lawmakers. But investors do.

As we've already discussed, investors take a back seat in the minds of the auditors and accountants, who set the accounting rules. Despite the obvious need for a completely different approach, accountants have pushed the one-size-fits-all solution. Without any significant protest from investors, they've merely tinkered with their model instead of making fundamental, but supposedly costly, changes in reaction to changing corporate and economic conditions.

Canadian and US accounting followed a similar path for a short while but diverged decades ago when the US adopted a more robust approach. While Canada adhered to the one-size-fits-all approach, US accountants established more specific guidelines for industries with different fundamentals than conventional retailers and manufacturers. Initially, Canada followed this path for two reasons: naivety and greed.

Naively, Canadians want to believe that we are good people and, by extension, better people than Americans. We want to think we are more honest, peaceable, and sensible. We return lost wallets, help our neighbours, and ensure honest financial reporting within a wide-open accounting framework based on a few simple ideas, but without many specific prohibitions, and with loopholes big enough for a Zamboni. If we constructed a criminal code on the same premise, it would boil down to one simplistic statement: "Be good."

Accountants and auditors remind us constantly that we behave differently than Americans, then turn around and laugh all the way to the bank. By adhering to a so-called principles-based approach to accounting, and claiming that honest Canadian executives do not need hand-holding, accountants and auditors avoid the costs of laboriously updating accounting rules, applying prohibitions, and closing loopholes. The myth of the good Canadian might inflate investors' egos, but it does little to protect their wallets. Basic evidence, including the list of financial failures in Appendix A, shows that the Canadian pretence of greater honesty is simple rubbish.

Recent changes to the one-size-fits-all approach have merely added to the confusion. By adopting IFRS, Canada takes the one-size-fits-all mentality and spreads it across the world, ignoring significant differences in basic culture, corporate ideology, regulation, taxation, and a host of other issues. Some countries produce disproportionate amounts of consumer products, others export raw materials, such as metals, oil, gas, fertilizers, and forest products. Applying a one-size-fits-all approach may simplify the task of the accountants, but it produces wildly unrealistic results.

Within Canada, the same concerns arise whether we apply a one-size-fits-all approach to shoes or accounting. A bank and a nuclear power plant operate in hugely different ways, with vastly different priorities. Banks have to focus on day-by-day cash flows, whereas a nuclear facility focuses on long-term safety and maintenance. An accounting system such as IFRS addresses the lowest common denominator between a bank and a nuclear facility. How can this possibly make sense? To work effectively, the accounting system has to consider the emphasis by the bank on cash and the enormous capital expenditures of the nuclear facility. To do this, the system needs to apply different controls and monitoring techniques to each operation.

Investors must consider the basic restrictions of Canada's financial reporting system in making investment decisions. The more a company's assets and liabilities extend beyond accounts receivable, inventory, accounts payable, and accrued liabilities, the less applicable the one-size-fits-all framework becomes. With the exception of some large-cap companies listed in the US and Canada, Canadian corporations have used this simplistic accounting approach to disclose much less information than their US counterparts for decades. As basic business transactions have become more complex, accounting has increasingly lagged behind.

Auditing also becomes more difficult under a one-size-fits-all approach because trivial transactions distract the auditors. Without understanding a business sufficiently, auditors often conduct pointless audit procedures, while the real essence of the business, including its high-risk areas, remains unexamined. A one-size-fits-all approach emphasizes receivables, payables, inventory, and the related balancing entries for revenue recognition, cost of goods sold, and expenses, which tends to downplay issues that affect long-term assets, long-term liabilities, equity, and financial statement notes. Auditors end up rubber-stamping irrelevant quantifications based on unreliable figures. With no incentive by auditors to look for them, related-party transactions and outright frauds occur with relative frequency in Canada.

The drive for simplicity under a one-size-fits-all mentality, and IFRS, underlies the long-standing problem of netting financial statement figures instead of showing gross amounts. Instead of separating cash receipts from cash disbursements, for example, companies provide only a net figure. This can sometimes create false conclusions, misleading investors into making mistakes.

Suppose, for example, that you are thinking of investing in a finance company that specializes in short-term loans. For simplicity, let's assume that the company has extended two loans in the current year. It made one loan to a fish-canning company for $10 million, and the other to a real estate company for $10 million. The fish company uses the $10 million to buy and can fish. By December 31, the cannery has repaid $8.5 million of the loan by selling much of the canned fish. It expects to repay the other $1.5 million in six more weeks, again by selling more fish.

In contrast, by December 31, the real estate company has repaid the full $10 million, but only by taking out a new loan from the finance company for $12 million. By netting the $8.5 million of cash receipts from the fish company against the $22 million in total loans, the finance company reports only $13.5 million in loans as of year-end.

That figure is very deceptive.

In fact, the real estate company has not repaid the original $10 million loan from its business operations. Not only has it not repaid the loan, the finance company has lent it an additional $2 million, perhaps to pay interest due on the principal $10 million loan.

Of the two companies, the fish cannery has behaved with greater clarity and integrity. It has repaid most of the $10 million by doing what it was supposed to do, selling canned fish.

The real estate company, on the other hand, had to borrow another $2 million. Why? Perhaps some of the leases expired on its rented buildings and the tenants moved out. It now needs the extra $2 million to attract new tenants and cover operating expenses. The finance company, in essence, has refreshed its original $10 million loan and provided a further $2 million.

In its financial report, the finance company can make two choices:

| | (in millions) |
|---|---|
| (A) No netting: | |
| Loans made ($10 + $10 + $2) | $ 22.0 |
| Loans repaid (ignoring the faked $10 million from the real estate company) | 8.5 |
| Net increase in loans | $ 13.5 |
| (B) Netting (as allowed under IFRS): | |
| Increase in loans ($10 + $2 + $1.5) | $ 13.5 |

When the finance company uses no netting, the investor sees directly that the company has collected only $8.5 million from the total of $22 million in loans. The investor can then ask why the short-term finance company hasn't collected more of the $22 million.

Using a one-size-fits-all approach permitted under IFRS, management can hide, in the financial statements, the fact that the loan to the real estate company could be a bad one. And, under IFRS, the finance company can avoid reporting the impairment of such questionable loans for years. On its balance sheet, it can report the $12-million loan to the real estate company as a legitimate asset, when in all likelihood it is not, and investors will never know the difference. At one time, Canada took action to prohibit this specific financial reporting trick, but that prohibition will be washed away under IFRS, along with other restrictions designed to help investors.

Over the past twenty-five years, many Canadian banks, finance, trust, and insurance companies have had to legally defend their decisions to report netted loan figures in court against investors, many of whom had lost considerable capital after making decisions based on these elusive financial reporting practices. Most of these cases were settled out of court and, as a result, few specific rules exist to prohibit the continuation of netting of figures in the future. While Canadian accounting rules prohibit some netting of transactions, those prohibitions generally do not exist under IFRS. Therefore, Canada seems doomed to repeat the past, and investors seem doomed to get taken once again for a ride.

Without accounting rules aimed directly at non-retail and non-manufacturing companies, investors will face crucial information gaps. The recurring problems will likely involve insurance companies, banks, and investment companies in particular. The problems will arise from questionable valuations, derivative instruments, guarantors, and counterparties.

Valuation concepts are vague to begin with, and will be made much worse if companies are permitted to provide only the basic information required under such flimsy financial reporting guidelines. A company may apply a value to property, for example, by considering recent comparable sales, the replacement cost of an equivalent building, or cash anticipated from renting the available space. Each of these choices varies the valuation considerably from the others.

To avoid misleading investors into making costly, inappropriate conclusions with such excessive simplicity, companies need to follow clear rules that determine when they can use each valuation technique. Under current rules, and under IFRS, companies can use techniques that rely heavily on assumptions about future cash flow, interest rates, and other variables. If the assumptions are off target, the value will be affected, possibly by a significant amount (see Appendix F).

Under a simplistic one-size-fits-all approach, for example, companies can make pie-in-the-sky estimates for the expected revenue and costs of a building. In fact, occupancy and cash receipts might be low for a few years because of a business disruption, such as construction in the neighbourhood. In time, the net cash receipts of the building may rise to reflect greater rental occupancy. Rents may rise, as well, as a shortage of comparable space develops. Unless the valuation made today on the rental building appropriately reflects the improved conditions two or three years in the future, it will be unreliable.

The situation may get worse since financial statements under IFRS do not have to explain in detail how a company determines net cash receipts, discount rates, and other conclusions. In the midst of this one-size-fits-all thinking, the loser is the investor. If inaccurate valuations depress asset values, investors may sell their shares at a price well below their intrinsic value.

The same unfortunate situation applies in reporting derivative-based or other complex transactions. In such transactions, businesses buy and sell packages of debt obligations, for example, without always knowing the identity of their counterparties. Since the largest risk in investing in a business is the possibility of default on its securities, the absence of information about the calibre of counterparty management can cause concern for investors, because one-size-fits-all accounting does not deal with the problem of unknown counterparties.

While securities commissions in Canada ignore the changing nature of business, our governments and lawmakers continue to cave in to corporate and auditor lobbying pressures. Auditors have crammed a one-size-fits-all accounting approach down the throats of other industries such as financial institutions, real estate corporations, and resource industries, which has produced some disastrous results for Canadians. Some of the largest corporate failures in Canada tied to inadequate financial reporting have occurred in financial institutions and real estate companies.

Having blindly trusted the auditors for too long, and ignoring the need for a tough national securities commission, our lawmakers have worked themselves into a very tough corner, one they will need to fight their way out of, if they have any interest in protecting investors.

CHAPTER SIXTEEN

# Cooking the Books, Feathering the Nest, and Other Lessons in Manipulation

*"There are more fakers in business than in jail."*

MALCOLM FORBES

**YOU MIGHT** have gathered by now that accounting involves at least as much art as science. Depending on their circumstances, two companies can report the same transaction in different ways, which, in turn, results in different profit figures. The different results arise from choices in the way the companies account for the transaction, and from assumptions made by management in computing the results.

Sometimes a company has little or no choice in the way it accounts for a transaction. For example, cash spent on paying a phone bill is clearly an expense. Cash spent on new furniture, however, is reported as an asset, because furniture lasts for years and can be used to help the company to earn revenue in the future.

Conventional accounting practices measure income by matching accrued revenue against accrued expenses. Furthermore, a company may allocate accrued expenses to a certain time period regardless of when it actually spent the cash. For example, a company will likely report cash spent on furniture as an asset and then report the depreciation of the furniture's value in future years as an expense.

Sometimes, though, a company cannot make such a clear distinction between an expense and an asset. It may spend cash on maintenance, for example, then have to decide whether the cash simply kept the asset in working order or added value to it. If it added value, then the transaction will produce an asset and lead to depreciation against future revenue. This is where the complications begin.

Companies also make assumptions in reporting profits and cash flows. Two companies might account for sales in the same way, but then make different assumptions about the percentage of product that will be returned in the future. This assumption will have a direct impact on each company's revenue and reported profits.

While companies make assumptions about the way they report transactions, investors make assumptions when they interpret the reports. Even when management does not try to deliberately mislead investors, investors may simply misinterpret, or underestimate, the impact of accounting inequities. A wide chasm exists between the needs of investors to value a company properly and the rules and conventions of accounting and financial reporting. In order to bridge the gap, investors must make decisions based on incomplete or misleading information and fill in the gaps with their own assumptions.

In our experience, the values reported by most companies need adjusting to compensate for one-size-fits-all accounting rules, and to clarify management assumptions. To compensate for such inadequate information, investors have to make their own assumptions, and quite often their assumptions are wrong. Investors routinely misinterpret figures and miscalculate the value of the companies whose shares they own. A seemingly innocuous accounting choice can carve 10% to 20% off the value of a stock, so it pays to know how to make some common adjustments when evaluating a company.

To help you understand the basic ways in which companies can manipulate accounting rules, and the way investors can misinterpret the results, we use the acronym CHOICE, which stands for:

Capitalized expenses
Hidden asset impairments
Off–balance sheet liabilities
Inflated revenue
Cookie jar liabilities, and
Executive compensation

*Capitalized expenses.* By capitalizing an expense, a company records it as an asset on the balance sheet rather than an expense in the period in which it was paid. Capitalized expenses might include interest paid on debt, overhead expenses, such as a portion of management salaries and bonuses, and customer acquisition expenses. Two companies in the same industry may make different choices about whether or not to capitalize the same transaction. In particular, companies may choose to capitalize the cost of new facilities or significant research and development initiatives very differently. By comparing the accounting choices made by several companies in the same industry, investors can determine if one of them has capitalized an expense unduly to make its reported results appear more impressive.

*Hidden asset impairments.* When it comes to estimating the fair value of assets, executives sometimes make overly enthusiastic assumptions to hide impairments. Under IFRS, management will have even more opportunities to overinflate the value of assets on their balance sheets. IFRS will enable them to keep asset values inflated, even if those values become impaired, and when, in fact, a write-down expense should appear on the company's income statement instead.

By choosing the appropriate valuation technique and making the appropriate assumptions, management can inflate the value of anything, from financial instruments to real estate to capital assets to inventory. Even something as simple as an overly optimistic discount rate in a cash-flow model can wipe millions of dollars in expenses from a company's income statement.

To protect themselves against such manipulation, investors should compare the accounting choices and assumptions made by several companies in the same industry. Investors should also analyze the specific valuation techniques and assumptions employed by each company. For instance, a chosen valuation method, or discount rate, may not make sense for a company in its current circumstances. A company that is undergoing significant turmoil, or industry upheaval, might need to record some of its equipment at reduced values rather than assuming that future cash flows will remain uninterrupted for the next ten to fifteen years. Potential obsolescence considerations are important to manufacturing, industrial, media, communications, and technology companies, to name but a few.

*Off-balance sheet liabilities.* Off-balance sheet liabilities include items such as operating leases, pension liabilities, asset securitizations, contractual obligations, and future commitments. By definition, off-balance sheet liabilities remain hidden from obvious view on a company's financial statements. By removing them, a company can make its balance sheet appear much healthier than it should. To track down these hidden liabilities, investors have to read the notes to the financial statements closely, no matter how innocuous they might seem. Investors should also acquire a good understanding of the company and the industry involved.

Investors can use several methods to place a value on a company, and off-balance sheet liabilities will influence most of them. This influence will likely become even more extensive under IFRS. For example, a company may have removed most of its pension obligations from its balance sheet by using a high interest rate on future payouts, yet these obligations have not disappeared, and the company will still have to meet them at some point in the future.

*Inflated revenue.* A company's revenue influences its entire income statement. By making an unreasonable assumption about revenue, a company's management can distort its gross margin, operating income, and net income. Although it's one of the least transparent areas within accounting, revenue recognition can also be the most important factor in an investor's valuation and analysis of a company.

Companies can also play games with their revenue recognition in many ways: stuffing the channels, carrying uncollectible receivables, swapping revenues, setting inadequate return allowances, inventing fake customers, and recording revenue too early to boost a current period's results. Investors must understand how the company does business and how it receives cash flow in order to put its revenue recognition policies into a meaningful context.

Investors can search for clues by examining the revenue recognition notes of comparable companies. But sometimes a company operates in such a specialized niche of its industry that there are no comparable public peers, and the complement of deliverables might be a mix of proprietary technologies, multi-year installation and construction contracts, and servicing and maintenance services. Examples might include satellite and aerospace, flight simulation, and certain entertainment companies. In such complex situations, the only solution for retail investors may be to avoid the company altogether, if they feel they do not adequately understand how the company makes it sales. Better to be safe than sorry.

*Cookie jar liabilities.* We use the term cookie jar to describe a company's non-cash reserves. These are liability amounts that the company sets aside to protect itself against future accounting losses. The amount in the cookie jar can be raised or lowered depending on management's assumptions about the future. A small change in reserves can have a big impact on the company's bottom line, because an increase or decrease in liabilities usually flows directly to the income statement.

For example, during bad times when investors are expecting poor results, a company might make a pessimistic estimate of the cost of a restructuring program, or future insurance claims, thereby increasing the company's cookie jar liabilities. When its circumstances improve, the company lowers the liabilities, improving its income statement and making its recovery look more impressive than it is. Recording extra losses in bad times is known as taking a big bath.

Sometimes a company will record unwarranted losses in overly good times, as well. They do this so that, when bad times hit in the future, the company can use the accounting reserves to make the bad times look better. In this way the company's results appear smooth and more predictable. Investors then reward the company with a higher valuation in the marketplace.

*Executive compensation.* Executive compensation drives a significant amount of misleading financial reporting, and executives can take several approaches to line their own pockets. If an executive feels secure in his position, for example, he might deliberately depress a company's results, then set artificially low performance targets that he can easily meet by reversing a few liability reserves or resetting a few critical accounting assumptions.

In an accountant's world, the manipulation of financial statements usually follows, like night after day, the introduction of a management profit-sharing plan based on before-tax income or a similar measure. Especially in smaller public companies, a friendly board of directors will approve such a profit-sharing arrangement, almost without question, on the assumption that it will encourage management to work harder to the benefit of everyone.

A poorly constructed management contract can raise serious problems, especially when a business takes a turn for the worse. When times get tough and customer volumes decline, management can still ensure their bonuses by applying weak financial reporting and accounting rules to fabricate a quick turnaround, or to squeeze out a few more years of profitability.

Investors should always focus on the incentive and bonus schemes of senior executives, especially those who control the company's accounting and reporting choices, estimates, and assumptions. These schemes may not be readily apparent, but you can find clues scattered throughout company disclosures, such as the management proxy circular, the annual information form, insider trading records, the company's MD&A, and the notes to the financial statements.

At Nortel, for example, the company stopped making a profit long before the first serious decline in its share price. Under a bonus system based on net income, Nortel executives would not have earned any bonuses at all. Clearly, this would have displeased the executives, so Nortel's board of directors approved a plan to add expenses back to the company's net income until it reached an amount sufficiently high enough to justify the bonuses.

The extra cash going out the door in the form of outsized bonuses contributed to Nortel's losses. Even though Nortel reported the losses in its financial statements, investors ignored them and relied on the fabricated profit figure instead. Nortel shares continued, at least for a while, to increase in value before they finally plummeted into a freefall.

Although Canada requires senior executives of public companies to disclose their salaries and bonuses, investors cannot easily identify the manipulation of accounting and financial reporting. You may find some clues, though, by looking at some of the following areas:

1. *The type of accounting system adopted by a company.* As previously noted, US GAAP is much stronger than Canadian GAAP in helping to prevent financial trickery. IFRS, which will soon replace Canadian GAAP, is exceedingly weak, as well.

    Some companies may choose IFRS over US GAAP because of their European ownership. But they may also choose IFRS because the international standards give management a much better opportunity to manipulate the figures by writing up the value of assets, for example, according to management estimates.

    Investors should pay particular attention to a company that replaces reported net income with an alternative performance metric such as pro-forma earnings, cash-based earnings, or distributable cash. Such metrics enable management to enhance profits and make the company appear more successful than it is. In such cases, the company then offers shares to the public at inflated prices, while executives increase their bonuses based on the fake profits and rising stock price.

2. *Large shareholdings by executives nearing retirement.* Executives may pump up stock prices before selling their personal holdings and cashing in on stock options and other share-based schemes. They may do this by playing revenue games, for example, and shifting would-be expenses to the balance sheet to increase reported profit.

3. *Majority control by a parent company or large shareholder.* When a large shareholder or parent company controls a majority of the shares, it may try to get rid of a troublesome minority without paying a fair price to do it. The parent company may raise the price of goods and services supplied to the subsidiary, for example. The subsidiary's sales then magically decline, especially sales made to the parent company or its other subsidiaries. Related companies may also levy a variety of other charges against the majority-controlled company. All these manoeuvres function to force a decline in the results of the majority-controlled company.

Through additional accounting manipulations, the majority-controlled company may also report further losses. Each time the parent offers to buy out the minority shareholders, it makes a lower offer to remind them that only one buyer wants their shares. Such oppression against minority shareholders occurs commonly in Canada. But since investors have to prove in court, through expensive litigation, that such tactics were excessive or needlessly vindictive, you should avoid getting cornered as a minority shareholder.

4. *Potential violations of agreements with creditors, including banks.* As part of their agreement, creditors may insist that a company maintains minimum levels of net liquid assets and equity capital at all times. Since a period of cash losses can eat away at both liquidity and equity, companies may breach these covenants. To detect management deceptions, investors should look closely at notes in the company's financial statements that describe these covenants.

Companies may use weak accounting rules to circumvent these covenants. Since violation of the covenants may drive the company into bankruptcy or force a sale at bargain-basement prices, management has little to lose by applying weak accounting rules to enhance liquidity or reduce losses. Companies may appear to have turned themselves around when, in fact, they've simply used the techniques of revenue enhancement, expense deferral, and cash-flow gimmicks to fake compliance with covenants and restrictions.

5. *Insurance and regulatory requirements.* By regulation or agreement, construction companies, trust companies, banks, and insurers may have to maintain minimum capital or equity balances to withstand economic downturns or company-specific problems. Insurance companies provide surety bonds to construction companies that guarantee the completion of a job, if the company encounters financial problems. The surety bond provider will insist on adequate equity capital to reduce the risk that the construction company will go bankrupt. Likewise, trust companies, banks, and insurers have to maintain minimum levels of equity capital to meet regulations that protect depositors. Investors need to assess the financial cushion that such companies have in place above the minimum requirement. Especially

in bad times, they may use accounting games to try to manipulate revenue, and inflate profits and equity.

6. *Purchases and sales of other companies.* Two merged companies likely adhere to different accounting policies. Unscrupulous management can pursue its own objectives under the guise of developing a new set of financial reporting policies and procedures common to both.

   The first few periods of financial reporting after a major merger or acquisition may not raise any red flags. Investors should pay close attention to later accounting adjustments, when income statements, in particular, may contain extensive adjustments for inventory, receivables, and warranties, allowing management to pursue its own agenda.

7. *Purchase price based on earn-outs.* Some companies are difficult to value because much of their worth depends upon future events such as commodity prices. An acquiring company may base the purchase price of such a business on an earn-out formula, such as a multiple of the average of the next four years' net income. The purchaser of the company, who controls the accounting records, can easily reduce net income over the next four years through various accounting means. The seller then has to launch a costly lawsuit or swallow the loss. Given the vast array of accounting tricks that the purchaser can use after the fact, an earn-out formula is nothing more than a disaster waiting to happen.

8. *Income or other taxes.* Motivated by tax considerations, companies may play with their financial numbers, organizational structure, offshore locations, and more. When tax authorities allow companies to make accounting choices and apply them consistently, management teams may choose to gamble by taking a risky tax stance. If the tax court rules against them, investors get hit with a large tax bill. Investors should read the notes to financial statements that mention tax assessments. You should also keep in mind that many companies expect to win such cases, at least according to their financial statement notes.

   A final word on taxes: because they allow companies to revalue assets constantly, IFRS will likely produce very unusual numbers at times. Investors can conduct a useful reality check of a company's net income by calculating taxable income based on taxes actually paid.

Applying the open and vague assumptions allowed under so-called principles-based accounting rules like IFRS, management can create financial statements that put a favourable spin on bad decisions, such as troubling acquisitions or a poor choice of product mix. Thinking they need just a few quarters to right the ship, management may use all available accounting means to hide the gravity of a situation. Management may even justify their chicanery by claiming that they are doing a service to investors, while reaping benefits for themselves before the ship finally sinks.

Companies with several divisions may charge the expenses of a losing division to another division that is profitable, making a strong-performing division suddenly appear to have weakened. Investors may conclude, erroneously, that the strong division has encountered a negative trend, when, in reality, management simply transferred the expenses from a losing division. Investors may spot such peculiarities by reading the segment-reporting note to the financial statements.

A variation of this cover-up may occur when the company puts a restructuring charge on the income statement, supposedly to clean up a mess and restore the company to its former glory. All too often, the restructuring charge is excessive, and the extra amount is used in the next financial period to reduce expenses and give the appearance of an impressive turnaround. Then, in the following period, when the excess has already been used up, more financial losses might appear unless the company has made real and lasting operational improvements. This practice of holding off the wolves is all too prevalent in Canadian financial reporting. And unfortunately, too many investors end up getting duped.

It's imperative for investors to recognize management's objectives when analyzing a company's financial statements. To get the most accurate picture of a company, investors need to look beyond the accounting and financial reporting and try to understand the motives behind the numbers.

CHAPTER SEVENTEEN

# Cash Is Trash

*"Nothing succeeds like the appearance of success."*
CHRISTOPHER LASCH

**FINANCIAL ANALYSTS** and investors think they can uncover the real story about a company through its cash-flow statement. In truth, a company can manipulate its cash-flow statement as easily as its income statement. The fundamental problem is that many people mistakenly believe a cash-flow statement reflects actual cash flows. In fact, the adage that cash is king applies much more to a pawnshop than an investment philosophy.

You can thank accounting-speak for the misconception. Just as the word "cost" in accounting does not necessarily mean the amount that was paid for something, cash flow means something different to accountants than to investors, who must interpret a company's financial statements.

Most investors expect the figure for cash flow that appears in a company's cash-flow statement to represent the company's cash receipts minus its cash disbursements. But it doesn't have to. Much depends upon the design of the cash-flow statement. Investors and analysts can be easily deceived if they take shortcuts to determine a company's cash flow without analyzing the company's financial statements and the accompanying notes.

Investors often make a crucial mistake when reviewing accounting and financial reporting: they focus on what has happened and not on what did not happen, but should have happened. This may seem understandable, because if a transaction hasn't occurred, if there's no sale, no purchase, and no cash involved, then a company has nothing to report on its cash-flow or income statement. Nevertheless, the implications for the company's future might still be significant, because what ought to have happened did not.

For instance, a company that stops spending on advertising could soon experience a drop in sales. In the meantime, however, the company appears more profitable, because it's spending less cash on advertising and seems to be generating more cash from operations.

Likewise, a company may employ consultants who help it to generate revenue during a quarter but postpone paying for the consulting services until the following quarter. The company posts the consultants' bill to its accounting system as an account payable. Having collected the additional revenue in cash without paying the consultants' bill, the company appears to be more successful on a cash-flow basis than on an income basis. Yet the income-based figure, not the cash-based figure, more appropriately reflects the company's condition. (Read more about the effect of current assets and liabilities on cash flows in Appendix D.)

A CFO may manipulate a company's cash flows for several reasons. A company in financial trouble may need to borrow cash, for example, so the CFO approaches a banker who believes that a cash-flow statement tells a realistic story about the company. The CFO then devises a six-point plan to obtain the critical cash infusion from the bank. Under the plan, the company will:

1. Spend no cash over the next six months on repairing buildings and machinery, unless they're absolutely necessary to keep the company in operation.
2. Reduce spending on advertising by at least 50%.

3. Offer discounts of 10% to customers who pay cash, and additional discounts for lump-sum advance payments.
4. Delay for an additional 30 days, or longer, payments of outstanding accounts to all suppliers that do not offer discounts for prompt payment.
5. Pay all employee bonuses 60 days later than usual.
6. Decrease inventory by making special bulk sales for cash, at reduced prices.

According to the company's cash-flow statement for the period, it has saved cash by cutting spending on repairs and maintenance, and advertising. Using discounts to accelerate cash receipts can bring in cash more quickly, but reduced prices will also reduce revenue. Unless an investor or lender looks more closely at the company's previous financial statements, by comparing expenses on the income statement over several years, for example, the manipulated cash-flow statement reveals little of value.

Since management can choose the quarter or year in which it reports some types of bad or good news, deletions or deferrals can distort a company's cash-flow statement. Based on a misleading quarterly cash-flow statement, the company may succeed in enticing new lenders into the company. By the time the company reports the bad news about reduced revenue and lower income, it has completed the borrowing agreement and received the cash.

Management's actions or inactions can affect the reporting of cash on a cash-flow statement in other ways, as well. Management may choose to sign a contract on April 1 instead of March 31, for example, and push the financial reporting into the second quarter instead of the first. If one quarter isn't enough to persuade a lender or investor, management can roll forward the manipulated figures or escalate them to show two consecutive quarters of cash-flow growth.

Since management has so many opportunities to manipulate a company's cash-flow statements, investors must continue to pay close attention to the balance sheet and income statement to avoid being misled.

In assessing a company's cash-flow statements, investors need to consider three sections:

1. Cash generated by regular operating activities, such as providing goods or services, usually called cash from operations.
2. Cash obtained through financing activities, such as borrowing.
3. Cash spent on, or recovered from, investing activities.

The most important of the three sections is cash from operations. If a company uses money to sell its products at a loss, it will record negative cash flow from its operating activities and will need additional money to compensate for the cash loss. In other words, a company must offset a deficiency in one section of its cash-flow statement with money recorded in the other two sections. That money has to come either from financing activities, such as selling long-term debt or equity, or from selling its land, buildings, and other long-term assets. If a company records negative cash from operations beyond one year, investors should proceed with caution. They should watch carefully for such divesting, which will appear in the investing portion of a company's cash-flow statement. A shrinking company may indicate a shrinking future, as well.

Companies sell land and other assets out of desperation. In the late 1990s, for example, Canadian Airlines International tried desperately to survive by selling its aircraft. As a consequence, it had to lease aircraft and reduce its travel routes. In this case, the strategy worked; instead of going into bankruptcy, the airline managed to merge with Air Canada.

Companies may also offset negative cash from operations by selling short-term or long-term debt. Buyers of the debt, however, need to make sure that the company does not squander their cash on the unprofitable operating side of the business, or by making exaggerated cash distributions. They must also make sure the company does not use their cash to pay back previous lenders. Investors can find clues to such Ponzi schemes in the section of the cash-flow statement where the company records its financing activities.

Companies in difficulty may also try to obtain loans or share capital, and they'll use their cash-flow statement to do it.

If companies reported cash flow directly, it would appear in a format similar to this:

Cash from operations:
Cash increases (listed by category)            $ 1,000
Less:
Cash decreases (also listed by main categories)      840
Net increase in cash                              $   160

In this example, a company lists only cash on its direct cash-flow statement.

Unfortunately, few companies report cash flow in this way. Most of them use indirect reporting instead, which looks like this:

Cash from operations:
(in millions)

| | |
|---|---|
| Net income for the period | $ 120 |
| Add (subtract) non-cash items (examples would be amortization of intangibles) | 180 |
| | 300 |
| Changes during the period in current assets less current liabilities: | |
| Receivables | (380) |
| Inventory | (440) |
| Accounts payable | 450 |
| Unearned revenue (and similar) | 160 |
| | (210) |
| Cash provided by operations | $ 90 |

Like a conversation with someone who doesn't speak directly but beats around the bush, indirect cash-flow reporting is wide open to interpretation. Unless investors are careful, they can be misled.

At first glance, a company that reports $90 million in cash from operations, as our indirect cash-flow statement does, appears strong. But that figure may conceal all sorts of deceptions, including:

1. The figure of $120 million for net income: this figure can be manipulated by falsely increasing sales revenue, reducing expenses by placing them on the balance sheet as assets, or overstating assets such as receivables and inventory instead of writing them down.
2. A one-time extraordinary gain on the sale of extraneous equipment included in regular, recurring income as a reduction of an expense: this gives investors the impression that expenses will remain lower by a similar amount in future years, even though the company may have no more spare equipment to sell.
3. An inflated figure for accounts payable of $450 million: by reporting this inflated amount, management offsets $380 million in receivables, some of which may not be collectible, and $440 million in inventory, some of which may be obsolete.

Management can manipulate the company's accounts-payable balance at the end of a period to reduce the total change in current assets and current liabilities, which must be subtracted from net income to calculate cash from operations. In our example, the inflated accounts-payable figure helps to reduce total changes in current assets minus current liabilities to $210 million. When this is subtracted from $300 million in net income, it leaves a positive figure for cash from operations of $90 million. If management had reported accounts payable of only $250 million, instead of $450 million, it would have reported cash from operations as a cash loss of $110 million.

Knowing that it would alarm investors, management has deliberately avoided reporting negative cash from operations. Investors would draw an entirely different conclusion about the liquidity of the company if management suddenly expensed many of the receivables and the inventory costs, reported the extraordinary gain on the equipment sale outside of regular operations, instead of netting it against expenses, and kept accounts payable at normal levels.

To detect such trickery, investors should:

1. Compare the increase in accounts payable during the period with purchases, if reported, and cost of goods sold over the past period and

over the past three to four years. Is the increase in accounts payable out of phase with other numbers?
2. Compare the increase in inventory during the period with purchases and cost of goods sold. Companies sometimes accumulate many months of inventory that cannot be sold at cost. Balance sheet comparisons over three to four years might indicate such inventory build-ups. If the increase is not in line with cost of goods sold, investors should track down the reasons for the inventory increase. The company may provide an explanation in the MD&A section of its annual report. It might have purchased another company, for example, which would affect inventory. Without an adequate explanation, investors should dig deeper and perhaps consider selling the stock.
3. Analyze the company's financing transactions. Investors should identify lenders of cash to the company and the terms of their loans. In particular, investors should note high interest rates on new borrowings, additional pledges of assets as security, and tough restrictions on further borrowing.
4. Pay special attention to management compensation schemes. Investors should satisfy themselves that such schemes do not represent a culture of management and board myopia that could indicate financial manipulation.
5. Evaluate whether too much was paid for another company. Typically, a company pays for such an acquisition in stock, not cash, in order to acquire some cash flow from the new company's operations. Investors should also determine when the sellers of the acquired company are eligible to sell their shares, as such a sale may depress share prices.
6. Examine the notes to a company's financial statements to determine the profitability of its different operating segments.

In order to ensure there has been no manipulation of the cash-flow statement, it's important that investors refer to several different sources to gather all the evidence. It should be noted, however, that investors who rely too heavily on cash-flow figures are usually looking for quick answers, and at worst, asking for serious trouble.

CHAPTER EIGHTEEN

## Death By Nortel

> "Markets as well as mobs respond to human emotions; markets as well as mobs can be inflamed to their own destruction."
>
> OWEN D. YOUNG

**GREED, HUBRIS,** pride, denial, and sheer gullibility on a national scale pushed the value of Nortel's common shares up to $374 billion at their height. Now, as Canadian investors know, those shares are worthless.

For a brief moment, Nortel found itself on top of the heap, and not just in market hype, but also in actual business acumen. As Internet growth exploded, the company correctly timed the market for its optical networking gear. But once that moment passed, and the dot-com bubble collapsed, Nortel fell harder than its peers. While most of them recovered to prosper another day, Nortel embarked on a slow death march that led to a second embarrassing collapse and bankruptcy that wiped out investors amid allegations of accounting fraud.

From 1998 to 2001, Nortel used its bloated share price to purchase more than a dozen companies that added little to its product suite in the short term. Its workforce ballooned beyond 90,000 people, many of whom pursued research and development initiatives that would not produce revenue, never mind profits, for years to come.

Facing the costs of its acquisitions, and with a large part of the company generating no revenue, Nortel did not produce net profits. Yet the company still managed to convince investors to ignore the large losses and focus instead on net earnings from operations, a figure that the company basically invented for the purpose of distracting investors. In 2000, for instance, Nortel reported revenue of $30.3 billion, and "net earnings from operations" of $2.3 billion. In subsequent press releases, Nortel continually trumpeted revenue and earnings from operations, noting in particular, the seemingly impressive percentage increases from quarter to quarter.

Everyone from docile, starry-eyed media to investment analysts swallowed Nortel's story. As they regurgitated this figure over and over again, they drove up the share price for the purposes of their own ego and prestige, not to mention the brokerage revenue it brought their firms. When Nortel reported in 1999 that third-quarter earnings from operations had increased by 61%, a headline in *The Wall Street Journal* blared, "Nortel Tops Forecasts as Net Rises 61%." In days gone by, the world's most respected business publication would have reserved the word "net" to imply "net income." Now it meant something different, and the difference was enormous.

Only rarely did any of these enthusiasts mention that Nortel did not actually make any money. In 2000, for instance, the company lost $3.5 billion. To account for the $5.8-billion difference between its net loss and its so-called earnings from operations, Nortel referred to "Acquisition Related Costs." It defined these costs as "in-process research and development expenses and the amortization of acquired technology and goodwill from all acquisitions subsequent to July 1998, stock option compensation, and certain one-time gains and charges."

Now there's a mouthful.

Neither the company, nor its supporters, bothered to explain why Nortel had deducted these specific charges. Nor did they explain why investors should ignore these charges when valuing the company.

We would be the last people to advise investors to take a company's net income, produced in accordance with GAAP, at face value. But even we find it beyond the realm of belief to think that a company could express a $3.5-billion net loss as $2.3 billion in earnings. Keep in mind that Nortel ignored these "acquisition costs" not just once, but quarter after quarter, year after year.

The very fact that the company referred to its made-up performance measure as "earnings from operations" speaks volumes. Depending on the industry, a company might exclude certain one-off charges in calculating normal operating earnings. Nortel excluded far more and then referred to its calculation as earnings from operations, which was similar enough to the normal measure to leave investors hopelessly confused.

To add insult to injury, Nortel's management argued that "acquisition-related costs" were non-cash items and could therefore be ignored. Then they calculated their bonuses to a significant degree on the made-up performance metric of "earnings from operations." Yet the acquisition-related costs were incurred in acquiring assets that would eventually produce revenue for the company. If the company had developed the acquired products internally, how could it have justifiably ignored the cost of the acquisition?

Nortel supporters argued that the company had paid for the acquisitions in shares, not cash, which only created additional problems. All of the shares issued for the acquisitions had diluted the value of stock held by existing shareholders. At its height, Nortel was trading at more than 100 times its made-up "earnings from operations." Either way, investors were way out on a limb.

Defending Nortel became an issue of national pride. When we argued that investors should not ignore the company's net losses, Nortel CEO John Roth told the *National Post* that we were undermining "Canadian technology companies' efforts to secure investment, driving them to the United States where valuations in the sector are better understood." In the same article, published in July 2000, just months before the start of the company's ignominious slide, the headline said that Nortel's earnings had risen by 64% during the quarter.

Nobody questioned the figure, and nobody drew attention to Roth's performance bonuses and stock option grants, which were largely based on Nortel's made-up "earnings from operations."

That year, Roth also criticized Canada's tax treatment of stock options. Because the US treated them less harshly, he said, Nortel executives were leaving in droves to work at US companies. Without favourable changes to Canada's tax system, he added, Nortel's Canadian workforce would continue to shrink.

Again, nobody seemed even slightly bothered that Roth, as the single largest holder of Nortel stock options, had the most to gain from a change in tax treatment. Instead, he received accolades as a catalyst for change. *Time* magazine called him "the most successful businessman in modern Canadian history." *National Post Business* magazine featured him on the cover twice in 2000, first in caricature as a flying superhero over a caption, giving him credit for making investors more than $250 billion, and again, just three months later, crowning him as CEO of the year.

Less than twelve months later, the value of Nortel's shares had sunk precipitously, its prospects looked dim, and Roth had disappeared as CEO. If he'd received as much blame for scuppering Nortel as he did for building it into a global corporate titan, the media should have, at least, accused him of personally destroying hundreds of billions of dollars in shareholder wealth. Canadian business magazines should have portrayed him on their covers as the Grim Reaper, using his scythe to cut down scores of investors, but, perhaps, they were too ashamed to draw attention to their own sycophantic fawning.

Naturally, Roth didn't see it that way, nor did many others. Roth blamed Nortel's decline on Canada's failure to "create a culture of winners." In the meantime, Roth had successfully cashed out of his Nortel options, stuffing his own pockets with several hundred million dollars before they collapsed in value. Most other Canadians were not so lucky. Many lost everything that they had bet on the Nortel dream.

Investors had to shoulder some of the blame, too. They had put their faith in a made-up performance measure. They had regarded a company executive as a national hero. And they had ignored the net losses that Nortel itself had published in plain black and white. Within twenty-four months, Nortel's shares fell from their high of $124.50 per share to a low of just $0.67. Frank Dunn replaced Roth as CEO, and the company embarked anew, or so it seemed.

Amazingly, many people still held high hopes for Nortel. In mid-2002, the company raised $1.5 billion by issuing new shares. In the following months, their value slid downward by 70%. The company reported disastrous results for 2002, then surprised everyone by reporting a profit in the first quarter of 2003. And it was an honest-to-goodness net profit, at that, not made-up "earnings from operations." Nortel's shares started climbing once again, and the company's top executives and managers, including Dunn, collected millions in bonuses based on the company's "return to profitability."

Unfortunately, Nortel had once again betrayed investors' trust. Warning signs emerged in 2003 and early 2004. Even as Nortel reported its surprise profits, the company's board initiated an internal review to examine its balance sheet accounts and expense reserves. In October 2003, Nortel announced it would restate its financial results for 2000, 2001, 2002, and the first half of 2003, including the period of so-called return to profitability.

The market paid little attention to the announcement, and Nortel shares continued to climb. In early 2004, they exceeded $11 a share, and investors patted themselves on the back again. Those who had bought in to the new issue in mid-2002 had enjoyed handsome gains of more than 400%.

In March 2004, Nortel announced further restatements. The company also fired Dunn and several top executives for cause. As it turned out, the company had inappropriately manipulated expense reserves to orchestrate a quarterly profit and trigger executive bonus payments. Using one of the oldest accounting tricks in the book, Nortel's management had arbitrarily reduced liability reserves in order to book gains on the income statement. Nortel also had to correct revenue figures reported incorrectly in 2000, the heyday of John Roth. Not only were Nortel's "earnings from operations" based on bogus numbers, the company's reported increases in revenue were bogus, as well.

Nortel restated its financial results twice more in 2006 and 2007. For long periods over these years, the company's stock continued to trade, even though investors could not examine a recent financial statement— because the company didn't have one. With any other company but Nortel, authorities might have disallowed the stock from trading at all until the company got its house in order. But this was Nortel. Apparently, Canadian securities regulators treat a company differently after it becomes a national embarrassment.

Nortel never really recovered from the initial accounting scandal. It spent months of management time, and roughly $400 million, attempting to reconcile its figures with what actually happened in the early part of the decade. In the process, it completely lost its focus on the future. In the US, the Securities and Exchange Commission pursued the company and fined it $35 million. In Canada, regulators politely asked the company to pay nothing more than a few costs related to their investigation.

As Nortel limped into 2009, the company sought bankruptcy protection from creditors. Nortel had carried a considerable amount of debt for years and needed to make drastic changes to survive, but the market had little interest in major restructuring stories. To satisfy its creditors, Nortel would have to be broken up and sold in pieces. Nortel shares were delisted on June 26, 2009, at less than 2¢ a share on a split-adjusted basis, marking a disgraceful ending for Canada's 125-year-old telecom pride and joy.

Perhaps investors could forgive themselves for getting burned once by Nortel's accounting scams. To get burned twice by accounting scams at the same company seems a bit harder to explain. It seemed that many Canadians could not abandon their love affair with Nortel, nor could they stop defending the company even as it went down for the second time. Afflicted with some sort of Stockholm Syndrome for abused investors, they defended Nortel to the bitter end, seemingly unable to face the idea that they'd ploughed their money into a fundamentally flawed investment.

But Nortel certainly wasn't the last time investors would fall victim to a deadly combination of their own investment hubris, seriously deficient securities regulations, and lax accounting and financial reporting oversights.

CHAPTER NINETEEN

# Lessons from the 1920s to the Present

*"The most destructive criticism is indifference."*
EDGAR WATSON HOWE

**INVESTORS COULD** have learned more from the Nortel fiasco if federal and provincial governments still held judicial inquiries into such failures and publicized the findings. But since they stopped holding such inquiries in the 1980s, investors have had fewer opportunities to learn about the methods being used to dupe them. The media fell into a similar slumber, content to report on press releases that contained little in substance, yet were trumpeted by regulators and authorities as major advancements in financial reporting.

The Hercules decision in 1997 was the icing on the cake for investors. The decision by the Supreme Court of Canada made it extremely difficult for investors to sue auditors successfully, even if they had signed off on bogus annual financial statements. With this decision, an annual audit became close to meaningless for investors. Nevertheless, lawmakers continued to consult the auditors on financial reporting matters, even though the auditors had abandoned their traditional role and were no longer independent, nor capable of fairly considering investor needs.

By the mid-2000s, Canada had suffered financial reporting disasters on a monumental scale. First at Nortel, where they reported profits based on made-up earnings from operations, and then from low-quality business income trusts, which based favourable-looking reports on unreliable distributable cash figures. The worst was yet to come, however.

While our lawmakers again remained silent, Canada's auditors unilaterally decided to adopt IFRS, despite serious reservations about the new accounting rules from our largest trading partner, the US.

Canada has made some improvements to auditing and accounting rules that worked to the benefit of investors. Many of the changes occurred between 1950 and 1975, as a result of efforts made by a few dedicated people. Until the 1970s, governments stayed out of the picture, even ignoring the frauds related to the 1929 stock market crash. In the 1970s, companies and securities legislation incorporated GAAP by name. Yet, by the middle of the decade, when faced with more financial reporting problems, our lawmakers once again decided to ignore the situation. Instead they left the problem in the hands of conflicted accountants and auditors, who decided to deal with the situation in their own way.

During the recession of 1980 to 1982, it became clear that auditors did indeed have their own way of operating, but it had little to do with the well-being of Canada's investors. A new type of auditor had assumed power, one that stressed the marketing of accounting services over the interests of investors.

Meanwhile, the provinces staffed the accounting departments at their securities commissions largely with people who supported the auditors in whatever they wanted. While, nationally, Canada remained without an investor-oriented national securities commission to offer a different opinion. During this period, the integrity of financial reporting began to depend to a greater extent than ever on what auditing clients would pay for.

It took only a few auditors to seize control and impose their self-serving, anti-investor postures upon the rest of Canada. As lawmakers remained silent, one corporate failure after another followed the change of attitude by auditors after 1982. Fifteen years later, the Hercules case went a step further, giving unwarranted protection to auditors, who were offering audits of even lower quality than before.

Even though no government or regulator will ever draw their attention to it, investors must recognize the serious deterioration of financial reporting integrity that has occurred in Canada since 1982. Auditors and accountants have now imposed the vastly inferior International Financial Reporting Standards upon investors and creditors in Canada in a gesture that is both amazing and disgraceful. Viewed against the situation that existed in the 1920s, before the great market crash, Canada has made a stunning lack of progress in the way its public companies report their financial activities.

All of us would be rich if we had a dollar for every market pundit, economist, or politician who has said that the market crash of 1929 could never happen again. But exactly what part of the crash are they talking about? The prevalence of financial dishonesty that preceded the crash? The size of the market losses? The Great Depression that followed? Or the time it took to emerge from that depression?

If they are talking about the financial shenanigans that preceded the crash, they couldn't be more wrong. Much of the deceit and trickery that existed in the 1920s is still with us in Canada today, for the simple reason that we have not taken sufficient steps to curtail these deceptive practices. We have not seriously bothered to hone our skills to protect ourselves. Canadian market regulators do not appear to be aware of, or want to address, many of the basic bread-and-butter financial abuses and the warning signs that accompany them. Just look at the dismal record of prosecutions in this country and the excuses made by authorities for not proceeding with cases. Nonsensical statements like "Canadians don't want US-style regulation" pass unchallenged by the media, politicians, and investors alike.

Consequently, regulators are heavily overmatched against financial manipulators, and their inexperience in dealing with these scams has compounded itself over the years. Canadian regulators are in no shape to discover scams in their infancy. Even after scams are uncovered, our regulators are not equipped to ensure a successful prosecution. Oversight, warnings, and prosecutions with respect to accounting manipulations simply do not exist in Canada.

Accounting aside, our regulators still find it hard to address the needs of investors on even basic levels. In one of their most common tricks, a company will pull the wool over investors' eyes by informing them on, say, page 99 of a prospectus, in a footnote, that future dividends depend heavily on finding new investors to pour capital into the company. Regulators know that the average investor, or investment advisor, does not read a prospectus from front to back. So why do they let companies get away with burying crucial facts in the fine print of their financial documents? This kind of behaviour by companies amounts to nothing more than a regulator-sanctioned pyramid scheme. The underwriters certainly do not care enough to stop such a fiasco. And the issuers can always argue that they provided full disclosure. Somewhere, at some point, someone has to take the responsibility for acting on behalf of investors.

The mere presence of even an insufficient warning buried deep in offering documents can make prosecution of the offenders far more complex. Canada has made some improvements over the years to dig these warnings out of footnotes, requiring them, instead, to appear on page one of a prospectus, but we still have a long way to go. We need, for example, a regulated list of essential disclosure to warn investors about specific risks, as opposed to boilerplate nonsense that gets copied from one prospectus to the next.

In addition, a footnote on page 99 of a prospectus should not be sufficient enough to keep regulators and prosecutors at bay. Yet it does, because our laws are weak and our will to prosecute, even weaker. Even an unsuccessful prosecution would be better than no prosecution at all. It would, at least, function as a warning to serial offenders to change their ways. Prosecutions might also finally prompt some overdue regulatory and legislative changes.

Despite the monumental advancements in accounting and financial reporting practices that have occurred in the US, the situation in Canada hasn't really changed much since the 1920s. In those primitive days of accounting and financial reporting, many public companies engaged in flawed reporting practices. While some companies, like US Steel, published adequate reports, given the times, many other companies, like the railroads, issued flawed financial statements that amounted to nothing more than management pipe dreams. Inflated asset values were commonplace, and unfortunately, were believed by many investors during that era.

After World War I, money was needed for construction projects and general expansion, and the inflated financial numbers helped to attract naive investors. As the 1920s progressed, exaggerations of assets and profits became more extensive and stock prices remained bloated, thereby turning the financial market into one giant pyramid scheme.

Profit and asset exaggeration play an important role in pyramid schemes and Ponzi frauds. To attract money from newer creditors and equity investors in order to repay initial creditors and investors, a company spreads lies about its success based on financial and accounting trickery. The slacker the reporting rules, the more easily a company can con its investors. In Canada today, supporters of so-called principles-based financial reporting cannot grasp that such reporting plays directly into the hands of fraudsters. And matters will only get worse under IFRS.

As they did in the 1920s, unscrupulous Canadian companies continue to search for new ways to inflate profits. Just in the past ten years, companies have used bogus metrics and so-called cash-based reporting, while ignoring the obvious expenses of doing business. Changes in accounting rules have enabled companies to eliminate the cost of intangible assets and other expenses, while the broad scope for interpretation and assumptions has enabled companies to bamboozle investors into thinking they're profitable when they're not. IFRS encourages this kind of evasive financial reporting and will likely contribute to more than a few pyramid schemes over the next decade by allowing management to revalue assets and manipulate income. IFRS could actually set investors back fifty years before improvements start to be made.

Since the 1920s, Canada has lived with grossly inadequate investor education and protection. Similar activities that preceded the 1929 stock market crash prevail in Canada today and should not be ignored by investors. During the 1920s, cash-flow statements that actually focused on cash receipts and disbursements did not exist. Thus, investors could not compare a company's income and profit statement with its cash generation and usage. It was much easier for companies in the 1920s to bloat profits and ignore non-existent cash receipts, which eventually led to the disastrous drop in stock prices in 1929.

Conditions have changed since then, and accounting rules have been tightened, but given the tricks that have been successfully used in the past decade alone, Canadian investors still do not know what to watch for. Management provides investors with only selected information—partly to finance bonuses to undeserving executives—yet they continue to pour money into these unworthy companies at high prices.

For about twenty-five years after the 1929 stock market crash, only minor protections for investors were built into Canadian financial reporting legislation. In the early 1950s, small groups of accountants and auditors became concerned with needless diversity and began issuing bulletins to provide guidance on financial reporting, primarily for retail and manufacturing industries. During the 1960s, the auditors' umbrella group made some progress in aiding communication between companies, creditors, and shareholders. Research resulted in guidance to practitioners, and a number of key reference books were written.

But by 1980, financial reporting in Canada had taken a significant turn for the worse. Accountants and auditors no longer focused on improving financial reporting for investors. Forthright reporting was no longer a priority. Instead, accountants and auditors emphasized the marketing of their services to corporations. Especially after the recession of 1981 and 1982, shell-shocked auditors kowtowed to their client corporations to the detriment of investors. As sheer monetary greed took over, a series of high-profile corporate collapses ensued. Two banks collapsed in Alberta, Northland and Canadian Commercial, essentially from substandard auditing. Throughout this period, Canada's lawmakers continued to maintain that all was well. They wrote off the bank failures as minor exceptions to the rule. Underneath the collapses, however, severe problems were brewing.

By the 1980s, Canada's lawmakers at the federal and provincial levels had amended their companies and securities legislation to embrace the version of accounting known as Generally Accepted Accounting Principles. GAAP had been developed over the previous twenty years or so to give greater credibility to the reporting of some types of transactions. Lawmakers could have given the task of setting accounting and auditing rules to an independent body; instead, they assigned responsibility for setting these principles to the country's auditors. By law, auditors acquired unchecked power to set the accounting rules, despite any conflicts of interest that might exist with their corporate clients.

Canadian GAAP differed from US GAAP in several important respects. In Canada, the adoption of accounting rules depended heavily upon the approval of powerful Canadian companies. Canadian GAAP also downplayed the importance of detailed disclosure, leaving investors guessing at what was happening in many companies. Eventually, when Canadian companies needed financing from the US, and had to meet US reporting standards, comparisons between the two countries were drawn, revealing Canadian financial reporting requirements to be seriously deficient, even primitive.

US companies operated within a much stricter regulatory environment, as well. The Securities and Exchange Commission had been established within five years of the stock market crash in 1929. Canada had no equivalent regulatory body, and still doesn't. The current effort to form a national regulator in Canada seems poised to fall well short of investor needs. Unless enforcement efforts and skills are seriously improved, and investor needs given priority over corporate wants, Canada will remain significantly behind the US SEC.

The enforcement efforts underlying Canadian GAAP were also weak and too frequently required tough negotiations between auditors and their corporate clients. With no Canadian SEC to bring both sides into line, improved financial reporting for investors was not forthcoming. All too often, rule changes were accepted only after they had been sufficiently watered down by corporate interests, dropping investor interests to the bottom of the priority list. As more financial collapses continued, our lawmakers remained silent.

During the recession of the early 1980s, the watering down of investor interests gained steam. The age of financial tricks blossomed as some accountants used their training to assist companies in bamboozling investors. Companies weakened by the recession were made to look better for a few years, thereby attracting investors who did not understand accounting's lack of precision and, all too frequently, its lack of reality.

Still, our lawmakers chose not to legislate a Canadian SEC. Instead, they left all power over financial reporting in the hands of companies and their auditors. Not surprisingly, since the early 1980s, Canadians have seen a flood of accounting and auditing-based financial failures. Worse, our lawmakers have essentially condoned these white-collar games by pretending that they do not exist. The fear of backlash from the country's large corporations has apparently intimidated them into silence.

## CHAPTER TWENTY

# Junkyard Blues

> *"Our great error is that we suppose mankind more honest than they are."*
>
> ALEXANDER HAMILTON

**SOMETIMES A** company swindles investors right in front of their faces, without using many accounting tricks at all. Like the emperor's new clothes, they just tell investors a story and, if they're convincing enough, collect their money.

A company in Quebec once attracted investors with an apparently foolproof and advanced computer system for translating English-language statutes into French. The swindlers demonstrated the system at their offices for investors and bankers. They asked their guests to choose ten pages at random from a book written in English that was sitting beside the terminal. After the guests identified the pages and scanned them into the system, it produced a perfect French translation. A translator invited to attend the session from a local service bureau then attested to the quality of the translation. The investors and bankers could not line up fast enough to persuade the company to take their money. None of them realized that the swindlers had translated the book in advance and loaded it into the computer, in English and French versions.

When rent came due on the office the next month, the swindlers had disappeared, along with the computers and the book. Refusing to believe that he'd fallen for such an obvious scam, one investor wondered whether someone else had bought the technology or, perhaps, even stolen it.

The owner of another company called VisuaLabs, based in Calgary, attracted a market value of more than $300 million by convincing institutional and individual investors that it had developed several groundbreaking consumer technologies. The company's founder, Sheldon Zelitt, claimed that VisuaLabs would produce a 3-D television that did not require special glasses or other apparatus, and another technology called GroutFree that would allow several small and inexpensive plasma screens to be stitched together to create a much larger viewing surface.

The company went public in 1997. Five years later, Zelitt said he would present both technologies to investors at the company's annual meeting. Zelitt did as he promised, unveiling the 3-D TV and a GroutFree prototype. But after the meeting, suspicious board members discovered that the prototype was actually a store-bought TV that Zelitt had etched with a glass cutter to make the screen appear as if it had been assembled from smaller screens. And the magic behind the 3-D technology turned out to be a compilation of trick photography on a VHS tape. The market value of VisuaLabs was obliterated overnight.

Perhaps the biggest scams of all occur in the film business. There's a popular saying: people don't invest in the film business, they make donations. That's because few films generate a profit, and rarely a cash profit, once a film company's accountants have added up the columns. And that's why film company scam artists tend to pay themselves a percentage of revenue, because even a two-thumbs-down film generates some of that. By the time producers, directors, actors, film companies, and individuals, who have advanced the funds, have divided up the revenue, the company has little left to pay the remaining expenses. As a shareholder, you may receive a percentage of the profit, but only if there is one. Generally speaking, you have a better chance of earning a profit at the racetrack than on a film project. At least the horses are honest.

Metal recovery firms, more commonly called scrapyards, are a perfect example of how companies can cook their books and financial statements to disguise frauds over several years. Such frauds occur in other industries, as well, but they seem to flourish in the scrap metal business.

In a company that buys scrap metal and sells the finished product in a cleaned-up state, the main assets are accounts receivable and inventory. The company might also have contractual obligations to deliver quantities of metal at fixed dates and fixed prices in the future.

Here's how such a company operates:

1. Trucks are sent to different locations that provide the scrap, such as building demolition sites. Before the building is knocked down, the company pulls the copper wire out of every room, along with other scrap metals.
2. As each truck returns to the scrapyard to dump its load, it's weighed. The supposed difference between a loaded and an empty truck is the weight of scrap metal that the truck picked up from the customer. However, room exists for con games, depending upon (a) who weighs the trucks and keeps the records, and (b) who estimates the proportion of non-copper elements mixed in with the copper scrap.
3. Copper wire, for instance, comes in a covering that has to be stripped off. Until the stripping process occurs, the copper is usually stored in tangled piles many metres high.
4. After stripping the covering, the scrap dealer sorts the copper by grade. Selling prices depend on the percentage of copper in the wire.
5. Scrapyards often chop up the copper and store it in large barrels until they sell it. This means that a scrapyard, at any point in time, has on-site large piles of unsorted scrap metal, piles that contain only one type of metal, in-process piles from which the waste material has not been stripped, stripped metal awaiting chopping, chopped metal in barrels ready for sale, and metal already sold, but stored temporarily until shipment.
6. The price at which a dealer buys and sells scrap affects the success of the scrapyard. Metal inventories represent large sums of money. Banks place a limit on the amount they'll lend to finance unsold

inventory. Yet if a company can increase its inventory of certain metals before the price of the metal rises, it can make big profits. Ideally, a scrapyard can store piles of scrap metal while the prices rise. Although it also runs the risk that prices will drop before it can sell the metal.

7. The scrapyard has to protect the metal, and to do this, it needs more than a couple of junkyard dogs. The scrapyard can purchase insurance, but coverage for anything but basic theft by employees can cost a lot of money, and even basic theft has to be proven before a company can collect. Depending on metal prices, a scrapyard has to make continual trade-offs between the cost of materials and possible losses if the price drops.

Having a scrapyard up and running, with shares issued to the public, management can now make choices that benefit themselves and ultimately deprive shareholders of their profits. Here's how:

1. Suppliers of scrap, who do not estimate the likely recovery of metal, are identified and then shortchanged. The difference between the price paid and the value of the scrap is then credited to a company that executives of the public company own indirectly.
2. Lower grades of metal are then delivered to less knowledgeable customers, who are charged for a higher-quality product. The additional profit is credited to the executive-owned company.
3. The high-quality metal is sold to companies owned by family members, who are charged low prices. The family-owned company then either sells it to other customers, or sells it back to the public company at a higher price than it paid.
4. Scrap metal is also sold for minimal value to friends, who provide kickbacks to executives, such as free vacations, recreation equipment, and golf-club memberships.
5. The public company, and companies owned by the executives, sign joint contracts to purchase metal in the future at a fixed price. If the price of the metal rises in the meantime, more volume is assigned to the executive-owned companies and less to the public company. If the price drops, they do the opposite.

6. Metal is traded among a group of companies, with kickbacks generated by each trade.
7. Inventory is stolen from the company. Then inventory is borrowed at year-end from other dealers, to give the appearance that no inventory is missing.
8. Arrangements are made with friends in the business to sign letters declaring that some scrap-metal inventories in their yards belong to the public company.
9. Inventories are overstated by filling barrels with lower-priced metal and claiming that it is of a higher quality than it is. If an auditor is knowledgeable and diligent in checking the inventory, a layer of higher-grade material is placed on top of a barrel full of lower-grade scrap.
10. Expense accounts are padded, excessive bonuses are taken, salaries are collected from more than one payroll, and other similar, more conventional tricks are carried out.

Regardless of the industry involved, bankers and shareholders recover little or nothing after one of these frauds. Such swindles have occurred frequently in Canada. As the company grows, shareholders receive dividends every quarter, and audit reports confirm the company's good health. Shareholders assume all is well and remain oblivious to the lurking danger. Then, one day, the media suddenly reports, "Environmental Services Firm Bankrupt." As creditors restructure the remaining pieces of the business, investors walk away with nothing.

How does this happen? How can a crook pay himself a fat salary and collect share options, as well, over several years without getting caught? The crook might even have donated some of his shares to charity at high prices, collecting a nice, fat income tax deduction and a reputation for selfless philanthropy. By the time the shares collapse in value, the crook has sold off his holdings and the charities are left with nothing. Unfortunately, these kinds of scams happen over and over again.

Auditors assume little or no responsibility when such scams occur, and securities commissions seldom take meaningful action. As usual, shareholders are on their own when it comes to protecting themselves.

CHAPTER TWENTY-ONE

# What Happens if You Sue?

*"Agree, for the law is costly."*
WILLIAM CAMDEN

**SOME CANADIAN** companies are cross-listed in Canada and the US, and they publish financial statements in accordance with US accounting and auditing principles and rules. For Canadian investors, these often make the wisest investments, especially if they encounter financial deceptions and try to recover their losses.

That's because the Securities and Exchange Commission monitors Canadian companies that trade in the US. This doesn't guarantee that every trick will be caught, but it certainly discourages many scams that succeed repeatedly in Canada. Canada's abysmal record of prosecuting and convicting companies that engage in financial malfeasance just encourages companies to keep doing it, because they know they have little to lose.

With the presence of SEC behind the cross-listed companies, investors stand a better chance of recovering some of their losses from financial scams. In Canada, under our current regulatory regime, they stand little chance at all.

Exceptions do occur, however. In Manitoba, for example, unit holders of the Crocus Investment Fund recovered a portion of the money they invested on the assumption that the fund was more than a glorified Ponzi scheme. The settlement was made out of court, which is par for the course in Canada. Even in the rare cases when investors recover some of their money, they'll seldom receive an admission of responsibility.

Canadian shareholders achieve more success in reaching a favourable settlement if US lawyers, through class-action proceedings conducted in the US, and under tougher US laws, arrange it. In fact, when lawyers bicker in such cases over the jurisdiction of a class-action lawsuit, defendants argue strongly that the case should be heard in Canada, because they know they stand a better chance in this country of winning.

Most investors who try to recover their losses from an investment in a financially deceptive company soon discover that they cannot afford the legal fees. As an alternative, they may choose to pursue a class action, so that many shareholders can share the cost of the litigation. Before they can proceed, however, a lawyer must convince a judge that each of them has suffered a loss in the same way, for the same reason, over the same period, at the hands of the same company. The greater the number of shareholders who suffered financial injury, the better the chance of convincing the court that they acted on false or misleading financial information.

The jurisdiction in which a case is heard will influence its outcome, as well. Courts apply the law differently in different states and provinces. Quebec, for instance, seems tougher on securities crimes compared to other provinces. But, matters can change quickly, which makes an experienced lawyer even more essential. In most jurisdictions, class-action lawsuits succeed only if the plaintiffs can prove fraud or negligence. Even then, shareholders may recover only a portion of their losses.

Just to get the case off the ground, plaintiff shareholders must find a law firm willing to accept their case, which isn't easy. Lawyers are hesitant to take on such cases because, depending on the circumstances, they may not collect a fee unless the case succeeds. Lawyers will also have to foot the bill for expert testimony, as well as their own time and expertise. They may also have to pay some or all of the defendant's costs, if they lose. That's why most law firms need to feel pretty confident that they'll succeed before they'll take on a class-action lawsuit.

Since many Canadian law firms generate substantial fees from defending corporations and their auditors, shareholders may have to consult several law firms before they find one to represent them. When they do find one, they'll often end up with a smaller firm, especially in Canada.

For their class-action case to interest a lawyer and then persuade a court that it should proceed, shareholders involved in the case have to consider the following factors:

1. Do shareholders have enough in common to justify a class action rather than individual lawsuits? An experienced lawyer can make this assessment quickly.
2. Based on the merits of the case, do the plaintiffs stand a better-than-even chance of winning? If not, they may not find a lawyer to represent them.
3. Is there enough money at stake to warrant a lawyer's enthusiasm for the case? Most lawyers charge a fee of about 30% of the eventual proceeds after expenses.
4. Can the case be settled prior to trial? Most lawyers prefer to settle rather than proceeding to trial because it keeps their costs down.
5. Will representatives of the shareholders assist in preparing the case? Lawyers rely on these representatives to help draft a convincing statement of claim to present to the court.
6. Will the action succeed only if the court rethinks a previous decision? It requires time and money to persuade a court to change its mind about a previous decision. With the exception of Quebec, most courts will adhere to the Hercules Managements decision, for example, in cases involving shareholders proceeding against auditors who have signed clean audit reports on a company's bogus annual financial statements.
7. Is one of the intended defendants close to bankruptcy? If so, the plaintiff shareholders will have to identify other defendants with deeper pockets, such as auditors and insurance companies, whose policies cover directors and officers. Otherwise, they won't recover enough to justify the expense.
8. Have the plaintiff shareholders considered the effects of litigation fatigue? Defendants commonly try to increase their opponents' costs

and delay a court decision with a flood of motions and other legal tactics. Canadian investors must have the stamina to pursue a case to the bitter end, if necessary.
9. Is there anyone left to sue? Many Canadian Ponzi schemes involve fraudsters who simply take the money and spend it, leaving investors with no money and no hope of recovering a penny.

If a law firm takes the case, it then has to draft the lawsuit, alleging that the defendants owed duties of care and other responsibilities to investors, were negligent or fraudulent, and directly caused financial losses. The lawyers have to gather alleged facts from investors and others, who have to be cooperative. Basic matters such as what documents investors saw, and when, from the company, brokers, and others before investing can become important.

Such cases usually involve multiple defendants, such as directors, officers, and auditors, and many will have their own teams of lawyers to slow down and complicate procedures. After they file their defences, a round of clarifications, examinations, and questioning occurs, all of which takes time.

Discussions among lawyers will occur about the possibility of a settlement, sometimes involving mediation or arbitration. Shareholders will have to decide whether they want to accept a settlement, usually for a fraction of the amount they lost, or whether they want to pursue the case and risk losing in court.

If the case goes to court, the trial date may be months, or even years, away. The trial itself may take several weeks. It will take time to prepare written arguments and even more time for the judge to render a written decision. If one side decides to appeal the decision, it can take one to three years for a higher court to hear the appeal.

In addition, extensive hearings and appeals on a variety of procedural legal matters can take even more time. In short, those who want to drag out a civil trial and avoid paying investors for many years have plenty of opportunity to do so in Canada.

Anyone who says that Canadian investors can always sue a company that deceives them has obviously never endured a class-action lawsuit. As the Hercules decision demonstrates, Canada's legal system does not favour investors. The playing field is heavily tipped towards the defendant underwriters, directors, officers, and auditors. A class-action case may take several years to resolve, and even then, investors will seldom get most of what they want.

As always, an ounce of prevention is worth a pound of cure.

CHAPTER TWENTY-TWO

## Tired Mussels

*"Honesty pays, but it don't seem to pay enough to suit a lot of people."*

KIN HUBBARD

**IN THE** early 1990s, a public company called Cross Pacific Pearls said it had a proprietary method for stimulating mussels to grow pearls. It planned to transport 350,000 mussels from the southern US, dump them into a northern California lake, apply a proprietary technique to the bivalves, and eventually harvest a pearl from each mussel. Listed on the Vancouver Stock Exchange, Cross Pacific raised $6 million in debt and $5 million in equity to establish its mussel farm. To demonstrate its revolutionary technique and to promote itself to American investors, Cross Pacific planned to grow a pearl as big as a bowling ball inside a giant clam at a Hawaiian shopping centre.

Before shovelling $5 million into Cross Pacific, investors should have studied the company's prospectus, dated May 15, 1990, and a technical report of March 15, 1990. According to the prospectus, Cross Pacific offered 550,000 common shares at $3.35 apiece. It planned to spend $933,336 on farming operations and another $791,380 on general corporate expenses.

This seemed straightforward enough, although investors should have made note of the purpose of the funds, according to the prospectus, and the way in which Cross Pacific eventually spent the money. For instance, if they found that Cross Pacific used the proceeds for executive bonuses or loans to related parties, investors should have become concerned.

Of more interest to investors, however, the prospectus showed that other companies had an interest in Cross Pacific. With this knowledge, investors should have investigated these other companies in further detail. Pineridge Capital, for example, owned more than 50% of Cross Pacific, but its ownership would drop to 44% after various transactions occurred, including the sale of the Cross Pacific shares.

Of even more importance, the prospectus qualified 1.5 million shares for issuance to specific people and another 800,000 shares registered for share-transfer purposes at a price of $2 per share. Given these signs, investors and auditors should have been aware of potential problems at Cross Pacific.

To confuse matters further, of the $3.35 at which Cross Pacific planned to sell shares to the public, about $3.05 would be assigned to the existing shareholders, who had acquired their shares at much lower prices. This should have alerted investors and auditors, as well, especially considering that Cross Pacific had earned no profit and generated no cash from its operations.

In the company's audited financial statements for the year ended May 31, 1989, and for the three months ended August 31, 1989, the company recorded a deficit and a net loss—which is not uncommon in a start-up company—no revenue from sales, and cash payments primarily for wages and benefits, office and administration, and consulting fees. It had invested only a minimal amount in its farm facilities.

If the prospectus caught investors' attention, the technical report should have reassured them. Prepared earlier in 1990 by Cross Pacific's auditors, BDO Dunwoody, the fifty-page document supported the company's assertions about the economics of the pearl farm. It quoted specialists in the field of growing pearls and claimed that they'd approved Cross Pacific's methods. It also listed several advisors to the company, who seemed on paper to have credible credentials. The report included impressive, although unsubstantiated, financial projections for the company, as well. And since the company's auditors had prepared the report, in their capacity as consultants, investors probably assumed that they'd performed adequate due diligence.

After its initial share offering, Cross Pacific started issuing press releases. "The company has signed a contract worth US$3.8 million," it said in July 1990, "to provide a Japanese company with implant beads used for the production of cultured pearls. The contract is with Pearl of the Orient Akashi Company of San Francisco."

In March 1991, it reported, "To date the company has implanted approximately 250,000 clams with about 1,000,000 nucleus implants, a figure which equates to 720,000 implants after taking expected mortality into consideration."

By then, according to its audited financial statements, Cross Pacific had lost $729,179 over the previous ten months, increasing its deficit to $1,608,838. Again, for a start-up company, these figures did not look alarming, although a note to the financial statements might have caused some concern. It read, "As economic levels of production have not been attained, continued operations are dependent upon the ongoing support of shareholders and/or third parties." In other words, Cross Pacific needed more outside money to keep operating. Yet the auditors apparently saw no other serious problems at Cross Pacific.

Cross Pacific's management initially believed that it would take eighteen to twenty-four months to determine precisely the number of commercial pearls the company might harvest from its captive herd of clams. Management initially expected its first harvest in the spring of 1991, but when that date passed without a single pearl in the hopper, the company issued another press release to explain that the mussels had fallen asleep in the cold northern California lake and were hibernating.

Six months later, management-prepared financial statements showed that Cross Pacific had total assets of $8,744,898, including $7,734,791 in cash. It reported a net loss of $788,022 for the period and a deficit of $2,396,860. Once again, not a surprising number for many start-up companies.

The picture changed radically over the following twelve months, however. By the end of September 1992, Cross Pacific's deficit had skyrocketed to $11,583,761, an increase of more than $9 million, while its assets had fallen by more than $7 million, to $1,001,412. Its long-term debt and equity of more than $11 million had been wiped out. In just one year, its cash reserves had dwindled to less than $10,000 from $7,734,791.

What happened?

If investors had looked closely at the company's audited financial statements prepared six months earlier, in March, they might have seen disaster approaching. Assembled with the help of the company's auditors, the financial statements contained some particularly glaring warning signals. One note to the statements said Cross Pacific had written off more than $7 million in loans to three companies, including Pineridge Capital Group, which owned more than 50% of the company. According to the note, Cross Pacific would "continue to make every effort to collect these amounts." Apparently, by September, the company's efforts had failed.

Another note in the audited statement said that Cross Pacific had advanced $93,000 to its president in the form of an unsecured and non-interest-bearing loan with no fixed terms of repayment. Presumably, he too made every effort to repay the loan, but by September, he still hadn't done it.

When the Vancouver Stock Exchange and the British Columbia Securities Commission received copies of the audited statements in September, they issued a cease-trade order almost immediately.

So here's what really happened: over the previous year, Cross Pacific had advanced $7 million of the $11 million it had raised from issuing shares and debt to two companies in Panama, as well as the company that owned more than half of the business. The two Panamanian companies promptly disappeared. The auditors, who had helped to draft Cross Pacific's financial statements, were fully aware, as the notes indicated, of these transactions. Meanwhile, the stock continued to trade for another six months, finally collapsing in value to 57¢ from a high of $4.30 in January 1992.

As for the pearl-producing mussels, they weren't just hibernating. Nine out of ten of them were dead, and the survivors weren't living up to Cross Pacific's promises. The scientists who had apparently approved Cross Pacific's pearl-growing technique later denied that they'd ever visited the pearl farm or approved the processes involved. The advisors listed in the report also later denied any involvement in the venture.

Pearl of the Orient Akashi Company of San Francisco, the company that had signed a contract with Cross Pacific for the company's pearls, turned out to be a local jewellery store, whose proprietor, Mr. Akashi, had never signed a contract with Cross Pacific, even for $3, let alone $3.8 million.

How could investors have known any of this? Securities regulators never tested the accuracy of Cross Pacific's press releases. Apart from a footnote, the company's financial statements never raised an alarm over the company's loans to Panama or another loan to the company's president. Apparently, the auditors did not investigate the truth of the company's claim about sleeping bivalves, either. Company management pumped up the value of its stock by making bogus claims about non-existent contracts, spurious scientific practices, phony advisors, and sleeping mussels, then rewarded itself with share options. With nobody monitoring the press releases, the company could say anything it wanted to a gullible public.

Why were these misrepresentations approved for a public share offering? Did anybody at the BCSC consider the adequacy and completeness of Cross Pacific's prospectus disclosure? Or did regulators dump full responsibility onto prospective investors? In any case, neither regulators nor auditors had to worry about repercussions of their oversight. As it stands, shafted investors cannot easily sue a regulator for dropping the ball, nor can they sue auditors for signing off on bogus annual financial statements.

About eighteen months after the collapse of Cross Pacific, journalists asked the company's auditors if they would have reported the bogus contract with the San Francisco jewellery store if they'd discovered the deception. "No," said one of the auditors, "I don't think we would report that." Asked about the misstatements in the auditing firm's supporting technical report, he said, "the normal procedure is to talk to the experts directly." But he never explained why no one contacted the marine biologist whose name was used in the report. As for the $7 million in loans that Cross Pacific wrote off, he said, "It's accounted for. We know where it is. We just don't know, we have no way of knowing, whether this is a good loan or a bad loan."

In the aftermath of scams pulled by companies like Cross Pacific, the provincial finance minister investigated the practices of the Vancouver Stock Exchange and the regulators who oversee it. Any small successes of the VSE in bringing new companies to market, he said, were completely overshadowed by "the continuing occurrence of shams, swindles, and market manipulations." The minister castigated regulators for allowing rampant insider trading, issuer conflicts of interest, general market manipulation, and the misuse of funds raised on the VSE.

Despite being tarred by the damning report of the province's elected finance minister, the long-time chairman of the BCSC, which vetted numerous VSE schemes (including Cross Pacific), was recently rewarded with an appointment as the transitional head of Canada's proposed national securities commission. Doug Hyndman, chair of the BCSC from 1987 to 2009, has more influence than any other individual in Canada over the eventual regulation and enforcement of the securities industry in this country.

In the meantime, scams like Cross Pacific's continue, although they've become much more sophisticated. Investors who lost money to Cross Pacific can only console themselves with a few pearls of wisdom:

1. The term "shareholders' auditor" means nothing. Perhaps, "management's toady" would be a more accurate term. According to the auditors, it is up to the directors to protect you. So, remind us again of why we have an audit? Why do companies and securities legislation specify an audit requirement?
2. Besides doing a financial statement audit for Cross Pacific, the auditor also prepared a technical report for the company to accompany the prospectus, in which some particulars were evidently misleading. Why is such a seeming conflict of interest allowed?
3. Both the securities commission that oversaw the prospectus filing and the company's auditors apparently saw fit to do nothing of consequence for investors, even when suspicions became more acute and the company's stock started to plummet as a direct result.
4. Apparently, the company's directors did nothing for shareholders, despite the increasing suspicions about large loans made to foreign companies. Other than a few lines in a footnote, the loans didn't merit any mention at all.

CHAPTER TWENTY-THREE

# No Trust, No Income

*"Whoever said, 'If it ain't broke, don't fix it,' probably never heard of preventative maintenance."*

STEVEN KASPER

**THE FIASCO** of business income trusts could have occurred in no other country but Canada. In fact, the mass-market swindle of the mid-2000s represents the questionable essence of Canada's largely unregulated capital markets.

Overwhelming evidence indicates that misleading brokerage sales practices, a lack of oversight by securities regulators, auditors, and lawmakers, and the Canadian media, which turned a blind eye to the problems of many business income trusts, all conspired to swindle investors out of billions of dollars. Lawmakers, auditors, and securities regulators stood mostly on the sidelines while investors, including many income-oriented boomers and retirees, fell victim to an enhanced variation of a basic Ponzi fraud.

Business income trusts promised outsized returns while deliberately confusing a return *on* capital (income) with a return *of* capital (simply giving back money previously invested in the company). Having seen this happen, no one could possibly believe again that financial deregulation would solve market problems in Canada.

Income trusts began in the real estate and oil and gas sectors as a way to return cash flows from an operating company directly to investors on a tax-advantaged, regular basis. Such trusts made sense for resource companies with depleting reserves. Instead of reinvesting cash in the company's operations, the company could distribute its excess cash to investors and receive a tax break in the process. Investors understood that the cash they received left nothing for the upkeep of the company. As soon as the company depleted its assets, the company would have no value. In essence, the cash distributions had only a limited life span. By comparison, companies pay dividends based on their income, and they usually leave enough cash in the treasury to reinvest in the business to keep it operating.

The distinction between dividends and the distributions of income trusts became obscured in the early 2000s, when underwriters looked for ways to replace the fees they'd reaped before the world's high-tech sector imploded. Sensing a way to peddle more equity to investors, while generating another batch of hefty fees, they turned their attention to income trusts.

Since the income trust structure had worked so well for real estate and oil and gas companies, they said, why not apply the same structure to companies in other sectors that spin off significant amounts of cash but need only small amounts for reinvestment? The result was the business income trust (BIT).

These structures worked well when applied to suitable companies, but there were only a limited number of these companies in Canada. Soon underwriters and opportunistic management started shoehorning less suitable companies into the structure, aggressively selling units in these BITs to investors by offering ever-larger amounts of cash. By 2002, income trusts accounted for roughly 80% of the capital raised in Canada through initial public offerings, and most of them were BITs.

Investors flocked to these structures, lured by the prospect of receiving tax-advantaged cash distributions far higher than they could hope for in the form of dividends or interest income from competing investments. They made their investment decisions according to the distribution yield of the trust, and not on the fact that their own capital was being partially returned to them in many cases.

Everyone from the BIT's management to the investment dealer to the broker to the media calculated distribution yield by dividing the cash distributed by the market price of the income trust unit. But even though everyone accepted it, that number was highly misleading, since the distribution usually consisted of a combination of the operation's income and a return of capital. Nevertheless, the distribution yield of most BITs far exceeded the dividend yield of most conventional public companies, and it far exceeded the yield on a corporate bond, as well. If a company had to tap into its own capital to come up with the distribution, most investors didn't care. Few of them knew the difference.

As time passed, numerous media reports led investors to believe that—because of the regularity of distributions—income trusts worked in the same way as bonds. Investors usually regard high-rated bonds as a safe haven, offering greater capital protection than equities, and the greater predictability of interest payments. If the media had told the story more clearly from the start, and if the investment community had clarified the confusion, investors would have realized that BITs carried far more risk than a corporate bond, and more risk than a stock, because BITs had to distribute as much cash as possible to remain competitive. When a trust scaled back its distribution, its market price could fall by 25% to 40%. These cuts occurred with far more regularity than with dividend-paying stocks.

For most of recorded business history, a yield has implied a return of income. It does not include the return of an investor's original capital. If it does, then the distribution constitutes something more than a simple yield, and that additional fact must be expressly stated. In the case of many BITs, their so-called cash distribution yields bore no comparison to a dividend or bond yield. But with a few exceptions, no one bothered to mention that: not the BITs' management, nor its auditors, nor the regulators, nor the media. Instead, they began to value BITs according to their distribution yield, even though no company, whether it's a BIT or a conventional public corporation, can indefinitely continue to distribute more cash to its investors than it earns from its operations. (Please see Appendix E for more on yield distortion.)

At this point, regulators and auditors should have stepped in and stopped the scam before it started. But auditors, of course, owe no duty of care to investors. And regulators, once again, heavily favoured the demands of corporations to operate freely to the detriment of investors needing a marketplace that is not rigged against them. Hobbled by corporate lobbying power and the lack of an organized investor voice in Canada, investors once again got the short end of the stick.

If anyone noticed the obvious disparity between cash being distributed and income being reported, BITs found a new metric to explain it: distributable cash. Distributable cash almost always amounted to more than reported income and was usually higher, as well, than the total cash being distributed. That implied that a BIT wasn't distributing every available penny but was prudently keeping some in reserve. Investors gained a false sense of security from the concept of distributable cash and the apparently prudent way in which BITs managed this dough. All looked rosy in BIT-land.

Unfortunately for investors, individual trusts calculated their own distributable cash by the seat of their financial pants. There were no guidelines and no standardization and no attempt to verify the distributable cash by an outside party. The auditors never really bothered, since they had no interest in helping investors.

Among the many major flaws in the concept, distributable cash ignored conventional accounting measures such as depreciation and amortization expenses. Instead, management estimated spending to maintain the assets of the company. During the height of the trust boom, so-called maintenance capital expenditures (as estimated by management and verified by nobody) amounted to only 14% of total distributable cash in the average business trust. This meant that a BIT calculated the cash that it could pass along to unit holders by subtracting 14% from its total distributable cash. (And that figure in itself was questionable.)

By contrast, the more conventional measures of depreciation and amortization amounted to an average of 42% of distributable cash. If a BIT had subtracted that measure of asset wear and tear from total distributable cash, it would have appeared to have much less to dole out to investors. Over the long term, across numerous trusts, the 14% and 42% figures should have been roughly equal. Obviously they weren't even close. The huge disparity was a major sign that financial reporting games were being played to dupe investors. Red flags should have been flapping across the sky. But no one seemed to care.

Like a Ponzi scheme, many BITs confused the distinction between income and a return of capital, either by accident or by design. Such BITs were mislabelled and mis-sold by many in the industry to resemble investment vehicles that delivered a straight return of income. Not only did investors not appreciate that many BITs were distributing their own capital, they also believed that these BITs could generate such a return in perpetuity.

To be fair, some BITs were honestly governed. Resource businesses, for example, that don't intend to reinvest their capital assets can logically distribute cash in excess of income because they have only a limited quantity of ore, oil, or gas to extract. Why invest in additional extraction assets if the resources will soon be depleted anyway, and the company wound up? Why not give back the money that investors put into the company in the first place, along with a share of the income? Even in these cases, though, companies very clearly inform investors about the proportion of the distribution that is merely capital that's being returned to them and how much represents earnings on their capital investment.

Few, if any, BITs had the intention of winding up their operations after they'd exhausted a limited resource. Yet these businesses had to reinvest cash in repairs, replacements, research, and similar revenue-generating activities to generate future cash earnings. By failing to adequately repair and replace worn-out equipment and assets, for example, because it has distributed all its available cash to investors, a company soon denies itself any hope of attaining the same level of future profits.

Market regulators, auditors, corporate lawyers, and stockbrokers cannot have missed the distinction between an ongoing business and a business that was not investing adequately for the future. They must have known, as well, that the distinction was of critical importance to investors. But provincial securities commissions and auditors ignored the irregularities contained in many of the BITs' financial reporting for too long.

Although the rules of accounting have for decades very clearly separated investors' capital funds from the income earned on that capital, the rules were essentially thrown out the window. In the process, the term income trust became highly misleading, since distributable cash was not income, and investors could hardly put their trust in that.

BITs eventually represented 70% of the income trust market, and most of the businesses were small, with capitalizations of $250 million or less. By 2005, underwriters of income trusts had nearly exhausted the supply of decent companies. They'd turned even mediocre companies into income trusts, and they had almost no more appropriate businesses to scrape off the bottom of the corporate barrel.

When a BIT distributes more cash to unit holders than it brings in from normal operations, it has the following options:

1. It can save cash by not keeping its assets in good form.
2. It can squeeze working capital for more cash.
3. It can borrow more cash.
4. It can sell more trust units and use the proceeds to pay distributions to both new and existing unit holders until the cash runs out.
5. It can sell its productive assets and rent them back.
6. It can reduce its cash distributions.
7. It can go bankrupt.

Most low-quality BITs chose to cut their distributions drastically once all the options, except bankruptcy, had been exhausted. In the process, they obliterated the market value of their units. But borrowing or selling productive assets would eventually have had the same ultimate effect: shrinkage and, finally, bankruptcy.

All of the above was well understood by the BIT underwriters, specialist fund managers, and their consultants, including many auditors and lawyers. Further, they knew that many of the low-quality business trusts would not be able to pay distributions for more than a few years at best. Rather than warning investors, they did the opposite. Many BITs issued more units, raising more money, and generating more fees for the underwriters, while company founders disposed of their remaining holdings before the axe fell.

The axe fell in 2006, but it fell in such a way that trust promoters could convincingly blame the government for the carnage. To attract investors, conventional income trusts in the real estate and resource sectors had enjoyed favourable tax treatment. BITs qualified for the same favourable treatment, even though they didn't really need it, and they used this advantage to explain the disparity between their extraordinarily high distributions and more conventional dividend yields.

Few investors thought to look further to see where the rest of the cash came from. Nor did they heed warnings from some fund managers that the tax relief would not last forever. The sheer number of companies converting, or announcing their intentions to convert to trusts, should have indicated that something would have to change. When the government decided to tax the trusts at a rate similar to corporations, the sector died, but the perpetrators, aiders, and abettors of the scam escaped unscathed.

BITs appealed, in particular, to income-oriented investors such as boomers and retirees, because they distributed so much cash on a regular basis. Unfortunately, few understood the nature of the cash payments. By comparing them favourably to share dividends or bond coupons, they bid up the price of the trusts' units. Encouraged by many financial advisors and marketing specialists, they created a market that should never have existed in the first place.

The BIT market had been grossly overinflated by the deceptive practices of numerous greedy parties, and a collapse was inevitable without any change in tax status. But since the federal government initiated the tax change, and received the blame for the collapse, it has avoided a closer investigation of the BIT fiasco. If ever we needed a judicial inquiry, we could have used one to illuminate the deceptions and delusions of the BIT market. But that will never happen, unless the government suddenly swallows a dose of courage.

To avoid falling for a similar scam in the future, here's what you should keep in mind about business income trusts:

1. Distributable cash was a misleading, unverifiable, incomparable figure that varied significantly from trust to trust, but was nevertheless used as the primary basis of valuation in the sector.
2. The reported distributable cash figures were collectively inflated by billions of dollars.
3. Neither the auditors nor the securities regulators stepped in to mandate a change to the calculation of distributable cash. Any efforts

were too little, and came much too late, to help investors. Once again, the self-regulatory conflicts of interest did serious harm to investors.
4. Many underwriters, brokers, and specialist fund managers used deceptive sales practices to take advantage of investors' ignorance of the new concept of distributable cash.
5. Numerous other parties were complicit in the deception, including some major Canadian law firms and most major Canadian media outlets.

As mentioned at the outset, the business income trust scandal comes close to encompassing all that is wrong with Canada's largely unregulated capital markets. It was a complete letdown for investors, including many income-seeking boomers and retirees, who were run over roughshod by deceptive underwriters, brokers, and specialist fund managers. Those parties were aided by ignorant commentary from the media and many professionals (including many law firms), which simply ramped up the unwarranted hype about trusts. As always, the auditors and securities regulators stood idly by, handcuffed by their conflicts of interest, not to mention their self-interests.

As with other wildly popular investments that seem too good to be true, investors placed far too much reliance on business television and print media hype of BITs. Endless endorsements, including special advertising supplements in newspapers, encouraged people with little understanding of BITs to depend on them for a steady income. Even today, many people still think that changes to income tax legislation caused the low-quality business trusts to collapse in value. While the tax change simply hastened the process, the losses were inevitable. In fact, losses were sealed at the very moment the flawed business trust units were purchased.

Investors fell for something that was too good to be true with many of the BITs. They thought they could get income returns and cash flows that well exceeded returns from other sources. The tax savings also proved too good to be true, and the warning signs were there, if investors had known where to look.

CHAPTER TWENTY-FOUR

## Insured Confusion

> "Insurance: an ingenious modern game of chance in which the player is permitted to enjoy the comfortable conviction that he is beating the man who keeps the table.
>
> AMBROSE BIERCE

**THE CONFEDERATION** Life Insurance Company was placed into liquidation in August 1994, subject to a court-approved wind-up order. The company had been experiencing financial difficulties for several months. As with most situations where the audited financial statements depart from cash reality, a liquidity crunch was the final blow.

Confederation Life had operated for more than 100 years, and its failure came as a major surprise to many people. A related company, Confederation Trust, collapsed at the same time. It's a familiar story: if a company cannot pay its debts, the creditors take control, and equity investors get taken to the cleaners.

With life insurance companies, though, the sequence of events doesn't occur so predictably. Insurance companies usually have time to dig themselves out of financial holes before creditors step in. That's because people pay premiums on their life insurance policies for many years before they die. These payments flow into the life insurance company, allowing it to accumulate and grow cash for years before it has to make a payout.

So, why did Confederation Life fail so abruptly even with this built-in cash cushion? Bad investments? Inappropriate financial reporting? Bad cash management?

The answer is all of the above.

Confederation Life invested in weak mortgages on properties that did not generate enough cash to pay mortgage interest and principal. A recession in the early part of the 1990s also did not help the company's liquidity situation. The company's loan officers, however, received bonuses for meeting their targets for loans, so they kept on lending without paying too much attention to the quality of the loans. This happens with lending institutions; when economic conditions worsen, mediocre loans become bad loans. But bad loans were not Confederation Life's only problem.

As a financial institution, Confederation Life's success depended on its cash position and liquidity. Unfortunately, Canada's auditors have persuaded insurance companies to adopt the same type of reporting model as companies in other industries. Rather than emphasizing cash and liquidity, the auditor-advocated reporting model focuses on accrual accounting. The deterioration of a company's cash position can go unnoticed more easily with this style of accounting. The investors and policyholders of Confederation Life certainly didn't notice anything was amiss.

Life insurance companies have to invest their insurance premium money each year, after operating expenses, in order to produce sufficient cash to pay contracted death benefits. Stock market and other gains have to offset losses over the insured time period. In an important sense, accounting in life insurance companies is rough and ready. Annual profits are the result of two huge financial estimates: (1) the value of invested assets in bonds, shares of other companies, and property held by the insurance company, and (2) the estimated liability, in today's terms, for death and disability benefits to be paid in the future. Actuarial estimates of the assets and liabilities are loaded with assumptions, especially about the future expected investment success of the life insurer, often called the expected return on investment, or investment yield.

The types of policies that insurance companies are writing is an important concern to investors. Group insurance policies for risky employers, or guarantees of rates of return, have caused financial difficulties for large insurers in recent years. The problem for life insurance companies is that their financial numbers are usually full of disputable estimates. Trends may not prove reliable for investors because management's level of optimism can easily change from period to period.

Like Confederation Life, an insurance company or a bank can report profits even when they don't receive cash. Unless investors are on guard against such situations, and carefully examine whether reported income is out of phase with cash receipts less disbursements, they may not realize that those profits do not represent cash earnings. In fact, they may believe that a near-bankrupt company is doing well. Using its cooked-up financial figures, the company then issues more debt to unaware investors.

In the case of Confederation Life, investors should have concentrated on the cash value of the company's investment portfolio. Mortgages that were not fully collectible in cash should have been expensed down to the level of their cash value. In turn, the cash value could have been determined by considering:

1. Were cash receipts overdue for interest and principal payments, and by how much, and for how long?
2. Was the collateral, resale value of the mortgaged land and buildings below the mortgage amount that was shown on the company's balance sheet? If so, an expense should have been recorded immediately.
3. What costs would the company incur in realizing on the property so that it could be sold to others? Were these amounts accrued as liabilities because they would soon have to be paid in cash?

Unfortunately, Confederation Life's auditors did not adequately respond to cash shortfalls in the company's mortgage portfolio by requiring the company to record adequate expenses or losses. Instead, the company's publicly available, audited financial statements appeared to provide inappropriate assurances.

Before life insurance companies adopted the same reporting model as other companies, they distinguished admissible assets from non-admissible assets on their balance sheets. Admissible was defined as assets available to pay liabilities, including to policyholders. Hence, cash and equivalents were admissible, necessary assets. Cash and liquidity were given a place of prominence. Non-admissible assets included head-office land and buildings and other investments that could not be readily sold and, therefore, were not cash equivalents.

During the 1960s, regulators lost full sight of the need for insurance companies to emphasize cash and liquidity. By adopting the auditors' one-size-fits-all approach to reporting, cash and non-cash items became blurred, and the vital cash and liquidity needed to manage an insurance company was de-emphasized. The adoption of IFRS will only make the situation worse.

Confederation Life's problems extended beyond the inappropriate valuation of mortgages and other loans, though. The two largest assets and liabilities on a life insurer's balance sheet are investments and reserves. Insurance companies acquire bonds, as well as mortgages, to earn cash interest revenue. Many of these bonds may mature twenty years in the future and generate 6%, or so, in annual interest. The insurance company may or may not hold the bond until it matures. The bond's price in the market can fluctuate wildly over twenty years, as well, responding to changing interest rates. Even the currency can differ from what the insurer uses for financial reporting purposes. By holding the bond until its maturity date, the insurer receives a consistent interest income of 6% per annum.

If an insurance company intends to sell its twenty-year bonds within the next year at a loss, instead of holding them for twenty years, it should record the value of the bonds according to prevailing market prices on its year-end financial statements. But if the insurance company's management wants to play financial tricks, they can say they intend to hold the bonds to maturity. That way, they can avoid recording losses this year even though they intend to sell the bonds early next year. If bond values are high compared to their cost on the financial statements, management can do the opposite, saying they intend to sell the bonds next year, even though they intend to hold them to maturity to improve the company's reported financial results, and possibly to offset other realized losses.

Logically, insurance companies should hold most of their bonds to maturity to diversify the interest rates payable on the bonds. But political interference may force them to adopt accounting rules that value their bond portfolio at a particular moment rather than assuming that the bonds will be held for a period such as twenty years. Such mark-to-market financial reporting could result in artificial value swings as interest rates and currency fluctuations occur, creating drastic fluctuations in the annual results. The introduction of IFRS will have just this effect.

Different accounting systems have different rules. So-called principles-based accounting, for example, gives management leeway to interpret many rules for itself. Investors have to determine which accounting rules apply, especially when they evaluate an insurance company's investment portfolio. The company's intentions to hold or sell securities can affect the application of rules under several of the different accounting systems. Unless compelled by the rules to tell the whole story, management may provide only the information that makes it look good.

Insurance companies also have to account for reserves set aside to pay claims. For this purpose, they employ actuaries to estimate losses based on such variables as a person's age, sex, smoking habits, and location. Actuaries attempt to combine history with assumptions and predictions in order to estimate liability reserves. Minor tampering with reserve liabilities can therefore have a devastating effect on reported insurance company income. A variation of 5% in reserve liabilities of $1 billion, for example, could raise or lower a company's income before taxes by $50 million.

Overall, investments in life insurance companies should only be made by investors who understand some of the fundamentals of life insurance reporting. Confederation Life was largely brought down by cash and liquidity problems that arose from questionable investment strategies, but investors who didn't know where to look would never have known this. Similar investment problems can exist in non-life insurers, as well, but the magnitude of difficulty is usually lower, because they place less cash in long-term investments.

The prime method employed to cook property and casualty insurance books is to understate loss reserve liabilities. Three components of loss reserves are:

1. Estimated costs to settle a reported claim, less any amount that has been reinsured and will be recovered from other insurance companies.

2. Losses that have been incurred but not reported.
3. Claims adjustment expenses such as fees to be paid to lawyers, adjusters, and doctors.

With automobile insurers, for example, repairs to vehicles usually have to be paid fairly quickly, so cooking the books would have only a short-term effect. But head and spinal injuries, or other severe injury cases, may take years to settle. Executives may instruct in-house claims adjusters to keep low liability estimates on any claims for bodily injury. That way they can keep profitability high by recording inadequate claims-reserve liabilities.

To keep claims reserves low, companies can take several steps, such as:

1. Not seeking up-to-date medical reports on the gravity of the insured's injuries.
2. Consulting doctors who are always optimistic about the prospects that the insured will recuperate fully.
3. Obstructing attempts on behalf of the injured party to settle cases quickly.
4. Closing claims files without justification, opening them up again briefly only when payments have to be made, and then closing the file again.
5. Deliberately recording minor dollar liability reserves until overwhelming evidence piles up.
6. Placing misleading memos in claims files in order to mislead regulators, internal auditors, and reinsurance companies.

Using such tactics, insurance companies may hide understated loss reserves for several years. At an insurance company's financial year-end or quarter-end, estimates have to be made of losses that likely occurred before year end, but which have not yet been reported to the insurance company. Actuaries typically calculate these sums based on a sample batch of claims. Deliberately understated claims reserves can easily lead to understated calculations for unreported losses. Companies may also understate reserves by adjusting expenses. They can do this by not paying invoices promptly or by dragging out assessments from medical specialists. Without tight supervision and controls to detect such manipulation, insurance companies may overstate profits for several years.

Detection of the schemes usually occurs when:

1. Reinsurance companies become suspicious while doing claims audits to determine their percentage of losses compared to the premiums that they earned.
2. The insurance company is sold and the new buyers realize what has been occurring.
3. A regulator notices a discrepancy when he calculates whether the insurance company is adequately solvent.
4. An actuary, who keeps several years of data to determine trends, notices a peculiar pattern of actual cash settlements in excess of loss reserves.
5. A new employee asks too many questions and blows the whistle.

Unfortunately, investors usually are the last to clue in to the problem. That's because insurance companies provide only selected information that makes adequate investor analysis almost impossible.

Especially compared to required US corporate disclosure, Canadian financial reporting is frequently inadequate, because:

1. Lawmakers refuse to legislate a national securities enforcer (as opposed to a mere regulator) and staff it with competent people who can stay abreast of ever-evolving financial schemes.
2. Provincial securities regulators repeatedly ignore investors' needs.
3. Auditors long ago abandoned their obligations and duties of care toward investors, with the apparent blessing of legislators and the courts.

Stated bluntly, investors are often at the mercy of one or two people in a company who are able to overcome antiquated investor protection systems. The evidence of these systemic problems continues to go unheeded because of the considerable advertising and lobbying efforts on behalf of those who are the cause of the investment losses.

Meanwhile, investors have lost hundreds of millions from the financial dishonesty of Canadian insurance companies. Not only do Canadian investors have to suffer through often useless, detailed financial disclosure of minor issues, but they have to listen to exaggerated claims about improvements made to financial reporting, including the adoption of IFRS.

The reality is, the current Canadian investor protection system is in shambles, and there is no serious effort being made to fix the problems.

CHAPTER TWENTY-FIVE

## Banking on Apathy

*"I have not observed men's honesty to increase with their riches."*
THOMAS JEFFERSON

**THROUGH THE** credit meltdown between 2007 and 2009, Canadians heard endless talk from politicians and the media about the safety and virtues of the Canadian financial sector. While they made some valid points, they also misled the public in several important respects.

Canadians need to better understand their financial sector. Most of us have a significant amount invested in the big five banks and other financial institutions in Canada, whether we realize it or not. In addition to the banks, Canada's financial institutions sector includes insurance and investment companies, regional banks, alternative lenders, and financial exchanges. Either through direct investments or through pension funds and mutual funds, few Canadians can remain unaffected by its machinations.

Financial institutions can be rewarding investments in Canada. However, they have also disappointed investors periodically. Before the credit meltdown, for instance, some banks suffered significant losses from investment banking and international acquisitions.

Investors should not assume that all banks are generally the same. Nor should they assume that all financial institutions are safe investments that present buying opportunities regardless of their share price. Sometimes banks represent buying opportunities, and sometimes they don't. The difference depends on financial analysis, and nowhere does it get much more complicated than it does with Canadian banks.

Compared to the US, Canada has proportionately far fewer banks. Yet we've suffered a number of collapses in the financial sector that have seriously hurt investors. A partial list of failures includes Canadian Commercial Bank, Northland Bank, Confederation Life, Confederation Trust, Standard Trust, Hercules Managements, Victoria Mortgage, Teachers Investment and Housing Co-operative, and Coventree, as well as dozens of smaller trust companies, credit unions, and finance companies. Generally, the banks survive for a few years, abetted by weak accounting and distorted financial reporting to investors. Ultimately, they fail for the usual reasons: excessive greed, egos, inappropriate lending, speculation, and failure to consider the economic cycle.

Since the failures tend to happen for similar reasons, our analysis of the financial fraudulence, and cover-up processes, should prove useful to investors who want to avoid such risky ventures.

Financial institutions deal in cash. Most accounting systems and financial reporting mechanisms deal with a combination of cash and non-cash adjustments, such as uncollected interest and loan loss estimates. Financial institutions and non-cash reporting rules are often not compatible. Not surprisingly, therefore, many financial institutions that have reported long stretches of audited profits have gone unexpectedly bankrupt in short order because their financial reports focused on accounting profits and not liquidity and cash. The clear message is that the audited numbers can be manipulated, and they are especially troublesome at financial institutions where the accounting is so complex and the financial leverage is often quite high.

Banks can have highly leveraged balance sheets, supporting considerable lending, with only small amounts of shareholders' equity. This can create impressive returns on equity during good times, but an economic downturn can reveal the risks of such leverage. Equity can quickly vanish because of bad financial decisions involving uncollectible loans receivable or financial derivatives.

Regulators watch banks to make sure they keep sufficient capital on hand, but they can be slow to react, especially if financial shenanigans are afoot. Investors have to remain one step ahead, so they can react long before a bank needs fresh capital.

Unfortunately, banks can easily cover up certain financial losses. Equity capital may appear to exist when it actually doesn't. Investors have to be on their toes to ensure that banks have not manipulated their audited financial numbers.

Similar cautions should be applied to other types of financial institutions, including alternative mortgage lenders and reverse mortgage companies. Reverse mortgage companies in particular face a variety of risks, especially with respect to how they are financed. They need sufficient equity capital to ride out economic swings, and they need cash upfront to acquire long-term mortgage positions. (See Appendix G.)

Whereas the inventory for sale in retail stores may be shoes and clothing, the so-called inventory of financial institutions is cash. Cash is bought and sold. "Follow the money," therefore, is a compelling credo for investors in financial institutions.

Unfortunately, financial institutions can use accounting and financial reporting to muddy cash flows. Emphasizing receivables, payables, and prepaid amounts, for example, financial institutions can draw investors' attention to profitability, when in fact investors should pay more attention to liquidity or cash availability, especially when the economy gets shaky.

Investors have to pay particular attention to the following aspects of financial institution accounting and reporting:

1. *Interest revenue.* Unless the interest is collectible in cash, it should not be recorded and reported on the company's financial statements. Investors must scrutinize notes to the financial statements for signs of the manipulation of revenue.
2. *Valuation of receivables.* Cash collectability of receivables is also important. The principal and interest on a loan can both turn into

losses when cash is not likely to be received. Banks can easily hide such losses by increasing receivables when they don't receive interest and fees in cash.
3. *Overdue loans.* Banks should not record interest revenue if they've received no cash for the most recent 90 days. When they restructure overdue loans, banks can pull numerous stunts.
4. *Valuation of financial instruments, including various derivatives and hedges.* In using derivatives and hedging instruments, financial institutions contract with counterparties that must be financially sound and reliable. If they're not, banks can incur huge liabilities. Banks with brokerage and underwriting subsidiaries can also experience bad times. Banks can also tamper with the valuation of securities held within the institution. Investors should compare this information in reports from prior years.
5. *The rogue trader syndrome.* Investors should determine the quality of a bank's financial controls, using its financial reports. Even when they claim to have good control systems, banks can incur large trading losses.
6. *Incentive plans for managers.* Bonus/reward programs repeatedly contribute to losses in financial institutions. When a manager receives a bonus based on the dollar volume of loans he makes rather than the quality of those loans, what else should we expect? As forensic accountants, we have encountered many atrocious lending practices and losses because managers had no incentive to make good loans that would enable the bank to recover principal plus interest.

Once a loan becomes trouble, a bank can hide the loss by restructuring the loan, using any of the following steps:

1. It might lend more money to the customer, possibly in a disguised manner, to allow the borrower to make interest payments on the troubled, overdue loan.
2. It may vary the terms of the loan to reduce or postpone principal repayments.
3. It may obtain worthless personal guarantees to give an illusion that the loan is good.

4. It can relax covenants and ratio stipulations so that the customer can borrow more money from third parties. The financial institution then receives cash, while the newly acquired creditor absorbs forthcoming losses.

As long as the borrower can pay overdue interest on the troubled loan, the financial institution can avoid recording loan losses, record phony higher profits, and attract more lenders and investors.

As a consequence, investor attention has to be placed on revenue and losses, and seeking out cash deficiencies and obligations. Notes to the financial statements that describe cash commitments, guarantees, and similar non-quantified liabilities can often provide investors with significant clues. Nowhere is it more crucial to follow the cash trail, to sniff out potential problems, than with banks and other financial institutions.

CHAPTER TWENTY-SIX

# Swimming with Sharks

*"In modern business it is not the crook who is to be feared most; it is the honest man who doesn't know what he is doing."*

OWEN D. YOUNG

**HOW DO** financial swindlers succeed so often? Primarily, investors let it happen. Some investors believe almost anything that is published. This makes it easy to sell them an investment based on a poorly researched media article or a hack brokerage research report.

Other investors, who just want to hear that someone else has invested in the same scheme, are the easiest to swindle. They can be talked into almost anything. Boomers and retirees, especially, can be their own worst enemies. Swindlers love them, because they encourage others by word of mouth to participate in investment ventures, and other questionable products, like certain reverse mortgages, without really understanding what they've bought. Friends usually describe only the perceived benefits, but none of the risks. Their misguided recommendations can spread like a virus, extending the life of a securities scheme.

Investors may take some consolation from the fact that almost no Canadian has avoided being duped by a misleading money manager, brokerage firm, or media outlet that lends credibility to their schemes. Given the serious regulatory shortcomings in Canada, such deceptions are inevitable.

To avoid scams altogether, you could leave your money in guaranteed investment certificates or other term deposits. That seems safe, until income taxes and inflation erode your capital over time.

Even when choosing something that falls in between investing in GICs and losing one's shirt in a Ponzi scheme, investors still fall victim to systemic misrepresentations. This middle ground is fraught with dangers, especially if investors choose the wrong broker or the wrong mutual fund. Many honest, helpful, educated brokers, investment advisors, and mutual fund managers work in Canada, but many are nothing more than manipulative salespeople. In fact, you're surrounded by people who want to separate you from your hard-earned money. You simply have to learn what to watch for.

In our experience, investors can sometimes discover, with only a little bit of homework, that a supposedly attractive investment is really an illusion.

Some of the more common scenarios that have to be watched for include:

1. *Unsuitable investments.* Brokers who just want to make money for themselves try to acquire control over as much of an investor's portfolio as possible. Beneficiaries of an inheritance, or sellers of a family business, make ideal victims. Intimidated by investing such large sums, investors give authority to the broker to make decisions on their behalf, within the limits of the investor's acceptable risk tolerance. A pushy broker will often persuade the investor to increase his risk tolerance level. Investors have to watch that a low-risk government bond portfolio does not get turned into a collection of fly-by-night mining companies that generates commissions for the broker. Investors must study their monthly statements carefully to note any unusual trading activity. Some investments might seem conservative and straightforward but have a twist that makes them much riskier. (Read about foreign currency preferred shares, for example, in Appendix I.)
2. *Switching mutual funds.* Investors have to understand the costs of getting into, and out of, mutual funds, especially when there are penalties for early exits. Even more important, you must learn how your broker is compensated. All too often, a broker or advisor suggests that the

investor sell mutual fund A and buy mutual fund B, for little apparent reason, when in fact the broker wants a fresh commission.

3. *Portfolio churn.* "You have to churn to earn" is an old expression amongst brokers. Frequent selling and buying of stocks and bonds certainly increases your broker's commissions. Investors should regard with suspicion brokers who pester them three or four times a week, week after week, to buy or sell without an appropriate reason. After all, who is really making money in this situation?

4. *Hot markets.* During the high-tech bubble and income trust frenzy, many rubbish stocks experienced unwarranted rises and inevitable crashes. Disreputable brokers placed pressure on investors to buy into weak companies, often on the ludicrous assumption that their share value would simply keep rising. When playing hot stocks and markets, most investors pile on the money but forget to take money off the table or even to rebalance their portfolio. Quite often, hot or volatile stocks are best left to day traders.

5. *New issues.* Often, offers to average retail investors to obtain a piece of a new share issue are not what they seem. Rarely do investors get an inside track on a new issue. A truly attractive offering usually is scooped largely by institutional investors. Only when an issue proves hard to sell do brokers start pressing their retail clients to take a piece. Always ask "Why me" when a broker hypes a new issue. Indeed, retail investors can often get into such share issues at the offering price, or below, by simply bidding afterwards in the secondary market. By doing so, they can also avoid the risk of having their funds committed to the terms of the offer for weeks until the issue closes.

6. *Inventory dump.* For any number of reasons, a brokerage might find itself with an excess of stock in its inventory. When a brokerage wants to clear out its inventory of shares, it has to find customers to buy the excess, and the victim may be you. As a general rule, say, "No thanks," and avoid buying the stock until you can make a thorough analysis and allow time for the stock, if it's a new issue, to settle in the market.

7. *Margin accounts and options.* If you have been a conservative investor, watch out for calls asking you to open a margin account. A broker may say that you can take advantage of a new issue by using margin, without raising capital by selling investments in your cash account.

A margin account at a brokerage firm operates much like a bank loan. The collateral is the stock that you hold in your account, and the interest rate could be much higher than a bank would charge. If the value of your stocks drops, then you have to find the money to maintain the value of your collateral. To do this, you usually have to sell some of your stock. In short, margin accounts can speed up your losses or winnings and obviously have to be managed carefully. Options can also accelerate your winnings and losses, and unless you understand how they work, stay away from them. In almost every case, the risk is too great. Just say no.

8. *Short selling.* The average investor should stay far away from short selling, as well. Short selling involves borrowing a stock and selling it, in the hope of buying it later at a cheaper price and pocketing the difference. If the price goes up, which it often does, you lose. Sometimes manipulators drive up the price then sell their shares quickly before the stock's price drops too fast. Regular cash investors get caught up in the hype and pay the price when the stock drops after the manipulation ceases.

With our lawmakers sitting on the sidelines, along with securities regulators and auditors, investors continue to lose money to these and other tactics. Meanwhile, swindlers and high-pressure salesmen roam free, looking for their next opportunity.

Despite what lawmakers may choose to think, many scams—but certainly not all—can be prevented. Basic regulation and education are not futile. Furthermore, excuses do not protect investors. Nevertheless, given that minimal improvements have occurred on behalf of investors in the past fifteen to twenty years, it seems that history will continue to repeat itself. Canada is, quite simply, years behind the financial swindlers in anticipating and heading off securities scams.

As an investor, you have to conduct extensive background checks into prospective brokers, their companies, their associates, their lawyers, their auditors, and all their affiliated companies. If you feel suspicious, do not turn over your money.

## CHAPTER TWENTY-SEVEN

# Too Good to Be True

> "There can be few fields of human endeavour in which history counts for so little as in the world of finance. Past experience is dismissed as the primitive refuge of those who do not have the insight to appreciate the incredible wonders of the present."
>
> JOHN KENNETH GALBRAITH

**TO WARN** against investment ideas that look too good to be true may seem obvious, redundant, or even downright condescending. Yet Canadian investors fall for these schemes with such frequency that the warning bears repetition. In fact, many investment traps are just slightly modified versions of schemes from investors' recent past, which makes them immanently avoidable in the future.

We've already covered several high-profile examples, including the rise and fall of Nortel and the tidal wave of low-quality business income trusts. In the case of Nortel, its market value, based on the price of its outstanding shares, reached $374 billion at one point. That figure alone, which exceeded the value of Canada's entire banking system, should have alerted investors to a potential skunk in the works. And if investors didn't smell it, their advisors should have. And if their advisors didn't, then what about the regulators or the media?

Instead of warning investors, however, the company, brokers, underwriters, and starry-eyed media alike convinced them to ignore basic reality and place their bets on the virtues of a made-up performance metric. Neither analysts nor most brokers helped investors to understand the deceptive nature of Nortel's numbers. Our securities regulators and auditors exhibited their usual disinterest in helping to clarify the matter for investors.

It seems that no one was paying attention. Everyone got caught up in the euphoria. Even investors who could have gotten out before the crash with just a simple check of financial reality were instead left holding practically worthless shares. The lesson to take away from it all: never trust an investment that requires net income to be ignored in order to substantiate its price in the market.

Just a few years later, the same thing happened again with business income trusts. Instead of issuing cold hard facts about their performance, trusts started issuing made-up metrics that made them look better than they really were. Many used the bogus concept of distributable cash to justify unsustainable cash distributions to unit holders in a way that made total sense to income-seeking boomers and retirees or anyone else who wanted a steady return on an investment. Not only did they receive steady returns, they also received higher so-called yields than they ever could have on corporate dividends and bonds. No one told them it was unsustainable.

The usual suspects, the underwriters, the regulators, the auditors, and the media had few bad things to say about BITs. When the government removed the tax advantage of the trusts, many investors blamed the change in tax law, rather than shady financial reporting, for the collapse of numerous low-quality trusts. To this day, many investors think the government alone caused them to lose money, even though they invested in something that was too good to be true.

Investors did it again when they bought non-bank asset-backed commercial paper (ABCP) without asking why it paid a premium over more conventional ABCP issued by Canadian banks. The complexity of these investments could overwhelm a brain surgeon, and the reasons why the market collapsed deserves a book of its own. But one simple fact remains unchallenged: investors fell once again for a product that was too good to be true.

Brokers sold non-bank ABCP on the assumption that it would provide a steady, reliable source of income to conservative investors. Some brokers might even have understood how the ABCP market worked. If they did, they'd have explained that investors were lending money to ABCP issuers, in much the same way as investors in bonds are lending money to bond issuers. While high-rated bonds are indeed reliable and secure, non-bank ABCP wasn't such a safe bet. In fact, some rating agencies wouldn't even provide a rating to non-bank ABCP in Canada.

Without going into the complexities, these rating agencies knew that if a disruption in the financial markets occurred, non-bank ABCP issuers might not be able to repay investors. And that's exactly what happened. As the credit crisis hit in August 2007, the market balked. The banks that had provided credit lines to non-bank ABCP issuers would not allow them to use those lines to repay investors. The risk that this might happen explains why non-bank ABCP carried a higher return in the first place. But by then, it was too late to clarify the distinction. Investors, once again, were left holding the ABCP bag.

The $32-billion Canadian non-bank ABCP market remained frozen for two years. Individual investors could not get their money back until the regulators, politicians, lawyers, banks, and brokers had argued among themselves over the best way to repay them. The people who should have warned investors in the first place about the pitfalls of non-bank ABCP, as usual, had better things to do.

As one decade rolls into the next, investors continue to be duped by promises of outsized returns that look too good to be true. Investors need to ask themselves: Where is the extra money coming from? At what additional risk?

Now they face the razzle-dazzle and attractive promises of leveraged Exchange Traded Funds (ETFs). Conventional ETFs are financially engineered investment vehicles that hold assets such as stocks, bonds, or options, and trade on a stock exchange. Many ETFs track an index of stocks such as the TSX, the NASDAQ, or the Dow Jones Index. Others track a commodity, such as oil, or a currency, such as the British pound. The variations are endless. ETFs charge a much lower management fee than most index mutual funds.

Leveraged ETFs go one big step further. According to the hype, leveraged ETFs provide investors with a chance to double, or even triple, the return of the underlying index or commodity. The problem is that such funds double or triple the return over just one trading day. If the market falls the next day, they provide double or triple the loss, as well. With such pervasive volatility in financial markets, investors who use leveraged ETFs to pursue longer-term investment strategies will not succeed. Indeed, they can lose their shirts, even when they correctly guess the direction that the underlying index will take over the longer term.

This is the shortest chapter in this book for a reason. It summarizes four well-known Canadian investment disasters that fall under the common theme of "too good to be true." Yet the real point is that they all bear striking fundamental similarities, which is the key for investors to avoid them in the future. Furthermore, they all occurred in the past decade, underscoring the short memory of investors and the impact of lax oversight.

Investors should also ask their broker, advisor, or planner to explain the risks involved in investment products, new or otherwise, especially in Canada where regulation and oversight are so lax.

## CHAPTER TWENTY-EIGHT
# Vanishing Yachts

> *"Deceivers are the most dangerous members of society.*
> *They trifle with the best affections of our nature*
> *and violate the most sacred obligations."*
>
> — GEORGE CRABBE

**BARRY SHERMAN,** founder of generic drug maker Apotex, and Michael Bregman, former owner of Second Cup coffee shops, have more in common than their considerable wealth. They were also victims in a luxury yacht tax-shelter swindle. By the time it collapsed, it had turned into the largest tax fraud in Canadian history. Not only did the investors lose their money, the taxman came after them, as well, demanding repayment of the tax losses they'd claimed on the phantom yachts, plus interest and fines to boot.

Sherman, Bregman, and hundreds of lawyers, businesspeople, and other wealthy customers paid Overseas Credit and Guaranty (OCGC) to build a fleet of eighty-foot luxury yachts with names like *You Only Live Once* and *Chasing Rainbows*. Founded by Einar Bellfield and Osy Minchella, the company said it would charter the yachts to wealthy clients in Europe and the Caribbean. According to the scheme contrived by OCGC's founders, the

Canadian investors could claim tax losses during construction to offset their income from other sources.

After a few years, the Canada Revenue Agency (CRA) started to question the validity of the tax deductions, and the existence of the yachts. OCGC had started thirty-six limited partnerships by then but had started construction on only one or two yachts. That's when the CRA started rejecting the investors' claims for tax deductions. As a result, not only did they lose on their investment, the CRA also demanded repayment of the disallowed income tax deductions, plus hefty interest and fines.

The CRA took several years to investigate OCGC. In the meantime, many investors made annual payments to the company. The delay before the CRA dropped its bombshell led some investors to believe that OCGC provided them with a legitimate tax deduction.

When the CRA suddenly announced that it had disallowed the investors' tax deductions and would not only demand repayment but impose penalties and interest, as well, investors stopped making their cash payments to OCGC. In the ensuing cash crunch, yacht-building stopped and the business folded.

As it did with the OCGC swindle, the CRA may allow your tax deductions for several years before it changes its tune. When that happens, you must cough up the tax, plus penalties and interest, even if you continue to believe that you've made a legitimate investment that has lowered your income tax obligations. When this happens, the CRA demands its money, and you have to pay, even when you no longer have the money. We have even seen cases of lawyers skimming off tax owed by their clients to the CRA, with the clients being none the wiser until the CRA auditor comes knocking. Swindled or otherwise, you have to pay the CRA. The rest is up to a court to decide, and the decision will likely take years.

For investors considering a tax shelter as a way to reduce their taxes, legal advice is essential. The CRA places the onus squarely on the investor to justify the deduction. If the investor's wrong, the CRA wants its money.

In the case of OCGC, Bellfield and Minchella withheld the advice they received from accountants that the CRA might disallow investors' tax deductions. In the subsequent trial, the court found that Bellfield and

Minchella had "misled, manipulated, and lied to" investors. Unfortunately, that didn't get the investors off the hook with the CRA.

The trial, which involved more than 500,000 documents, also revealed that Bellfield and Minchella had fabricated some of the information provided by OCGC to the CRA and investors. They'd created false financial statements, invoices, and tax slips. Bank statements recorded actual transactions conducted with funds recycled from other accounts to create the illusion of a much larger business. Bellfield and Minchella used some of the funds to purchase vessels but later sold them. They siphoned most of the cash away for their own personal expenses, including real estate purchases and brokerage investments.

In addition to all the usual investment risks, tax issues can add another level of complexity, so investors need to do their research. Tax shelters are frequently promoted by accountants or former auditors. Chartered accountants are supposed to declare possible conflicts of interest to buyers of limited partnership units if they have provided tax advice to shelters that they also represent as salespeople. But they don't always do this. With their qualifications and experience, they can easily talk the talk about income taxes, often persuading investors not to bother with independent income tax advice.

Tax shelters come in many shapes and forms, and they inevitably get investors into trouble unless they do their homework and seek independent advice. Donations to foreign entities can pose problems. So do business losses of joint ventures sold to investors as deductions against employment income. Charitable donations of used goods such as cars may trigger a tax deduction, but not if a for-profit business acts as an intermediary. The CRA will also disallow a deduction for a product valued above its fair market price.

Tax shelters exist primarily to encourage investment in socially worthy activities, such as building low-cost housing or scientific research. As government priorities change, so do the tax incentives that accompany them. Unless investors do their homework and look beyond the supposed tax savings at the underlying business, they can get into trouble. The initial attraction of income tax savings can quickly fade if the underlying business fails or the CRA disallows the deduction. Sometimes both happen at the same time.

Typically, a tax shelter subscriber pays some cash to a promoter and signs a promissory note, requiring additional payments per year, plus interest, until the note is paid off. The promoter may sell the promissory notes to others or use them as collateral to obtain other loans. In return, the tax shelter subscriber receives a document from the promoter stating that operating losses have been incurred in organizing the business, such as building yachts, and that these losses may be deducted for income tax purposes. In theory, an investor can postpone tax payments for several years and invest the savings to earn more taxable income.

No one knows exactly why the CRA initially opposed OCGC's tax shelter. Possibly the CRA objected to using the shelter to reduce Canadian income taxes while the company spent its investors' money on yachts built in other countries. Perhaps the CRA noticed that investors had based their deductions on expenses that Bellfield and Minchella had incurred for their personal benefit, and not for building yachts. Maybe the CRA was bothered by the fact that Bellfield and Minchella could determine their own salary, management fee, and other benefits in return for their management services, and spend the money as they saw fit. In the eyes of both the CRA and the jury, their own behaviour caused their downfall. At his criminal trial, the judge described Bellfield as "haughty" and "cunning."

Even though OCGC had formed thirty-six limited partnerships for income tax purposes, it had only one or two yachts available for rental. Shipyard problems had delayed construction of some yachts, and the CRA seemed displeased with the claims for tax deductions in light of the delays.

At the trial, considerable confusion arose over the exact definition of an expense for income tax purposes. Whether or not the jury understood the CRA's distinctions, it found Bellfield and Minchella guilty of swindling 613 victims into investing in thirty-six different limited partnerships promoted by their company. Both received stiff jail sentences.

As for the investors, the CRA's delays and the absence of clear warnings contributed to their losses. Yet the CRA also has an obligation to take its time and gather sufficient evidence before it pounces. Investors need to understand that they cannot rely on the CRA to tip them off if a tax shelter seems questionable. As always, investors have to do their homework and seek expert advice, if necessary.

CHAPTER TWENTY-NINE

# Stairway to Nowhere

*"There is nothing wrong with change, if it is in the right direction."*
WINSTON CHURCHILL

**AS PREVIOUSLY** discussed throughout this book, starting January 1, 2011, Canada will no longer use the Generally Accepted Accounting Principles (GAAP) that we have followed for decades, but will instead adopt International Financial Reporting Standards (IFRS) for use in Canadian public companies. It should be noted, however, that companies still have the option to report using more stringent US GAAP, if they so desire.

Auditors originally sold the idea of IFRS to Canadian lawmakers by claiming it was a one-size-fits-all approach to accounting that was applicable and relevant everywhere in the world, from a Russian resources conglomerate to a Canadian bank to a Brazilian hotdog stand.

In approving the use of IFRS, Canadian lawmakers acquiesced to the country's auditors, even though auditors made it clear in the Hercules Managements case that they owe little or no duty of care to shareholders in approving materially misleading annual financial statements. Given the complete disinterest of auditors in investors' needs, investors must take considerable care in interpreting IFRS financial statements.

Not long after Canadian lawmakers accepted the auditors' proposal to implement IFRS, the auditors stopped claiming that IFRS would allow for worldwide financial comparability. Instead, they simply turned to arguing that it was too late to turn back on the change. Like it or not, IFRS is here to stay in Canada.

The losers in the conversion to IFRS are Canadian investors because all companies in all industries end up getting pushed into the IFRS lowest-common-denominator framework. Investors will now have to take even more precautions to ensure that they are basing their decisions on reliable and accurate information.

Interpreting financial information under IFRS will be a nightmare for investors. It will force investors to address many assumptions, since management enjoys even greater freedom to manipulate the numbers under IFRS. The new system will make it critical for investors to determine earnings quality and income potential, for example.

IFRS is both overly permissive on certain issues and needlessly dogmatic on others. Excessive permissiveness, such as allowing reporting based on historical cost, fair value, or somewhere in between, destroys the possibility of a so-called accounting common language. Inappropriate dogmatic requirements are equally offensive, because they obfuscate transactions and their effects. For example, the netting of cash outflows with cash inflows can lead to misinterpretations about the quality and adequacy of cash inflows, which are critical to corporate survival.

Some Canadian companies will adopt US accounting and auditing standards instead of IFRS. It's also possible that, with many substantial improvements, IFRS will become more palatable to investors. Unfortunately, Canada has adopted IFRS prematurely, exposing investors to perhaps ten years of trial and error.

IFRS represents a significant watering down of the accounting standards in Canada. This will open the door to many more financial reporting tricks. IFRS also places much more audit responsibility on boards of directors, leaving auditors even less obliged to hold companies to a decent level of integrity, consistency, and comparability in financial reporting. IFRS effectively allows auditors to reduce their legal liability to shareholders and creditors, a process that has continued in Canada since the 1980s. Audits and auditors' reports in Canada under IFRS are in danger of becoming either misleading or meaningless. For years, auditors have verified the assertions that corporate managements have built into their financial statements to make sure they are fair and reasonable. This information is imperative to investors. Under IFRS, the verification of such assertions goes largely out the window, leaving investors with little reliable guidance.

Unless IFRS auditing standards are greatly improved, audits will provide little useful assurance to investors. Auditors will do no more than management, who will be able to put the most optimistic spin on corporate financial reports allowable under the loose rules of IFRS. This will give management extensive choice in making accounting decisions, which greatly increases the chances of manipulation. Under the rubber-stamp auditing philosophy of IFRS, corporate trickery will become more prevalent than ever.

How can an auditor disagree with management if they have followed one of the many acceptable principles of IFRS in preparing their financial statements? An investor certainly has the option of having the courts determine if management has materially misled him in its financial reporting, but that would take years. However, in the context of IFRS, no one knows exactly how the courts will distinguish a materially misleading report from one that's just a little bit misleading, or just a tad misleading, or misleading, but not enough to be materially misleading.

In the meantime, investors will have to endure years of IFRS waffling before court decisions clarify the interpretation of the standards. If Canada had waited to adopt IFRS, as the US has done, substantial improvements could have been made without inflicting doubt and confusion on the country's investors.

Written from a narrow viewpoint, IFRS provides little of use for investment decisions. The accountants who wrote IFRS made only a minimal effort to involve investors, regulators, or lawmakers in the process. Now that the decision has been made to adopt the rules in Canada, auditors have essentially handed over standards-setting to a foreign entity that will have even less interest in addressing the specialized needs of Canadian investors.

In our extensive correspondence with senior lawmakers and cabinet ministers, they have shown surprisingly little understanding of IFRS, or the major consequences of adopting international standards. They definitely do not know that IFRS reopens loopholes and gaps that were plugged years ago by Canadian GAAP, or that IFRS represents a substantial step backwards for financial reporting in Canada. Yet federal and provincial legislation governs financial reporting in Canada, and Canadian lawmakers should have involved themselves more thoroughly in the decision to adopt IFRS. By abdicating their responsibility, Canada's lawmakers have clearly shown that they have not learned from previous financial frauds. As usual, Canadian investors are on their own.

Legislators should have relieved auditors of their standard-setting duties years ago, when the Canadian Institute of Chartered Accountants argued successfully to the Supreme Court of Canada that investors could not rely on audited annual financial statements to make investment decisions. Despite the staggering implications, lawmakers did nothing. Since then, auditors have imposed even weaker auditing standards on shareholders under IFRS. Now investors will be stuck with these low standards until a courageous court says otherwise.

Given the political apathy about IFRS, Canadian and foreign investors have cause to feel great concern. Under IFRS, scams can be hidden for several years before they surface, resulting in losses to duped investors. But acting too late is a Canadian trait, as we have seen with the likes of Nortel, low-quality business income trusts, and numerous Ponzi schemes. If Canada's purpose is to discourage foreign and domestic investors, lawmakers have certainly taken the right steps.

In some countries, IFRS will improve previously existing accounting regimes. For North America, however, IFRS is a major step backward.

An understanding of IFRS has to begin with an examination of the fundamental assumptions made by its supporters in Canada. These include:

1. *"Comparability of accounting across the world is accomplished by IFRS."* This assumption is laughable for a number of reasons and was essentially abandoned by Canadian auditors and IFRS promoters once it became too late to turn the boat around on adopting IFRS in Canada. The extensive freedom given to management under IFRS to report in

one of several different ways prevents comparability even within Canada, let alone other countries. Comparisons to companies in other countries is ludicrous.

Differences in laws, regulations, taxes, cultures, education, ethics, training, traditions, enforcement, and optimism make uniformity an opium dream. Just ask the accountants who have prepared consolidated financial statements for multinational companies under IFRS. In some countries, local accountants believe that everything is fine, whereas in others, they view consolidated statements as complete rubbish.

2. *"Governance, honesty, and ethical behaviour are not issues that IFRS has to address in setting accounting standards; IFRS sets the principles; others must do the policing."*

Accounting and financial reporting have repeatedly been used to cover up frauds that have bilked investors out of billions of dollars. Basic prohibitions against specified, known accounting tricks are essential. IFRS cannot self-immunize and ignore the extensive problems that it has created.

Income tax legislation in Canada, for instance, has been written on the correct assumption that executives will manipulate the numbers to reduce taxes. If IFRS and Canada's auditors assume that corporate managers will not manipulate financial reports to shareholders and creditors, they've swallowed too much fairy dust.

3. *"Management knows its company best, and should be given the freedom to report its financial beliefs."*

In a world of totally honest management, with no egos to protect and no errors to confess to shareholders, such an IFRS assumption might make sense. But it doesn't make sense in Canada or anywhere else.

4. *"IFRS is principles-based, solving the problem of swindlers finding their way around specific rules."*

Fortunately, the supporters of IFRS eventually withdrew this unsupportable assumption. IFRS has now adopted many US accounting principles. In comparison to US GAAP, however, IFRS

   A. often imposes very weak rules in areas such as revenue recognition that leave significant room for massaging the numbers;
   B. does not deal with many technical issues, leaving company financial reporting open to significant management choices

and potential deceptions in areas such as related-party transactions;
C. ignores many industry-specific problems, especially in resource industries, on which Canada's economic prosperity depends;
D. is vulnerable to political interference, especially from Europe, in choosing what gets reported versus what remains hidden, and
E. provides inadequate guidance to corporate executives and auditors about many types of transactions. This cannot possibly encourage uniformity in financial reporting. Each country will fall back on its pre-IFRS methods of reasoning, resulting in highly different approaches.

5. *"IFRS will reduce a company's cost of capital."*
No proof exists for such an assertion. If anything, the opposite is likely in North America, because IFRS will create greater uncertainty and raise even more concern among investors and lenders about the quality of reported earnings.

6. *"IFRS provides greater note disclosure, which will counteract the effects of so much management choice and freedom."*
Based on IFRS reports that we have seen, much of the required IFRS disclosure is too trivial to be of benefit to investors. IFRS may evolve, but the standards require much improvement. Above all, unless IFRS explicitly prohibits conventional scams, it will not likely contribute to improved reporting for the benefit of investors.

7. *"Current fair market value figures are relevant, whereas historical cost figures are not."*
This assertion deals with the way in which companies report the value of their assets. In the absence of strong guidance, IFRS enables financial swindlers to pick the figure they want to see in their financial statements. The critical difficulty of current value reporting is selecting the appropriate method of determining value, such as discounted cash flow, resale price, replacement cost, reproduction cost, and value-in-use. In calculating income tax effects, for instance, both original cost and current resale value have to be known to investors. Reporting only one figure, while throwing out the old standard, is grossly deficient. Say what you will about historical cost figures, at least they contain an element of certainty.

IFRS allows even more latitude in quantifying the figures once the measurement standard has been chosen. For example, in computing discounted cash flows, the validity of the interest or discount rate requires considerable support and explanation. The estimated cash flow amounts are also vital, including the range that can be expected versus the average selected by management. Similarly, to calculate resale prices the range of disposal costs, such as commissions, and payment terms have to be known.

IFRS allows management to use fair values, or variations, for many items that were previously recorded at historical cost. Such adjustments to the reported figures will differ from company to company and even from asset class to asset class within each company. This will wreak considerable havoc on analysis.

8. *"To get countries on board for IFRS we had to make some concessions. That's the price of universality."*
The so-called concessions are better described as sinking to the lowest common denominator on several issues, such as cash-flow reporting. Accordingly, IFRS, at this stage of its evolution, is a significant step backwards for Canada. And for what possible benefit, when the variations in application of IFRS from country to country are so staggering?

9. *"Few implementation problems have arisen with IFRS."*
Not much can be said about such an assertion, other than it is nonsense. If problems are few, why do auditors continue to stress the need for their help, instruction, and training well in advance of IFRS implementation? Could it have something to do with the massive billings involved? Many complaints have been raised about implementation costs and the inadequate conceptual and practical material available to explain so-called IFRS principles.

More importantly, perhaps, the users of IFRS financial reports have encountered extensive interpretation problems. It could take years for bankers, mergers and acquisition specialists, financial analysts, and investors to understand the financial deceits made possible by IFRS, especially in its different iterations in different countries.

Despite these concerns, the IFRS juggernaut rolls on. At great cost, conversion to IFRS will have substantially negative effects for investors.

Canadian lawmakers and securities administrators not only seem oblivious to investor concerns, they also seem to have swallowed even the most inaccurate assertions about IFRS.

Supporters of IFRS claim that more than 100 countries already use these standards. A vast majority, however, are irrelevant to Canada's accounting and auditing environment. Many others merely proposed to adopt IFRS, or allowed IFRS as an alternative to their current standard.

Investors should also understand that IFRS emerged quickly in the early 2000s as a result of a directive from the European Commission to impose similar accounting standards on member countries. Since Europe already shared a common currency, common accounting standards made sense. Unfortunately, the European Union (EU) badly bungled the implementation of IFRS. Member countries had practically no time to get the job done. "When countries like those in the EU took International Accounting Standards, they did so with great courage," said the chairman of the International Accounting Standards Board (IASB), "and total ignorance of what was in them."

To reach agreement among many diverse interests, the international reporting standards incorporated many lowest common denominators. What was unacceptable in country A, for instance, suddenly became acceptable, because country B had used that approach for many years. The result was a systematic weakening of standards and the creation of so many choices that any previous sense of uniformity disappeared.

Europe adopted IFRS in 2005, but in a significantly weakened form. For countries that had followed abysmal financial reporting practices beforehand, IFRS was a step up. The others derived some benefit from an improvement in standards in some of their close trading partners, although they also weakened their own accounting standards in the process. In any case, what works for Europe may not work for the rest of the world.

Nevertheless, Canada has moved ahead with adopting IFRS, even though its largest trading partner, the US, sees major drawbacks with it, and has not even come close to adopting the standards. In fact, the US may never adopt IFRS. Instead it may follow a path of mutual convergence that will reduce the differences between US GAAP and IFRS from both sides. In the end, US GAAP could be a formidable alternative to the many different regional versions of IFRS that will emerge as investors, lawmakers, and regulators in all countries push for tighter standards.

Canada has claimed for years that its accounting standards bore more ideological resemblance to the UK's than US standards. As a result, Canada became drawn into the IFRS web, since the UK is the centre for IFRS in Europe. Canadian accounting was said, without much support, to be based on principles, as opposed to more prescriptive rules that moved beyond the one-size-fits-all mentality. Pinning down those principles was often difficult, however. Meanwhile, Canadian accounting standards gradually converged with several US standards, which made sense, since the US is Canada's largest trading partner.

Convergence with US standards stopped abruptly in the mid-2000s. Canadian accounting standard-setters announced instead that they would run full tilt to adopt IFRS. They said, at the time, again without adequate evidence, that Canadian accounting was principles-based and could only be aligned appropriately with IFRS. Auditors jumped on the bandwagon and made several other highly questionable claims, which we've already addressed.

In the end, though, the principles-versus-rules debate turned out to be a crock. Even the long-time chairman of the IASB later said that US standards are based on principles that are also backed up by rules. These rules provide specific industry guidance, for instance, and lay out clear prohibitions to prevent much of the financial-statement manipulation that occurs repeatedly in Canada.

Canadian lawmakers and regulators seemed indifferent to standards of any kind to protect the public's interests. Lawmakers should simply have followed the money to discover the auditors' real intentions. They should have known that auditors didn't care much about the benefits of IFRS to investors. Instead, lawmakers looked the other way and allowed IFRS to become the standard for Canadian accounting. Now, the worst is yet to come.

It's apparent that the auditors of Canada are going to benefit enormously from switching over thousands of companies to a completely new accounting standard, and they did as much as they could to deflect attention away from this fact for as long as possible. Eventually, they admitted that their reasons for adopting IFRS were financially motivated. Of course, this admission was once again made after it was too late to turn back.

"Retaining a unique Canadian GAAP is no longer cost effective," said Canada's auditors, confirming that standard-setting had nothing to do with the public interest and everything to do with the cost of doing business.

Canada's auditors, in fact, regard standard-setting as another corporate cost centre, with a minimal budget, staffed, if possible, by unpaid volunteers. Canadian courts and lawmakers had said that auditors did not have to answer to the public interest, so why would they spend their money improving standards? They would derive no obvious benefit, and they would risk a backlash from their corporate clients, many of which want less regulation, not more.

Now they've rid themselves of the problem even more effectively, handing over standards-setting to a foreign entity and relieving themselves of the cost of administering the accounting rules. Instead of a cost centre, standards have become a profit centre, since corporations will have to pay enormous fees to convert to IFRS. And guess who collects those fees?

As a secondary benefit, weak IFRS accounting and auditing rules allow auditors to shift considerable responsibilities to corporate management, further reducing their already negligible legal responsibilities to investors. Other motivations could also have existed, of course. Some of the key people involved in handing over Canada to the powers that control IFRS, for example, have now moved on to more senior positions in the international accounting body.

In the end, the spreading of falsehoods and gross exaggerations, combined with the apathy of lawmakers, has successfully opened the door for IFRS to enter Canada. Investors have no choice but to learn about the many loopholes and management choices that IFRS allows for the manipulation of financial reporting. Unfortunately, investors' general unfamiliarity with IFRS, combined with the cover-up tactics accessible through the new standards, will keep potential frauds hidden for years.

Under IFRS, the manipulation of financial reporting will become more troublesome in several areas: non-arm's-length accounting and auditing; revenue recognition; business combinations or mergers; cash flows; and general cooking of the books by reporting expenses as assets, for example.

With so many choices available to management under IFRS, they may simply perpetuate variations of the same old scams: faking higher profits;

hiding liabilities; covering up bad management decisions; obscuring declining cash flows; hiding self-dealing transactions; building up cookie jars for tougher times; burying covenant violations so that creditors do not call loans; buying other companies to hide the messes in the acquiring company; postponing losses to future years by assigning high values to dubious assets; and avoiding the writing-down of goodwill and intangibles.

Not only will management try to get away with deliberate obfuscation, but investors themselves will also run the risk of grossly misinterpreting the results. Based on recent experience, Canadian auditors have a hard time reining in executive optimism when it comes to fair-valuing assets, for example. When companies stopped regularly expensing the cost of acquired goodwill and certain intangible assets in the early 2000s, all sorts of inappropriate value approximations appeared. More critically, the disclosure that accompanied the wide-ranging assumptions and methods was laughable. If this is the low standard to which Canadian investors have been accustomed, it certainly does not bode well for IFRS in Canada.

Given that Canada has experienced many financial failures of banks, trust companies, finance companies, and real estate enterprises, whose financial statements, based on Canadian GAAP, hid cash deficiencies, investors face a much more severe problem of interpretation under IFRS.

Given the weak auditing standards and wide-ranging freedom of management choice under IFRS, additional analytical difficulties will arise in the following areas:

1. *Context.* Serious misinterpretations of IFRS will occur because people with knowledge of US, Canadian, or another country's GAAP will make inappropriate assumptions based on their previous experience. For example, North Americans may believe that sales of goods or services need to be collectible for revenue to be recognized on the income statement. Under IFRS, investors will have to determine whether a company will actually obtain cash, or a receivable, for the goods or services. They will also have to determine if a receivable will be collected in cash within a few months, or if it will bear interest or be factored for cash, or never be collected at all, because the receivable might become an investment in a near-bankrupt company.

IFRS downplays the importance of cash collection. Yet it will be up to the individual to interpret the extent to which a company downplays that element of its financial reporting. IFRS could allow for the quick recording of revenue, while ignoring cash. This encourages financial manipulators, who stress valuations based on revenue, and could seriously mislead many investors whose valuation models depend on revenue growth assumptions. A mere two quarters after a company recognizes the revenue, the entire receivable may become an expense. For many IFRS supporters, this absence of logic appears to be unimportant.

2. *Audit assurance.* IFRS auditing material seems to reduce the obligations of auditors to detect problems and address them directly. Compared to US auditing standards, for example, IFRS cops out, enabling auditors to "inform the board of directors," instead of refusing to sign the auditor's report until the materially misleading numbers are corrected.

   IFRS diminishes the auditor's role to a point where many audits will provide no value-added benefits. The reliability of numbers and accompanying explanations will surely become suspect under IFRS, unless a significant change in attitude occurs.

3. *Self-dealings and related-party measurements.* According to IFRS supporters, the reporting of fair market values is a cornerstone of the new reporting standards. But IFRS backs away from requiring the measurement of the fair market value of self-dealings, and from the further reporting of transactions that may be unfair to investors.

   Instead of addressing the possibility that corporate executives may sell goods or services at unfair prices to a public company through their own executive-owned companies, IFRS merely calls for a trivial note disclosure. Canada abandoned such trivial disclosures more than fifteen years ago.

   Unfair self-dealings can tip off auditors to other ethical problems. Yet under IFRS audit standards, auditors can stick their heads in the sand, depriving shareholders of vital information.

4. *Netting of numbers.* In many Canadian financial collapses, companies have hidden growing deficiencies in cash inflow until it is too late. Hiding such deficiencies becomes easier when a company can

offset gross payments or cash outflows against cash receipts. Knowing the amount of cash inflow from repayments of loans, for example, is vital in evaluating the quality of a mortgage company's loan portfolio. Bad loans do not generate much cash inflow. Under IFRS, a mortgage company does not have to report receipts separately, but can net them instead. This is another step backward from Canadian GAAP, and will make the recovery of cash stolen from investors much more difficult if the courts accept inferior IFRS as a Canadian standard.

5. *Burying expenses and using valuation choices to hide them.* With the choices allowed under IFRS, companies can value land, buildings, and equipment in several different ways. Many overhead costs and expenses, such as some executive expenses and compensation, could be extracted from the IFRS income statement and then buried in buildings and equipment as part of a disguised restructuring. Investors would have considerable difficulty detecting the scheme under IFRS because a generous valuation estimate could be used as a cover-up technique.

Such a scam could be used in different forms for several years. When combined with weak international auditing standards, it is not realistic to expect auditors to blow the whistle.

6. *Comparisons among companies.* The deeper an investor digs into the so-called principles of IFRS, the more depressing they become. It takes only a cursory reading to demolish the dubious claim that IFRS allows for worldwide financial reporting comparability. IFRS makes these and many other comparisons almost impossible, because management can choose to do what it wants in many situations, and in most cases, disclosure of management's choices does not provide adequate information to make adjustments. Accordingly, investors have to avoid making critical comparisons using IFRS.

7. *Historical cost versus current value.* To sign up many countries to IFRS, the body responsible for setting the standards had to grant numerous exceptions to the rules. IFRS could work in a totally different way in one country than another. Real estate, for instance, may be recorded at cost, or in one of several other ways available under current valu-

ation methods. All of the possibilities comply with IFRS. With so many choices available to management, comparability becomes impossible. The many differences in valuation inputs and assumptions will simply exacerbate the problem.

8. *Trend lines.* A trend line of profits, sales, or cash from operations that moves steadily upwards attracts investors. But investors may look twice at a trend that seems too steady, since it may indicate financial manipulation. Under IFRS, such steady trend lines will become rare. (See Appendix H.)

    Steady trends reported under IFRS, year after year, should prompt investors to investigate thoroughly. Unless the economy is in a boom period with no slowdowns, IFRS should generate somewhat erratic trend lines.

    Cooking of the books using valuation changes will likely become a new field of study for financial swindlers eager to find ways of avoiding detection under IFRS.

Based on our lengthy experience as forensic accountants, we expect IFRS will make life miserable for investors. In reaching this conclusion, we reviewed dozens of past litigation files for which we had prepared forensic analysis reports for the courts. We selected cases that involved allegations against directors, officers, and auditors for which our plaintiff clients had received financial settlements. Our clients in these cases were primarily creditors and shareholders who had allegedly been deceived by deficient or misleading financial reporting.

We posed this question: if IFRS had been used instead of Canadian or US GAAP, would the court case have been strong enough to produce a financial settlement to the benefit of the plaintiffs?

In general, courts require evidence of provable material violations of the rules and principles of accounting, auditing, or fair presentation before they will decide against directors, officers, and auditors. These decisions usually involve breaches of fiduciary duty or negligence.

According to our file review, weak IFRS principles, and the absence of specific prohibitions, would have made convictions or settlements either impossible or highly unlikely in many cases. To reach a favourable decision for the plaintiffs, a court would have to conclude that IFRS unfairly permitted deceptive or fraudulent reporting. To reach this decision, a judge would have to look beyond behaviour allowed under weak IFRS standards to conclude that such flimsy requirements were unacceptable to society. The British Columbia Court of Appeal made such a ruling in the Kripps case, in which investors relied on audited financial statements in a prospectus when they decided to buy the debentures of a mortgage company. But it will require a courageous judge or appeal court to conclude that IFRS imposes a standard of financial reporting and auditing that's unacceptable to Canadian society.

Will investors likely see many such court decisions in the next five years? Don't hold your breath. Given the insurance coverage carried by directors, officers, and auditors, they could easily wear down plaintiff creditors or shareholders, financially, in a lengthy trial. Swindlers could thus win by default.

Canadian lawmakers could step in to prevent such outcomes, but based on their track record so far, they won't. Meanwhile, the promoters of IFRS have retracted most of their sales pitches, such as worldwide comparability and principles-based advantages. Even they seem to admit that IFRS doesn't measure up to existing Canadian standards and will have to change drastically to catch up.

Meanwhile, shifty executives will find themselves in heaven, using vaguely worded IFRS principles to report figures that make them appear more competent. Even assuming the honesty of management, investors will inevitably make serious mistakes because of their unfamiliarity with the new rules and the implications of management choices, honestly motivated or otherwise.

CHAPTER THIRTY

# Moving Forward

> "Morality cannot be legislated, but behaviour can be regulated. Judicial decrees may not change the heart, but they can restrain the heartless."
>
> MARTIN LUTHER KING, JR.

**WE HAVE** focused in previous chapters on arming investors with the knowledge they need to avoid financial scams that occur in Canada because of our deeply flawed investor protection safety net. We now turn our thoughts to fixing the holes in that safety net.

Some of the following recommendations for improving investor protection in Canada are fairly obvious. For instance, the US got it right when it set up the Securities and Exchange Commission more than seventy-five years ago. Now that Canada has begun the process of establishing a pan-Canadian securities regulator, it is crucial that we establish something similar.

By appointing Doug Hyndman to lead the initiative, we got off to a very poor start. Hyndman argued for years that we didn't need a national regulator. He also headed the British Columbia Securities Commission during the two decades when financial dishonesty tainted the reputation of the Vancouver Stock Exchange around the world.

Canada might get a national securities regulator, but unfortunately, its function seems destined to merely cut a few costs for companies, such as listing, filing, and registration fees, along with the legal and other expenses now incurred with multiple provincial dealings. It's a nice gesture, but hardly worth the effort. It's also a serious slap to the face of investors.

What Canada really needs is a national securities enforcement agency. Ideally, it would operate completely separately from the regulatory authority that looks after listing requirements, cost cutting, and other interests of corporations. Also, such an agency would be independently funded, and it would place investor interests first, acting as a much-needed counterbalance to current provincial regulators who put corporate interests ahead of investor needs.

A national securities enforcement agency should have the authority to set and collect fees from public companies and to levy hefty fines. It should have an operating budget that enables it to train forensic accountants and fraud investigators to look beyond the brainwashed mindset that presumes that all executives are honest people incapable of allowing financial factors to influence their decisions.

At the moment, enforcement activities are conducted by a division of our provincial securities regulators, which greatly diminishes its independence and effectiveness. A national enforcement agency would abandon the current approach of provincial regulators, who prefer to slap companies on the wrist behind closed doors rather than punish them publicly for misbehaving. If the agency clamped down on financial reporting shams and imposed sizeable fines publicly, other offending companies would quickly correct their behaviour. Companies understand one thing, and that's money. Substantial fines would have a far greater impact on corporate deception than gentle persuasion.

Corporations argue that Canada does not need more regulation or enforcement, as if the mere idea impugns their personal honesty and integrity. Yet Canada has an abysmal record when it comes to securities enforcement. As we've clearly demonstrated through the case studies examined in previous chapters, the current approach is broken. We need significant changes to address investor concerns properly.

Corporate lobbyists push for cost reduction above all else, and they make their voices heard. When issues arise, such as the rampant misuse of distributable cash reporting by business income trusts, corporate interests push back. Compared to corporate lobbying groups, individual investor groups in Canada seem almost inconsequential.

There is something seriously wrong when the head of enforcement for Canada's largest provincial regulator says that Canadians have no interest in pursuing white-collar fraud more vigourously. Do Canadian investors really agree that "The attitude in Canada is that there is a lot more room for compassion and understanding and rehabilitation"?

Unfortunately, that seems to be the mindset underlying the formation of our new national regulatory body. Once in place, it will likely charge headlong into the abyss of principles-based securities regulation. As with accounting in Canada, principles-based securities regulation is long on ideals and short on reality. It assumes too much honesty and integrity on the part of the players involved. Other countries, such as the UK, have experimented with principles-based regulation and met with unmitigated failure. Yet Canada still has the audacity to think it can make the proverbial turkey fly.

The powers that be will not likely drop the ill-guided concept of principles-based regulation. Corporate interests will likely push for principles-based regulation, because it is the cheapest approach. If we had a national securities enforcement agency, however, companies might understand that, if they stray too far off course, they will be put in their place by tough, clear, and prescriptive judgments.

In addition, Canada needs to emulate the rest of the world and separate the duties of accounting and auditing practitioners from the duties of accounting and auditing standard-setters. This would eliminate the major conflict of interest that currently exists when the same group is responsible for meeting the desires of their client corporations and the contrasting needs of investors.

The US made this distinction when it established the Financial Accounting Standards Board (FASB) in 1973 to develop US accounting rules. In establishing the FASB, the US took responsibility for standards-setting out of the hands of the American Institute of Certified Public Accountants (AICPA).

The AICPA acts as the self-regulatory body of accounting and auditing practitioners in the US. It addresses professional and ethical standards, continuing education, advocacy, and similar issues. In Canada, the Canadian Institute of Chartered Accountants (CICA) is the equivalent of the AICPA. But Canada has no substantial equivalent to the FASB. The Accounting Standards Board (AcSB) sets standards in Canada, but it is a division of the CICA, and thus falls under its financial control.

The CICA has tried to create the appearance that the accounting practitioners of Canada did not completely dominate the setting of standards. In 2000, it established the Accounting Standards Oversight Council (AcSOC), supposedly to allow public input into the setting of accounting standards. Since 2005, the chairman of AcSOC has been Doug Hyndman. Enough said.

The AcSOC is staffed by volunteers, all of whom have full-time jobs elsewhere. With such a structure, AcSOC cannot possibly address the pervasive conflicts of interest that confront investors when accounting practitioners influence the substance of accounting rules.

With the adoption of IFRS, Canada has handed control of accounting rules to the International Accounting Standards Board (IASB). So why does Canada need a separate standard-setting body at all? The answer is that the basic rules of IFRS will inevitably evolve into a multitude of regional variations. The rules were left wide open by design, and a Canadian standard-setting body will have to interpret and clarify them.

Much of US GAAP, for instance, will continue in practice even if the US moves closer to convergence with IFRS. Given the large gaps that exist in IFRS, investors, creditors, analysts, and corporations will seek more prescriptive rules to accompany the primary IFRS principles. Such a process has occurred with Canadian and US GAAP over the past twenty-five years. But the IASB cannot possibly address all the regional issues that will crop up around the world. Local organizations will have to deal with the gaps.

By unloading responsibility for standard-setting onto the international accounting authorities, the CICA believes it has eliminated a long-time headache, when, in fact, it will enable investors to take the next step more easily in reforming accounting standards-setting in Canada. Since the CICA clearly wants no part of standards-setting in Canada, it will have a hard time arguing against the establishment of a completely independent accounting standards-setting entity by Canadian lawmakers.

Canada needs an organization to set accounting rules that puts investors, creditors, and other users of financial statements first. It will take several years to train a staff of competent investigators, including forensic accountants and fraud examiners, who understand the gaps in the current rules. Such an organization will need strong leadership, backed by political support and adequate long-term budgets. More importantly, it will not assume that all corporate executives are honest people.

A similarly independent body must set financial statement auditing rules in Canada. This organization would act in the same way as a national securities enforcement agency to counterbalance weak principles-based securities regulation, and undo some of the damage inflicted on investors by the vagueness of IFRS.

Canada also needs to stop listening to self-regulatory organizations for advice on how to fix the SROs. The SROs that govern accounting, auditing, and securities regulation in Canada have repeatedly hung investors out to dry. By their inactions, investors have lost significant savings to market schemers. Yet every time a major collapse occurs or a key issue crops up, Canadian lawmakers turn to those SROs for counsel on making changes to the status quo.

With the adoption of IFRS, for instance, we contacted dozens of federal and provincial legislators to object on behalf of investors, after we saw disaster looming. Lawmakers who did not pass the buck to other government departments suggested that we take our concerns to the CICA, the very group that sold investors down the river in the first place.

We need a clear alternative to asking the fox to fix the lock on the henhouse door. Among other things, we need to reinvigorate the lost Canadian tradition of judicial inquiries into financial collapses and large-scale market scandals. Only by seeking out the wise counsel of independent justices can lawmakers hope to find workable solutions to the problems that will continue to affect the environment in which Canadians save and invest their money.

Canadian lawmakers also need to institute legislation to fix the Hercules court decision, since investors need to be able to rely on annual audited financial statements when making important investment decisions. Since 1997, auditors have owed no duty of care to investors for approving misleading annual financial statements in Canada. Legislatively mandated audits have become not only a waste of shareholders' money, but also a dangerous red herring that leads investors to believe they enjoy more protection than they actually do. Without any audit function at all, they would at least relinquish their false sense of security. Canadian lawmakers should either eliminate the legislative requirement for an audit or force auditors to stand behind the quality of their work. If lawmakers intend to address this problem, though, they must look beyond the auditing community for advice. After all, the auditing community is part of the problem, not part of the solution.

In the 1950s and 1960s, individual Canadians regarded the financial marketplace with grave mistrust. It took a major effort to encourage the public to invest in equities. Are we heading back to those days?

Likewise, if weak regulation discourages foreign investment in Canada, what will happen to our standard of living?

To raise Canada to the standards that the rest of the world applies to protect domestic and foreign investors, we need to take the following steps:

1. *Establish an independent Canadian accounting standards board similar to the US Financial Accounting Standards Board that is free from the financial control and influence of the accounting practitioners of Canada.* Investors will need significant help in the years ahead to do this, once IFRS proves itself inadequate. We will also need solid regional interpretations and standards. The new body will need to be staffed with forensic accountants and fraud examiners initially, as traditional accountants are retrained.
2. *Establish a national securities enforcement agency to act as the judicial counterpart to the proposed national securities regulator.* The agency must have the ability to overrule any independent Canadian accounting standards board on accounting issues, in the same manner that the US SEC has the ultimate say over the US FASB's rules.
3. *Dispense with the concept of principles-based securities regulation altogether when establishing the framework for Canada's national securities regulator.* Such regulation has proven a failure in other countries. Vague principles are not enough to keep people in check, especially if the issue ends up in court.

4. *Establish an independent Canadian auditing standards board that is free from the financial conflicts of current audit practitioners in Canada.* The new board will act as the judicial, Canadian-controlled auditing counterpart to both the IASB and the newly proposed Canadian accounting board. Ultimate say, however, must be ceded to a national securities enforcement agency.
5. *Stop asking SROs for solutions to the problems they cause.* Canadian lawmakers need to find independent sources of information and analysis if they hope to fix the country's systemic investor-protection problems. Legislators need to look past the SROs, corporate lobby groups, and so-called defendant-bar law firms that exclusively defend corporations and their auditors. These groups seem solely interested in protecting the status quo for their own benefit. Canada needs to start conducting judicial inquiries again into the collapse of companies, investment products, and similar market scandals.
6. *Introduce legislation to fix the Supreme Court of Canada's decision in Hercules Managements.* This decision essentially absolves auditors from any duty of care to investors when they approve misleading annual financial statements.

Without these fixes as a minimum, investors will continue to be on their own when it comes to investing in Canada. In the meantime, they must continue to act as their own advisor, analyst, auditor, and securities police force to avoid falling victim to one of the many financial schemers who practise in this country. Canada has a long history of financial scams, and the people who perpetuate those scams have no intention of stopping now.

APPENDIX A

# Fifty Canadian Financial Fiascos

**ADVOCATES OF** maintaining the status quo in Canada, instead of adopting US-style legislation and enforcement to protect investors, often say that Canada does not have the same problems as the US. Such comments clearly run counter to the facts.

In addition to the examples of Canadian auditing, regulatory, and enforcement failures provided throughout the book, there are numerous others that could fill subsequent volumes. What follows is a partial list of Canadian cases in which investors have been seriously abandoned by our lawmakers, investigators, regulators, and auditors, and left to fight on their own:

> ATI Technologies
> Atlantic Acceptance Corporation
> Atlas Cold Storage Income Trust
> Berkshire Securities
> Betacom Corporation
> Bramalea Companies
> Bre-X Minerals
> Canadian Commercial Bank
> Cartaway Resources
> Castor Holdings

Churchill Forest Industries
Cinar
Confederation Trust
Corel Corporation
Crocus Investment Fund
Cross Pacific Pearls
Eron Mortgage Corporation
FMF Capital
Golden Rule Resources
Hercules Managements
Hollinger
International Nesmont Industrial
Investors Overseas Syndicates
Jevco Insurance
Livent
Merit Energy
National Business Systems
Nelbar Financial
New Cantech Ventures
Norbourg Asset Management
Norshield Asset Management
Northland Bank
Nortel Networks
Overseas Credit and Guaranty
Pacific International Securities
Philip Services
Pigeon King International
Pineridge Capital
Portus Asset Management
Principal Group
Royal Group Technologies
Shamray Group of Companies
Standard Trust Corporation
Sungold International Holdings
Teachers Investment and Housing Co-operative
Thermo Tech Technologies

Victoria Mortgage
VisuaLabs
YBM Magnex
Yellow.com Business Pages

Obviously, many more could be listed. Some of the above led to civil trials, ending with financial settlements that did not involve admissions of negligence or fraud. Too few of these cases involved criminal investigations. Nevertheless, billions of dollars of investors' money was lost.

By doing little or nothing about these cases, Canadian lawmakers are merely encouraging the financial swindlers to escalate and repeat their activities. In so doing, Canada has acquired a reputation among the rest of the world as a place where investigations are few, prosecutions even fewer, and penalties rarest of all.

## APPENDIX B

# Financial Statement Interpretation

**THE CONTENT** and design of a company's annual report to shareholders can differ from country to country, especially when comparing a corporation in North America to one in Europe or Asia. There tend to be some broad similarities, but much of the feel and specialized content of foreign reports takes some getting used to. Outside of annual reports, additional information can be very helpful to investors, such as supplemental annual information forms, management circulars, acquisition reports, and insider transaction and ownership reports, to name just a few. Quarterly reports (not available in all countries) can range from the very insightful to the barebones, virtually useless variety.

However, perhaps the most useful piece of information of all for investors is actually very basic: where the stock is traded, and therefore, what country or countries are likely to have the most regulatory and enforcement influence on the company. Investors are safest investing under the guard of US regulators, whether the company is Canadian, American, or otherwise. Canadian investors in particular should be wary of foreign companies that use Canada as a regulator of convenience. Many foreign mining or resource companies may choose Canada to gain access to greater capital in a lax regulatory environment. However, those companies may also choose to pull their Canadian listing after a while, leaving Canadian investors in the lurch.

A typical Canadian annual report for a publicly traded company has two main parts that are somewhat subject to regulation and oversight: (1) the audited financial statements, including the financial statement footnotes; and (2) the Management Discussion and Analysis section (MD&A). The general background information of the annual report and the MD&A sections are not audited. The MD&A comes under the purview of the securities commissions and their umbrella organization, the Canadian Securities Administrators (CSA). This organization attempts to regulate the MD&A by persuading companies to provide some standardized disclosures. Quite often, but not always, the MD&A is where companies will portray alternative financial metrics that they claim are of use to investors. Examples would be distributable cash reporting, cash operating figures, and so forth, which are generally referred to as "non-GAAP" measures.

The MD&A section can also be used by companies to put their particular spin or interpretation on the significance of financial activities. Thus, caution should be exercised when reading this section. Of special importance to investors is whether management's indications for the future relate logically to what has happened in the past. Various segments of the company may be successful, or they may be dragging down profits and cash flows. Investors need to be mindful of veiled promises of quick turnarounds in weak segments of a company. The financial numbers might be subject to manipulation through various games, such as converting expenses into dubious assets, and other schemes.

Audited financial statements tend to include most or all of the following individual financial statements:

1. Balance Sheet, or Statement of Position.
2. Income Statement, or Profit & Loss Statement, or Operations Statement.
3. Cash-Flow Statement.
4. Retained Earnings, or Retained Income Statement.
5. Statement of Comprehensive Income, or Changes in Comprehensive Income.
6. Statements of Changes in Specialized Equity or Capital Balances.

In addition, notes to the financial statements are vital in grasping the approaches or choices that a company has selected and their probable financial importance. Several permitted methods of recording a particular transaction may exist, and effects on income and reported cash flows may therefore vary appreciably. The seeming specificity of the reported amounts and figures can mislead investors into believing that the reported amounts are the only allowable amounts. Rather, investors should be analyzing them and considering amendments to account for corporate shenanigans.

Likewise, much financial trickery depends somewhat on people's belief that audited figures must be the "real" or "true" figures. In fact, auditors, based on their own loose rules, are fully entitled to accept any one of, perhaps, ten possible ways of accounting for a particular transaction. Unless the investor or creditor knows exactly which choice of reporting treatment the company has selected, the conclusions reached by the financial statement reader could be dreadfully inappropriate. Basic issues, such as whether management is optimistic or pessimistic, honest or dishonest, fully informed or clueless, can also affect accounting numbers. All-purpose accounting and financial reporting truths simply do not exist. The notes to the financial statements provide clues about the critical accounting choices that have been made.

What follows is a basic view of the components of a financial statement, an understanding of which is necessary to identify basic investment scams.

**BALANCE SHEET**
A balance sheet is a listing of a corporation's assets, its liabilities to others, and the residual owner's investment or owner's equity. Suppose that you just acquired a condo for $400,000 by signing a mortgage for $300,000 and paying $100,000 cash. The balance sheet would look like this at the date of purchase:

Condo Name or Other Description
Balance Sheet
October 31, 2010

|  | ASSETS | LIABILITIES AND EQUITY |  |
|---|---|---|---|
| Condo | $400,000 | Liability: |  |
|  |  | Mortgage payable | $300,000 |
|  |  | Owner's equity | 100,000 |
|  | $400,000 |  | $400,000 |

The balance sheet has to balance, with the assets equalling the total of liabilities and owner's equity:

$$\$400,000 = \$300,000 + \$100,000$$

All kinds of additional assets could eventually exist, such as furniture, rugs, art, and similar. Hence, by November 30, 2010, the asset total could be well above $400,000. Similarly, if credit cards were used to acquire the furniture, liabilities would increase by the amounts that are due to the credit card companies. An owner's equity would not change as a result of having used credit cards to purchase furniture and similar assets.

INCOME STATEMENT

An income statement shows revenue less the expenses of earning that revenue. When revenue exceeds related expenses, the company reports a profit (before income taxes). When the opposite occurs, and expenses exceed revenue, a loss results. Income and losses affect owners' equity. Net income gets added to owners' equity on the balance sheet, whereas a loss would be subtracted. The two statements are linked, and changes in one can often affect the other.

Suppose that the condo is rented on November 1, 2010, for $2,000 per month, but various expenses have to be paid (such as property taxes, insurance, condo fees, interest on the mortgage, etc.), totalling $1,450 for November. An income statement could be prepared as at November 30, 2010, and would show (ignoring income taxes and other accounting refinements such as amortization/depreciation):

Condo Name or Other
Income Statement
For the Month Ended November 30, 2010

| | |
|---|---:|
| Rent revenue | $ 2,000 |
| | |
| Expenses: | |
|   Operating | 1,450 |
|   Income (before tax) | $ 550 |

Usually, a detailed listing would be provided to show each of the individual major revenue and expense items. For example, interest on the mortgage would likely be large and a separate expense line, "interest on mortgage," probably would be shown on the income statement.

The November transactions (revenue and expenses) result in a change in the balance sheet as of November 30, 2010. For simplicity, we will assume that the $2,000 was received in cash and the $1,450 was paid in cash. If so, cash of $550 ($2,000 - $1,450) would remain and be added to the condo's assets. The November 30, 2010, balance sheet would thus show:

Condo Name or Other
Balance Sheet
November 30, 2010

| ASSETS | | LIABILITIES AND EQUITY | |
|---|---:|---|---:|
| Cash | $ 550 | Liability: | |
| | |   Mortgage payable | $ 300,000 |
| Condo | 400,000 | | |
| | | Owner's equity: | |
| | |   Capital | 100,000 |
| | |   Retained earnings | 550 |
| | | | 100,550 |
| | $ 400,550 | | $400,550 |

The cash of $550 belongs to the owner of the condo. It is not a liability to any person or company. Therefore, it appears on the balanced balance sheet as an asset (cash of $550) and an increase in owner's equity of $550. The original capital or equity of $100,000 is separated from the $550, usually because of corporate law requirements. An equity-type name, such as retained income or retained earnings, is often used for the separate earned profit.

One of the financial tricks mentioned in this book several times is that of increasing income/profit by reducing expenses (on the income statement) and creating fake assets (on the balance sheet). The financial statements still balance when a would-be expense item is turned into an asset on the balance sheet. The balance sheet would show additional so-called assets that are offset by increased retained earnings from the inflated income. The income was inflated as a result of the expense not being recognized as such, but rather being recorded as a fake asset instead. An example of an expense-turned-asset could be something like a typical repair expense. Instead of treating it as an everyday cost of maintaining the condo, it might be argued, within the accounting rules, that the repair actually increased the value of the condo, instead of simply maintaining it.

CASH-FLOW STATEMENT

Although the term "cash-flow statement" is commonly used in published annual reports, the financial statement itself often contains more than just cash transactions. Thus, investors have to be careful in their interpretations. For example, a strict cash-flow statement for November's condo transactions should show:

Name
Cash-Flow Statement
For the Month Ended November 30, 2010

| | |
|---|---:|
| Cash receipts: | |
|     Condo rent | $2,000 |
| | |
| Cash disbursements: | |
|     Condo operating expenses | 1,450 |
|     Increase in cash | $ 550 |

But, what is more commonly seen in North America would be a cash-flow statement along the following lines (except for several possible IFRS presentations):

Name<br>
Cash-Flow Statement<br>
For the Month Ended November 30, 2010

| | |
|---|---:|
| Operating transactions: | |
|     Income for month | $ 550 |
|     Non-cash items | 0 |
|     Total | 550 |
| Financing transactions | 0 |
| Investing transactions | 0 |
| Increase in cash | $ 550 |

The separation of operating transactions from financing and investing is valuable to investors, except when financial games occur (see Chapter 17 for more information). Financing transactions largely involve long-term debt borrowing and equity financing. Sometimes borrowing is legitimate, whereas other financings can be Ponzi schemes. Investing transactions are those that involve buying or selling long-lived assets such as land, buildings, plants, and equipment. But, intangible asset and goodwill acquisitions can also be called "investing activities."

Especially important to investors is the determination of how much cash is being generated by the regular operating aspects of the business (i.e., its sales and service activities less the costs of providing the sales or services). If cash flow from operating the business is negative, cash somehow has to be obtained through either financing or by negative investing (i.e., selling long-lived assets). Such processes cannot continue indefinitely. Thus, the operating activities portion of a cash-flow statement has to be studied very carefully to determine whether a business is viable over the longer term.

While it is important to recognize that the income statement figures may be tampered with, it is even more important to know that the cash operating activities portion of a cash-flow statement can also be cooked. When the operating activities section of the cash-flow statement starts with an income or profit figure (as it does the vast majority of the time), investors must be very careful. Cash losses can be covered up by financial reporting games, especially through manipulations that occur in producing the starting point "income" number.

OTHER FINANCIAL STATEMENTS

Depending upon the industry and the types of activities in which the company engages, other types of financial statements may also be prepared. Often, such financial statements merely show the continuity of funds from the opening balance of the period to the closing balance at the end of a year, half-year, or quarter.

Another financial statement usually provided is for reporting Retained Earnings or Retained Income. A corporation may show additions, like income and subtractions, such as dividends, to explain what happened to retained earnings during a period. Retained earnings should reflect the accumulation of net income and/or losses from all previous years (plus the current year), minus any dividends that have been paid to shareholders. Sometimes extraordinary adjustments to retained earnings may also be made, so these need to be watched for, as well. For example, corrections of previous years' figures (possibly from cooking the books) could be buried in adjustments to retained earnings.

Another financial statement that has only gained prominence in Canada within the past five years is the statement of Accumulated Other Comprehensive Income (AOCI). As its name implies, this is an accumulation of current and previous years' Other Comprehensive Income (OCI), which contains items that have not been attributed yet to net income. Examples of such items include unrealized gains or losses on available for-sale securities, or foreign currency hedges.

NOTES TO THE FINANCIAL STATEMENTS

Frequently, the best clues that financial deceptions have occurred arise from the wording of notes to the financial statements. For example, instead of using a conventional word or phrase, odd terminology may appear, or omissions might exist. Finance companies, for instance, may state that loan losses are recorded on a "multi-year rolling average basis." Alarm bells should ring for investors if they read something along these lines, especially when economic conditions are other than stable.

A so-called rolling average period could include months or years of good times, before the economy has turned negative. If so, the extent of bad loans will be understated, because the good times outweigh the bad times in a typical rolling average mathematical computation involving an economic decline or recession. The more conventional phrase for recording loan losses would be along the lines of "loan losses are recorded when a borrower has not paid interest and principal in cash for the past 90 days."

Investors who ignore the rolling average terminology that includes past good times could very well be investing in a declining finance company, which could go into bankruptcy should many more loans turn out to be bad. Cash businesses such as finance companies have to generate cash, or else. The 90-day rule focuses on recent events in deciding what constitutes a potential bad loan.

Various chapters of this book provide additional examples of clues arising from financial statement notes. Related party, or non-arm's-length, transactions (Chapter 3) are deliberately underreported by many companies. All kinds of financial games occur under the related-party umbrella, especially hidden management compensation.

Another goldmine of clues can be a note with a title such as "Contingencies, Commitments, and Uncertainties." Large liabilities can arise from lawsuits that are in progress, and which may not be resolved for several more years. Usually, not much is described in a note regarding pending, or potential, lawsuits, and a more extensive Internet search is necessary to get more details, including which parties are claiming how much, and for what alleged deeds.

Similarly, for financial instruments, derivative transactions, and similar hedging or other activities, the counterparties (meaning who the company is transacting with) may or may not be described in a note. Investors should be concerned about which of the transacting companies is absorbing the most risk, and whether the other company is financially strong. It is possible, for credit card companies especially, to be selling their best card receivables and to be retaining the dubious receivables with the accompanying probable losses.

The accounting and reporting choices that a company has made are often described in notes to the financial statements. Skimpy explanations of which accounting treatment is being used are often useful warning signs. When a reader gets confused by the wording, it is at least important to consider whether the words have been deliberately chosen to obfuscate.

WARNINGS

Considerable differences in financial results can arise not only because reporting currencies can differ, but because of significant differences between US GAAP, Canadian GAAP, and IFRS. Comparing two companies that are each following IFRS can be a nightmare because of management's freedom of choice to report what they feel is most appropriate for their company. Matters get that much worse when comparing US GAAP results to fuzzy IFRS reporting, because the latter tends to embed the overly positive biases of company management. Companies sometimes prepare separate financial statements: one US GAAP, and the other IFRS. These are valuable educational tools for investors, and differences should be noted and thoughtfully considered.

An alternative for certain other companies is a financial statement note that reconciles the numbers, of say, US GAAP and IFRS for the same financial period. Again, the comparisons can be instructive as to why differences have arisen.

But what cannot be done readily, or perhaps at all, is a comparison of two or three companies using different bases of reporting (i.e., US GAAP, Canadian GAAP, and IFRS). As is mentioned at various times in this book, IFRS is often quite troublesome for investors, because management tampering can easily get out of control. Sometimes, the cash-flow statements might prove useful for comparisons, but unexplained differences can also occur.

The differences between US GAAP and IFRS are much more complicated than comparing miles to kilometres. The philosophies of what constitutes a periodic profit, or income, are fundamentally different. It is vital to remember that when preparing IFRS financial statements, company management has extensive freedom to choose the reported amounts and the assumptions to support them.

APPENDIX C

# Significant Numbers: The Example of National Business Systems

**NATIONAL BUSINESS** Systems (NBS) originally reported to shareholders an income for 1987 of $13,696,000. According to the revised audited financial statements released later, NBS had lost $26,277,000 in fiscal 1987. As a result, the company had no retained earnings, but rather a deficit of $25,288,000.

Of the $39,973,000 difference between the income originally reported by NBS and the $25,288,000 loss, the auditors later attributed more than 80% to "fictitious sales" and "billings to customers for product not shipped until after year-end."

NBS had shipped more than $2 million in inventory to cover these fictitious sales. These shipments were then returned and placed back in inventory after the company's year-end, as if nothing had ever happened. NBS also overstated the value of assets by more than $5 million and executed other accounting manoeuvres that boosted the company's income by another $15 million.

Here are the details, as stated by the auditors, or as reported by the company:

APPENDIX C · 217

The previously issued consolidated financial statements as at September 30, 1987 and 1986 and our (audit) reports thereon dated December 28, 1987, and December 23, 1986, respectively, have been withdrawn. These revised consolidated financial statements reflect adjustments described in Note 1.

Note 1 to the revised 1987 NBS financial statements stated, in part:

Income (Loss) Before Extraordinary Items
The following reconciles the income before extraordinary items as reported in the Original 1987 Statements with the loss before extraordinary items reported in the Revised 1987 Statements.

|  | (In thousands of Canadian dollars) |
|---|---|
| Income reported in Original 1987 Statements | $ 13,696 |
| Gross profit on fictitious sales | (17,893) |
| Additional inventory obsolescence | (7,164) |
| Adjustment to reflect actual terms of sales contract | (1,648) |
| Write-down of fixed assets | (5,453) |
| Deposits which have no future value | (1,003) |
| Amounts expensed which were previously capitalized | (1,484) |
| Increase in bad debts and other items | (3,032) |
| Accrual of additional expenses | (1,862) |
| Costs related to lease guarantee | (865) |
| Write-off of deferred development costs | (3,384) |
| Legal settlement recorded as prior period adjustment | 2,564 |
| Gain on sale of shares previously credited to accounts receivable | 1,516 |
| Reduction in income taxes | 7,157 |
| Reorganization costs previously included as extraordinary | (16,378) |
| Equity gain on shares of subsidiary previously included as extraordinary | 11,792 |
| Other, net | (2,836) |
| Loss reported in Revised 1987 Statements | $ (26,277) |

Summarized below are accounts to which significant adjustments are reflected in the Revised 1987 Statements:

a) Accounts Receivable and Sales
Included in the adjustments to accounts receivable and sales are reversals of fictitious sales of $32,176,000 ($24,164,000 of which relate to sales recorded in 1987) and of $963,000. Other adjustments have reduced accounts receivable by $3,483,000.

b) Inventory
Inventory has been reduced to reflect increased provisions for obsolescence of $7,164,000. Inventory has been increased by $2,219,000 for the return after year-end of products, which were originally shipped to cover fictitious sales and the under-pricing of inventory of $557,000 attributable to fictitious credit notes. Other adjustments have reduced inventory by $841,000.

c) Fixed Assets
Certain fixed assets were written down by $5,453,000 to net realizable value. Also, $1,407,000, which was previously capitalized, has been expensed.

d) Other Assets
The various adjustments reflected in the Revised 1987 Statements led to a write-off of goodwill of $6,097,000 and a write-off of warrants to purchase shares of a partly owned subsidiary of $1,432,000.

Deferred development costs have been reduced by $3,591,000 for items having no further benefit and $1,650,000, which was previously capitalized. Other adjustments have reduced other assets by $1,836,000.

The major point that ought to be derived from the NBS example is that revenue scams typically involve very significant numbers.

Unfortunately, our lawmakers delegate virtually everything involving securities regulation to self-regulatory organizations that are essentially permitted to choose their own weak rules and regulations.

Certain facts cannot be ignored. Billions of dollars of investors' savings have been donated to financial tricksters in Canada. The serious deficiencies are not being addressed by our legislators, much to the detriment of foreign investment, jobs, and the Canadian standard of living.

## APPENDIX D

# Current vs. Non-Current Assets and the Cash-Flow Statement

**ON THE** balance sheet, a company often separates assets and liabilities into current and non-current categories. Current assets and liabilities involve cash flow that will occur within the next year, based on previous experience. Non-current assets and liabilities will likely occur beyond one year. In other words, a company's balance sheet, as well as its cash-flow statement, appears in three sections, as well: current assets and current liabilities; non-current assets; and non-current liabilities and equity.

In general, a company's operating activities affect the current asset and current liability sections of its balance sheet and are offset by the cash revenue and expense portions of the income statement. For example, a majority of sales revenue (on an income statement) should affect cash flows, or accounts receivable, or unearned revenue (all of which are either a current asset or a current liability).

Investing transactions should involve the non-current assets (such as land, buildings, equipment, and intangible assets) and reduced cash. Divesting reduces the non-current assets and increases cash or current receivables (i.e., the asset side of the balance sheet).

Financing transactions should increase non-current or long-term liabilities, or increase common or preferred owners' equity. Repayments of long-term debt use up cash but reduce long-term liabilities (i.e., on the liability and owners' equity side of the balance sheet).

## APPENDIX E

# Yield Computations for Income Trusts

**THE COMPUTATION** of yields, or returns on investment, have been seriously manipulated in Canada over the past ten years. For decades, the cash yield on an investment was computed as:

$$\frac{\text{Dividend received per year}}{\text{Average for the year stock market value}}$$

$$\text{e.g.} \quad \frac{\$500}{10{,}000} = 5\%$$

That is, your $10,000 investment in a company paid you back $500 cash in the year, which was 5% of your invested capital of $10,000. Such a calculation could thus be compared to alternate investments, such as a one-year GIC yielding 3% or, perhaps, a bond issued by a blue-chip company.

The greatest Canadian abuses of the definition of yield came from the promoters of many questionable business income trusts (that is, not really the resource, real estate, or infrastructure trusts; however, there were some exceptions). Yield computations by the promoters were based on so-called distributable cash and similar calculations. In essence, the cash payments were not based on the traditional idea of net income, like dividends are. Instead, cash might have been, and was in some cases, pulled from all available sources, including borrowed and raised funds, and to a certain degree, represented a kind of return of capital from the company.

For example:

| | |
|---|---:|
| Income trust's profit | $ 500 |
| Amortization/depreciation included in profit | 180 |
| Income tax effects of trust structure | 140 |
| Miscellaneous adjustments | (20) |
| | $ 800 |

Faked Yield: $\dfrac{\$800}{10{,}000} = 8\%$

The result was that when investors made a comparison of the 8% to a GIC yielding 3%, or a stock yielding 5%, they jumped and bought the phony income trust yield. Yield, and yield alone, seemed to be the reason for buying in many cases.

The moral of the story, therefore, is to do your own homework and calculations. Believing a broker who behaves like a used car salesman does not make sense. Far more analysis must occur, especially looking into matters such as how many more months the 8% cash payments can be sustained. When cash is drained from a company, future income is likely to suffer. Investors need to find out where the extra cash is coming from, and at what future price, consequence, or added risk.

## APPENDIX F

# Discounted Cash Flow under IFRS

**INTERNATIONAL FINANCIAL** Reporting Standards are not helpful in calculating value across a variety of situations and transactions. However, a favoured technique (based on one-size-fits-all thinking) is to employ discounted future cash flows (DCF).

DCF, because it focuses on the future, involves making estimates of many crucial variables. One critical set of assumptions involves the amounts that are expected to be generated from a project each quarter, or year, for the rest of its economic life. A second vital factor is the interest rate, or discount rate, that should be used to discount the future expected cash receipts to today's value. For a large rental office building, a significant number of costs have to be considered in valuation, and the effects can be huge given the building's potential future life of forty to fifty years.

For example, $1,000 invested at 10% should be worth $1,100 in one year (i.e., 1,000 x 10% = $100 of interest for one year, plus the original $1,000, totals to $1,100). Stated differently, $1,100 to be received in one year is worth only $1,000 today, if the discount or interest rate is 10%. To get to the $1,100 one year hence, the $1,000 would have to be invested, at least, at 10% interest per annum. Interest rates below 10% would not achieve $1,100, one year hence. Clearly, both the 10% rate, and the future cash flow figure of $1,100, involves making significant assumptions.

If either the dollar amount or interest rate is off target, today's value would be affected, possibly by a significant amount. Suppose only $1,060 of cash is generated one year hence (instead of $1,100) and the interest/discount rate is really 15% (instead of 10%), because of economic fluctuations. If so, today's value would be only:

$$\$1,060 \times \frac{1,000}{1,150^*} = \underline{\$922}$$

*The 1,150 represents 15% higher than the 1,000 for a one-year period.

Obviously, the more that the actual figures vary from the original estimates, the more the difference might be. Should the present value estimate involve five to ten years of future cash-flow estimates and be subject to changing interest rates, the calculated figures could vary considerably. The difference could easily reach as high as 25%, depending on the situation. As a consequence, blind adherence to a one-size-fits-all mindset that ingrains DCF for valuing so many different kinds of assets on the balance sheet leaves far too much freedom in management's hands.

APPENDIX G

# Reverse Mortgage Companies

**REVERSE MORTGAGE** providers have a limited role in society, being for those who are short of cash but hold equity value in their homes. Reverse mortgages, however, are fundamentally expensive ways of borrowing. For those who can meet monthly mortgage payments, a direct mortgage would be far less costly than a reverse mortgage.

A typical reverse mortgage on a property that is otherwise clear of debt usually operates as follows. People over age 60 can borrow up to 40% of the resale value of their home or condo. No monthly interest payments have to be made. The 40% cash is used by the homeowner for other purposes, like paying for vacations, repairs, gifts, or other luxuries.

The monthly interest is added onto the 40% reverse mortgage until the 80% or so level of the home's value is reached. Interest on the reverse mortgage may accrue at 8%–9% per annum, and not at, say, 5% for a standard mortgage.

In evaluating a reverse mortgage company's equity shares for possible investment, the investor must consider factors such as:

1. *The extent of possible declines (or increases) in property values due to recessions or real estate bubbles.* Does adequate equity coverage exist in each home?

2. *Operating costs per year for the reverse mortgage company.* Cash receipts arise only when the home is sold, which could be fifteen to thirty years hence. Thus, adequate cash may have to be borrowed just to pay operating expenses, particularly when volumes decrease.
3. *Interest rate spreads between what the reverse mortgage company borrows at and the 8%–9% (or whatever) rate it charges its customers.* The spread must be adequate and sufficient to provide a profit after expenses.
4. *General availability of cash to the reverse mortgage provider, either by selling more shares or debt.* Stagnation of the provider can occur when limited cash is available for potential new customers.
5. *The changing nature of prospective customers' education.* Volumes of business decline when customers recognize that reverse mortgages are costly ways of borrowing money.
6. *Differences in life expectancy in different regions of the country, and changes in economic status of geographical locations and attitudes toward borrowing.* These issues cannot be handled lightly, since reverse mortgages are often viewed as a fad, and interest waxes and wanes over time.

In effect, interest rate spreads of 3% or so, high mortgage turnover or property sales, and easy access to borrowed funds at low interest rates are crucial to the success of mortgage companies. However, investors have to watch out for interest revenue being recorded when chances of cash collection are low. Expected losses on the sale of specific homes (or other mortgaged assets) have to be recorded promptly. Otherwise, reported income becomes overstated.

APPENDIX H

# IFRS: Trend Lines and Cash Flows

**REGULAR CHANGES** in carrying values for assets and liabilities under IFRS that were previously not reported under US or Canadian GAAP could be huge. Thus, it is highly unlikely that IFRS should be reporting steady trends in income or profit.

IFRS has added changes in carrying values to the conventional combination of cash/accrual/non-cash amortization categories in a typical income statement (i.e., accrual is for such items as receivables and payables). Investors who want to determine cash effects using the income statement will have to perform the following arithmetic under IFRS:

| | | |
|---|---|---|
| Income | $ | 10,000 |
| Adjustments: | | |
| Add (subtract): | | |
| A. accruals/non-cash | | (2,000) |
| B. amortization | | 1,500 |
| C. valuation adjustments during the year | | (15,000) |
| Operating cash deficiency | $ | (5,500) |

IFRS also permits the reversal of previous write-downs of receivables, inventory, equipment, and so forth. Thus, the conversion of an IFRS-based income figure back into operating cash flow can become very complex. These can seriously affect cash from operations and the valuation of the company involved.

APPENDIX I

# The Risk of Foreign-Currency-Denominated Preferred Shares

**PREFERRED SHARES** in Canadian banks seem like a relatively safe source of income. However, a major exception exists when the preferreds are denominated in US dollars. The risks attached to such a twist on a standard investment are rarely fully explained to, or understood by, most income-oriented investors.

Take the example of a Canadian income-focused investor who purchases US$10,000 in preferred shares from a Canadian bank when the Canadian/US dollar exchange rate is $1.40/$1.00. The purchase would cost the investor $14,000 Canadian. Yields and cash flows are obviously affected by currency and exchange-rate fluctuations, and thus, a senior who has to spend Canadian dollars living in Canada is naturally affected by the exchange-rate value of any fixed monthly dividends that are denominated in US dollars.

The banks and their underwriters do not choose by accident the timing of preferred share issuances denominated in US dollars. If they expect the Canadian dollar to strengthen, they know the fixed payouts in US dollars will cost them less as time goes on. Conversely, investors relying on this income will be receiving less when it is converted into Canadian dollars for their everyday use.

However, the real hurt can come down the road. To avoid being set up for a significant future capital loss, investors must ask several questions, including: When can the bank redeem the preferred shares? Is it in five years, or ten years, or longer? Will the bank pay back my $14,000 Canadian, or the $10,000 US?

Not surprisingly, preferred share issues denominated in US dollars might have redemption dates as short as five years. The fact that the issue is a preferred share that can be redeemed by the bank when it suits their convenience cannot be ignored. In fact, it might be a big red flag.

After five years, the bank is free to pounce on the unsuspecting investors and redeem the preferred shares. And if the exchange rate happens to have dropped to C$1.10/US$1.00, then the bank definitely has a major incentive to pounce. The income-focused investor gets paid back the equivalent of $11,000 Canadian of their original $14,000 Canadian investment, and the $3,000 difference becomes a significant loss that more than wipes out even the combined dividends that were declining in value over the past five years. Summed up, the income-focused investors were ill-treated because the risks of the financing instrument were not adequately explained to them at the outset.

APPENDIX J

# A Letter to the Ontario Securities Commission

Open Letter to John P. Stevenson,
   Secretary to the Ontario Securities Commission
From Pamela J. Reeve, Ph.D., Member,
   OSC Investor Advisory Committee

23 April 2010

Dear Mr. Stevenson,

1. I am writing with questions and concerns about the OSC's Investor Advisory Panel (IAP). By way of background, I was previously a member of the OSC's Investor Advisory Committee (2005–2007). In 2006, I participated in a research study conducted by Professor Julia Black of the London School of Economics, "Involving Consumers in Securities Regulation" (June 30, 2006). This study was commissioned by the Task Force to Modernize Securities Legislation in Canada and informs my thinking on this topic. In 2008, I made a submission to the Expert Panel on Securities Regulation in Canada in which I recommended the establishment of an investor advisory

panel modelled on the UK's Financial Services Consumer Panel (July 15, 2008). A related submission to the Expert Panel was made by Professor Laureen Snider of Queen's University on the importance of third parties representing the public interest in regulatory environments (July 13, 2008). I believe that an independent investor advisory panel, which is able to represent the public interest in the development of regulatory policy, is an important form of protection for the large percentage of Canadians who currently have exposure to capital markets through the investment of their savings and RRSPs.

2. In February 2009, I testified to the Standing Committee on Government Agencies in connection with their review of the OSC, raising concerns about the Commission's dissolution of the Investor Advisory Committee in December 2007. Again, in this context, I recommended the establishment of an independent investor advisory panel to represent the public interest in the context of regulatory policy development. I was pleased that both the Expert Panel and the Standing Committee on Government Agencies supported this recommendation in their final reports, and that the Ontario Securities Commission has decided to implement the recommended panel. Nevertheless, I have certain concerns about the timing, process, and parameters of the OSC's current initiative involving the proposed IAP.

3. Although there are certain differences between the Canadian and UK regulatory environment, such as the use of self-regulatory organizations (SROs) in Canada, there are important aspects of the UK panel, such as its independence, which merit emulation in the Canadian context. As it stands, the OSC's Investor Advisory Panel is deficient in a number of respects, which I shall discuss in further detail below. In particular, there is a significant discrepancy between the claimed independence of the IAP, as per the comment in the Response to Enquiries, that the OSC Panel is "intended to operate independently at arm's-length from the Commission," and the actual structure and function of the Panel, which does not support such an operation. This will be analyzed in detail below.

4. A further concern, and the one I shall begin with below, is that there has been no solicitation of input on the Panel's design (structure,

mandate, funding, membership criteria, and Terms of Reference). This is inconsistent with the OSC's repeated acknowledgement of the importance of effective engagement with retail investors in relevant Commission initiatives. Although I am writing as an individual, I have spoken with several advocates in this area who are equally concerned about deficiencies in the proposed Panel and the fact that their views were not invited as part of the process of drafting the Panel's mandate and Terms of Reference.

LACK OF CONSULTATION RE: IAP DESIGN AND TERMS OF REFERENCE

5. The lack of stakeholder consultation about the design of this panel is a significant concern. It appears that the panel's Terms of Reference have already been "adopted" by the Commission as of April 6, 2010, without any preceding discussion or consultation with stakeholders. This is contrary to the assurance given by OSC Vice Chair Lawrence Ritchie to the Standing Committee on Government Agencies at the hearing on February 23, 2009, in which he stated that such discussions were already underway. In response to a question from the Standing Committee about the dissolution of the Commission's previous Investor Advisory Committee (IAC), Mr. Ritchie confirmed:

> "We have to find a better way of getting some input. So we're open for suggestions. We're talking directly to retail investors about how best to engage them and to find a more permanent mechanism to receive input from that perspective, from the retail investor perspective." (February 23, 2009)

I am a member of the Small Investor Protection Association, and have contact with many of the individuals doing advocacy work in this area. To the best of my knowledge, no discussions were underway at the time as per Mr. Ritchie's comment, nor was there any solicitation of input prior to the OSC's announcement of the IAP in February 2010.

6. In its most recent Statement of Priorities, the Commission acknowledged that stakeholders had emphasized in their submissions the importance of "open and inclusive consultation." It expressed the recognition that

> "Effectively listening to and communicating with interested stakeholders is essential to meeting the challenges we face in fulfilling our mandate and addressing expectations about what we can accomplish." (p. 2536, March 26, 2010)

Indeed, the need for effective engagement with stakeholders and retail investors, in particular, has long been recognized by the Commission, as indicated in the OSC documents quoted in my submission on the Statement of Priorities (February 15, 2010). Moreover, this recognition is clearly expressed by Mr. Ritchie in the above comment to the Standing Committee.

7. Yet, I have to question the sincerity of this commitment to stakeholder engagement, given that no input was invited from "interested stakeholders" prior to the Commission's announcement of the Investor Advisory Panel and its already "adopted" Terms of Reference. This approach is inconsistent with the Commission's express acknowledgement of needing to consult with interested parties, and is contrary to Mr. Ritchie's assurance to the Standing Committee that the Commission was "open for suggestions" about how best to engage retail investors, and that it was already engaged in such discussions in February 2009.

8. OSC Investor Secretariat. A further aspect of the present concern relates to the establishment, by the OSC, of an Investor Secretariat in order to facilitate this engagement. In his presentation to the Standing Committee at the hearing on April 7, 2009, Mr. Wilson gave assurance "we're well on the way to developing better channels of communications with investors" (p. 6, April 7, 2009). My understanding is that the Investor Secretariat was created by the Commission some time in the spring of 2009 to facilitate this development in communications.

9. This body is referenced in the OSC's written Response to the Stakeholder Presentations made to the Standing Committee on February 23, 2009. Under point 3: "Investor Input in Securities Regulation," Mr. Wilson responds:

> "We recognize the importance of effectively engaging investors in obtaining input on securities-related matters, particularly initiatives

that directly affect investors. We have been seeking innovative ways to obtain input from investors. We know that more needs to be done in this area. We are actively engaged in a rigorous exercise to identify the most effective ways to obtain investor input and to address investor interests. For example, we are establishing an Investor Secretariat as a coordinating body within the Commission to better identify and address issues of concern to investors...As part of this new Secretariat, we are also assessing the best ways to encourage and facilitate investor input recognizing the challenges investors face in commenting on regulatory proposals." (p. 9, April 7, 2009)

10. The Investor Secretariat is referred to again in the 2009 OSC Annual Report:

"In order to serve the interests of all investors, especially retail investors, the OSC understands how important it is to solicit and obtain their input and understand their concerns about regulatory matters. The OSC is developing better channels of communications with investors by building on the experience of earlier initiatives related to investor outreach and consultations.... One such initiative that has been announced is the establishment of the OSC Investor Secretariat. It is anticipated that the Investor Secretariat will function as a hub within the OSC to better coordinate its policy efforts and assist with identifying and addressing issues of interest and concern to investors, especially retail investors." (June 30, 2009)

11. In line with this, the mandate of the Secretariat, as stated at the OSC website, was "to assist with identifying and addressing issues of interest and concern to investors" and "to help foster more effective communication of investor concerns and issues to OSC staff so they can be reflected in our priorities and policies." To this end, the Secretariat was to focus on "soliciting comments from investors on Commission initiatives" (quoted from the Secretariat's webpage as of February 14, 2010, now removed). Yet, it appears that the Secretariat was recently abandoned, apparently without having solicited

any input on the new Investor Advisory Panel. This would have been an obvious project for such a body, given its stated mandate and the oft-repeated recognition by the Commission on the need to consult stakeholders on OSC initiatives.

12. In February 2010, almost a year to the day following the February 23, 2009, hearing, the Commission suddenly announced the creation of a seven-member Advisory Panel (February 26, 2010). The announcement states that part-time Commissioner Mary Condon worked on the development of the Panel. Nevertheless, there was no preceding discussion, nor any invitation from Ms. Condon, the Investor Secretariat, or the Commission to provide input on the Panel's design, structure, function, membership criteria, or Terms of Reference.

13. It is well known to the Commission that consumer advocates have been recommending the establishment of such a panel for some time. As mentioned above, in addition to testifying on this subject at the Standing Committee hearing in February 2009, I made a submission to the Expert Panel on Securities Regulation in July 2008 in which I recommended the establishment of a retail investor panel along the lines of the UK's Financial Services Consumer Panel. In this context, I attended an Expert Panel roundtable chaired by Ms. Condon in October 2008.

14. Following the announcement of the IAP in February 2010, the Commission published a Request for Applications in March, which included a statement about the Panel's mandate, operational structure, funding, and membership criteria (March 19, 2010). Two weeks later, a ten-page Terms of Reference was published, stating that it had already been adopted by the Commission as of April 6, 2010 (April 6, 2010).

15. At no point has the OSC invited input in the course of designing this new body, contrary to its repeated assurances, especially regarding retail investors, about "how important it is to solicit and obtain their input and understand their concerns."

16. The Commission had ample opportunity to obtain input in the year following the stakeholder presentations in February 2009, where significant concerns were raised about how it was engaging with

retail investors. Although the OSC created a special body, the Investor Secretariat, to solicit comments on Commission initiatives, this has now vanished, apparently, without fulfilling its function regarding the present issue. Instead of consulting, the Commission seems to have reverted to a command-and-control approach, rolling out the new Panel with everything already decided.

17. Why hasn't the Commission undertaken to solicit timely input on this new advisory panel when it was made aware of the interest and concern about this issue in the context of the Standing Committee's stakeholder presentations in February 2009?

18. The recommendation of the Standing Committee on Government Agencies was that the UK Consumer Panel was to serve as a basis for the design of an investor advisory panel. As I will show below, the OSC Panel falls short in multiple respects when compared with this model.

19. A fundamental notion governing any consideration of such a panel is the concept of "interest representation." The following self-definition of the UK Consumer Panel illustrates the incorporation of this notion into its mandate:

> "We are an independent statutory body, set up to represent the interests of consumers in the development of policy for the regulation of financial services."

20. The focus of interest representation with the UK panel is the individual consumer of financial services. The equivalent category in the present context would be the retail investor; an especially vulnerable group in need of properly resourced advocacy in regulatory policy development.

21. OSC Vice Chair Lawrence Ritchie specifically referenced the vulnerability of retail investors in his comments at the third Standing Committee hearing in April 2009, where he testified that:

> "The retail investor is the most vulnerable of market participants, and therefore protecting retail investors is and needs to always be in the front and centre of everything that the OSC does." (April 7, 2009)

22. Mr. Ritchie outlined a number of initiatives, which he claimed were then underway to address the concerns raised in the stakeholder submissions the previous February:

> "We're in the midst of working towards realizing three distinct but interrelated initiatives that we believe directly respond to much of what we have heard."

23. The first initiative involved the setting up of the above-mentioned Investor Secretariat, which Mr. Ritchie described as "a hub, interacting with the operating branches of the OSC to help them better identify issues of interest to retail investors and to identify and assess the impact of OSC projects on retail investors." Regarding the operational output of this body, Mr. Ritchie stated, "The secretariat intends to publish those assessments and encourage responses from the investing public."

24. Nevertheless, it seems this body produced no output, nor did it solicit any input from retail investors during the year of its existence. The only records of its existence are references in the OSC's testimony to the Standing Committee, the Commission's 2009 Annual Report quoted above, and the Secretariat's webpage. The latter was still posted until, at least, mid-February 2010, but subsequently was removed. (A pdf of the webpage may be downloaded at: http://www.pjreeve.com/pjr/blog/Entries/ 2010/4/23_osc_investor_advisory_panel.html).

25. As mentioned above, this Secretariat was identified by Mr. Ritchie as the "first prong" of three interrelated initiatives responding to the stakeholder representations at the February 2009 Standing Committee hearing. The third prong involved an initiative to establish a more effective means through which to receive input from retail investors. We've heard comments from stakeholders on this issue and, in principle, the OSC supports the concept of a funded, independent voice for retail investors.

26. Mr. Ritchie claimed that efforts were already underway to find an appropriate structure for this body. As quoted above, he testified to the Standing Committee in February 2009 that:

> "We're talking directly to retail investors about how best to engage them and to find a more permanent mechanism to receive input from that perspective, from the retail investor perspective."

Nevertheless, it seems this outreach was not underway at the time nor did it occur prior to the OSC's announcement of the Investor Advisory Panel in February 2010.

27. At the third Standing Committee hearing in April 2009, Mr. Ritchie again reiterated that consultations were underway regarding the establishment of the above-mentioned permanent mechanism:

> "We're currently in the process of reaching out to third party organizations and universities to assist us with this initiative.... [W]e are committed to hearing directly from retail investors to find more and better ways to serve and protect investors."

Yet, it appears this outreach never occurred and that the commitment to engage with retail investors and hear from them "directly" regarding this initiative was never kept.

28. The Commission would have been aware by February 2009 that retail investor advocates were contacting provincial government MPPs with their concerns about the dissolution of the Investor Advisory Committee in December 2007. In response, the Commission spoke about a new "Investor Secretariat," as a "hub" focused on retail investor issues. Although it appears this body was created to address the concerns raised by consumer advocates and MPPs at the February hearing, it produced no output, solicited no input, and was quietly dropped earlier this year.

29. As a consequence, the current IAP initiative does not reflect due process. In fact, the timing has raised questions as to whether the Commission may have received a "heads up" from the provincial government of several advocates' submissions on the OSC's Statement of Priorities, following the dissemination to government officials in February, and responded by rushing out the current IAP initiative.

### INVESTOR ADVISORY PANELS DESIGN FLAWS
In my estimation, there are multiple design flaws in the proposed IAP.

#### A SMALL PANEL WITH A DILUTED FOCUS

30. The expectation was that the Panel would be dedicated to retail investor issues. In his Standing Committee testimony, Mr. Ritchie expressed the recognition that this constituency is "the most vulnerable of market participants." Yet, the Commission is also inviting applications from "Institutional investors from the pension sector or other buy side." This inclusion is not justified and is problematic for several reasons.

31. The OSC decided without consultation, or justification, to establish a Panel with only seven members, including the Chair. This contrasts with the original Investor Advisory Committee, which had ten members, excluding the Chair, and the OSC's current consultative committees, which have twelve to twenty members. The UK's Financial Services Consumer Panel has twelve members, including the Chair.

32. The relatively small number of IAP members, together with the relatively broad Panel focus on retail and institutional investor issues, inevitably will dilute and weaken the focus on issues affecting "the most vulnerable of market participants." These issues need to be the exclusive focus of a dedicated Panel. I can attest to this based on my previous experience with the IAC.

33. Institutional and retail investors have significantly different priorities reflecting differences in their access to capital markets. Retail investors access investments through financial intermediaries (i.e., registered representatives with investment dealers). This circumstance gives rise to very different issues and concerns (e.g., relating to the client/advisor relationship, advisor fiduciary duties, high/opaque fees, mutual fund point of sale disclosure, dealer complaint process, restitution options, including the Ombudsman for Banking Services and Investments (OBSI), and different concerns relating to product suitability, e.g., involving investment vehicles such as Principal Protected Notes (PPNs) and leveraged ETFs).

34. In contrast, pension funds are currently focused on issues such as corporate governance, executive compensation, International

Financial Reporting Standards (IFRS), taxation, shareholder democracy, and voting rights. OSC Vice-Chair John Turner, at the third Standing Committee hearing in April 2009, addressed some of these issues. He specifically mentioned the submission of the Canadian Coalition for Good Governance, a well-funded organization that represents institutional investors. This is further evidence of the distinction between institutional investor issues and those affecting retail investors, which were considered separately by Mr. Ritchie.

35. Also, as I pointed out in my submission on the OSC's Statement of Priorities (p. 13, February 15, 2010), institutional investors already have an organization to represent their interests (i.e., the Canadian Coalition of Good Governance (CCGG). The CCGG is a well-funded, well-staffed organization with over forty dues-paying members, supporting an executive team, ten-member Board of Directors, nine-member Accounting and Auditing Policy Committee, and a seventeen-member Public Policy Committee. Moreover, institutional investors already have two representatives on the OSC's Continuous Disclosure Advisory Committee.

36. In contrast, individual retail investors—"the most vulnerable of market participants"—are left to fend for themselves with virtually no resources to represent their interests, either with the investment industry or the regulators. This is clearly illustrated by the preponderance of industry submissions responding to the OSC's request for comment on the mutual fund point of sale framework. The Commission is aware of this disparity and the lack of resources on the side of small investors. A few years ago, the Small Investor Protection Association submitted a funding proposal to the OSC, and even received assistance from Commission staff in developing the application, which then was turned down by the OSC Board.

37. One aspect of the vulnerability of retail investors is their strategic disadvantage, given their lack of adequate resources to undertake skilled and effective interest representation in the context of regulatory policy development. The inclusion of institutional investor issues on the relatively small Panel further skews the current imbalance of resources in favour of the institutional component.

### LACK OF ENGAGEMENT WITH SROS

38. A further problem with the design of the OSC Panel is the omission of any reference to engagement with self-regulatory organizations (SROs), such as the Investment Industry Organization of Canada (IIROC) and the Mutual Fund Dealers Association (MFDA). Evidently the intention is that the Panel will respond only to OSC regulatory initiatives. Nevertheless, IIROC and the MFDA develop regulatory policies, which have a direct bearing on retail investor interests.

39. The UK Consumer Panel provides the following standard regarding its engagement with regulatory policy:

> "We work to advise and challenge the FSA from the earliest stages of its policy development to ensure they take into account the consumer interest."

40. This early-engagement principle is extremely important. In the Canadian context, where SROs are used to regulate financial intermediaries, it is essential that retail investor representatives should be able to interface with SROs in the policy development process. In view of this, the lack of any provision for SRO engagement (by which I do not mean Panel membership) in the IAP's mandate and Terms of Reference is a significant shortcoming.

41. Moreover, this is also clear from the testimony of OSC Chair David Wilson and Vice-Chair Lawrence Ritchie to the Standing Committee on Government Agencies in February 2009. In the context of responding to questions about the dissolution of the previous Investor Advisory Committee, OSC management undertook to justify the discontinuation of the IAC on the basis of the perspective that the IAC was only engaging with OSC staff. The argument was proposed that because retail investor issues involve the SROs, it is necessary to have them at the table as well. This is the outlook behind the following comment by Mr. Ritchie:

> "...the concerns of retail investors transcend just the Ontario Securities Commission. It involves, for sure, the Ontario Securities Commission, but it transcends it because of our system of SROs and also other complaint-handling processes." (February 23, 2009)

42. When a member of the Standing Committee continued to raise questions about the dissolution of the IAC, Mr. Wilson responded:

> "Let me try to explain a little bit about how the system works, Mr. Prue. The retail investors, when they are touched by the system, are not directly touched by the Ontario Securities Commission. When retail investors get involved in the system of investing securities, their point of contact is through a registered representative. To really have a forum where retail investors' issues get to the core of who regulates investment advisers, IIROC has to be in the tent.... If the advisory committee is going to have its ideas land on fertile soil, it should have the IIROC people listening to it."

43. In fact, SRO staff attended about half the IAC meetings, as had been planned from the beginning. Since Mr. Wilson acknowledged the importance of the SROs being "in the tent" relative to the consideration of retail investor issues, the absence of any provision for their inclusion in the Investor Panel process, and the prospect that the Panel will be dealing solely with OSC regulatory issues, is a significant weakness vis-à-vis retail investor concerns. Although I questioned this in my comments on the OSC's Statement of Priorities, there was no response, and no provision for this engagement was incorporated into the IAP design.

### LACK OF INDEPENDENCE OF THE IAP

44. Another significant concern is that the Panel proposed by the Commission is not independent. The word "independent" is not used in the original news release announcing the Panel (February 26, 2010), nor does it occur in the Request for Applications, which describes the Panel's mandate and operational structure (March 19, 2010), nor is independence referenced at any point in the Terms of Reference (April 6, 2010).

45. Nevertheless, the following comment occurs on page 2 of the Commission's "Responses to Enquiries on the OSC Investor Advisory Panel" (April 6, 2010):

"The Panel is intended to operate independently at arm's-length from the Commission."

The mere use of the words "independent" and "arm's-length" in the context of this Response, and the reference to the Commission's undocumented intentions about how the Panel should operate, is insufficient to establish that the Panel is an independent, arm's-length body or that it has the capability of operating "independently at arm's-length from the Commission." The further concern is that the use of these terms in the Response to Enquiries is intended to quell legitimate concerns while nothing was actually changed in the Panel's structure and function.

46. In fact, it appears that the Commission has not created an independent, arm's-length body, but merely a variant of its current consultative committees. This reflects a shortcoming, given the recommendation of the Standing Committee on Government Agencies, that an investor advisory panel should be "based on the financial services consumer panel in the United Kingdom." This body is indeed independent as shown by several key features, which are lacking with the IAP. Moreover, the Expert Panel on Securities Regulation in Canada also recommended the establishment of an independent investor panel in its report.

47. The Commission has published documents in which the structure and function of the Panel is specified in some detail. These specifications and the lack of other key features provide a basis for determining whether in fact the Panel is independent and has an "arm's-length" relationship with the Commission.

48. The term "arm's-length" is a relational term with implications about how one party (person or organization) functions relative to another party. A discussion paper by Canada Revenue Agency (CRA) on the "Meaning of Arm's-Length" for the purposes of the Income Tax Act provides a helpful elaboration about the meaning of this phrase, which is applied analogously in different relational contexts (June 8, 2004). I want to emphasize that I am using this source in the present context to extract an analogical meaning for the purpose of determining whether the Investor Advisory Panel, as designed by the OSC,

is set up to function in an independent, arm's-length manner relative to the Commission.

49. The CRA discussion focuses on the nature of the relationship between two parties. It specifies criteria that determine whether or not parties have an arm's-length relationship. A major consideration is the nature and extent of the control or influence of one party over another. For example, in considering the adoptive relationship, CRA clarifies that the mere appointment of someone as a guardian does not constitute de facto adoption. It is a question here of determining the nature of the relatedness vis-à-vis relevant influence and control:

> "The factors to look for in determining whether a certain relationship between an individual person and a child constitutes an adoption in fact are actual control and custody, an exercise of parental care and responsibility on a continuing basis, dependency, and proximity to each other."

50. In a section on Corporations and other "persons," the issue of control is equally prominent in determining the nature of the relationship. Control here means de jure control,

> "which generally means the right of control that rests in ownership of such number of shares as carries with it the right to a majority of the votes in the election of the board of directors of the corporation."

51. In another section, which clarifies the notion of "control," the CRA observes that:

> "The courts have also held, in certain cases, that excessive or constant advantage, authority, or influence can constitute de facto control (i.e., effective without legal control). This situation can bring parties into a non-arm's-length relationship. It is important to note that this advantage need not be exercised to be a factor; the mere ability to do so is sufficient."

52. In a section under Partnerships, the CRA comments that a partner, which has "little or no say in directing the operations of the partnership" will be dealing at arm's-length with the partnership.

53. The question then, taking into account the above criteria relating to the general nature of an independent, arm's-length relationship, is whether the OSC has indeed established the IAP as such a body in relation to itself. As per the above considerations, this needs to be answered in view of the nature and extent of the Commission's authority, control, and/or influence over the Panel.

54. The Panel's Terms of Reference states that it is "an advisory panel to the Commission" (1.1). Yet, the extent of the control exercised over the existence, mandate, structure, and functions of the Panel effectively makes it an internal or relatively internal committee of the Commission rather than an independent, arm's-length advisory body to the Commission. In contrast, the UK's Financial Services Consumer Panel clearly would fall in the latter category relative to the FSA. This contrast will become clearer in the course of considering various constraints on the operations of the IAP.

55. Article 6.1 of the Panel's ToR states that, "The Secretary to the Commission shall serve as the general liaison between the Panel and the Commission and will serve as the Secretary to the Panel." This liaison through the Commission's Secretary does not per se establish the Panel in an arm's-length relationship with the Commission. The Secretary to the Commission is itself an office within the OSC, as indicated in the organizational chart. While it is true that the FSA provides the Consumer Panel with a secretariat, which is housed in the same building as the FSA, the Consumer Panel has certain operational features or capabilities, which effectively allows it to function independently of the FSA, which are lacking with the IAP.

56. Complete control over IAP mandate and Terms of Reference: a main emphasis in the CRA material with respect to determining whether there is an arm's-length relationship between two parties is on control. In fact, the Commission has designed the IAP in such a way that it has complete control over the Panel's mandate and Terms of Reference. Article 10.1 states that the OSC can unilaterally "amend, affirm, or rescind the mandate" of the Panel upon

review (i.e., without the need to seek the Panel's agreement). If agreement was required, this would have been included. If the mandate of the Panel were to be rescinded, it seems the Panel would cease to exist altogether. Also, the Commission has complete control over the Panel's Terms of Reference, which it can amend as it sees fit with 60 days notice to the Panel members. Again, there is no indication of any requirement of acceptance of such amendments by the Panel. On this basis alone, the Panel cannot be considered to exist in an independent, arm's-length relationship with the Commission.

57. Determination of IAP agenda & issues: according to article one of the Panel's mandate, the IAP has been set up as a responder to Commission initiatives including various kinds of requests for comment on a range of issues. While it is expected that the Panel would serve this kind of function, as does the UK Consumer Panel, it does not appear that the IAP is able to determine an agenda of its own regarding issues affecting retail investor interests (i.e., which it might think need a policy response on the part of the regulators). As a member of the OSC's previous Investor Advisory Committee, I recall that we spent quite a lot of time discussing and determining a set of issues that we felt needed regulatory attention. If the IAP is set up only as a responder to OSC initiatives, this will make the deliberations of the Panel *dependent* on Commission requests, effectively giving the Commission substantive control over the issues considered by the IAP. This form of control also diminishes the capability of the IAP to function as an independent, arm's-length body.

58. Inability of the IAP to speak out publicly on investor interest matters: on this point, there is a very significant contrast between the Investor Advisory Panel, designed by the Commission, and the UK Consumer Panel. This operational capacity has a direct bearing on the issue of independence and an arm's-length relationship. In general, if party A is independent of B, then A is able to act independently or, in this case, speak out independently of B. The header at the Consumer Panel website describes it as, "An independent voice for consumers of financial services." Clearly, the ability to speak out publicly is integral to the independence of the UK Panel.

59. Considered more closely, it is clear that in addition to its formal written responses to FSA requests for comment, the Consumer Panel has the ability to publicly express its views outside this context, and even has the ability to express its disagreement with the FSA. This ability is embedded in the Consumer Panel's Terms of Reference and, arguably, is an essential element of any body that operates in an independent, arm's-length relationship with another. The relevant passage:

> "10. The Panel can speak out publicly when it wishes to draw attention to matters in the public interests and when it disagrees with the FSA."

60. The Investor Advisory Panel designed by the OSC has no such capability. The only output envisioned by the Commission will occur when the Panel provides formal written responses in the context of the request for comment process, in which case its responses will be publicly posted together with others. The Commission also envisions an Annual Report, which is described as "a report to the Commission on its activities for the preceding year."

61. The ability of the IAP to publicly communicate its views is thus extremely limited, to an extent that it cannot be described as functioning, or having the capability to function, "independently at arm's-length from the Commission." The inability of the IAP to speak out publicly on investment matters affecting the public interest is a key factor supporting this conclusion.

62. When and why might the IAP want or need to speak out publicly on retail investor interests? The ABCP crisis provides an example of circumstances where the independent voice of a body representing the interests of retail investors would have been appropriate and potentially very helpful, serving to encourage the Commission to consider taking a different approach in the way it was addressing the investor protection issues that arose in the crisis. In its report, the Standing Committee on Government Agencies noted the critical comments of some stakeholders (re: the Commission's response to the ABCP crisis) and observed that:

"it is important that the agency charted with protecting the public interest be seen to be taking a leadership role when there is a major disturbance in the markets that threaten the interests of retail investors. In this respect, we have some concern that the Commission may have adopted a narrow interpretation of its public interest jurisdiction in responding to the ABCP crisis." (p. 10, March 29, 2010)

63. Control of communications: no website. Commensurate with its ability to speak out independently, the UK Consumer Panel has its own website, independent of the FSA. The OSC-designed Panel lacks this functionality entirely, which provides further evidence that the Panel has not been provided with the requisite capability that would allow it to operate "independently at arm's-length from the Commission." Overall, the communications of the IAP are controlled to an extent that effectively nullifies its claimed independence and arm's-length relationship with the Commission.

64. Coming back to the IAP's Annual Report: this is described as a report to the Commission on the Panel's activities for the preceding year. In contrast, the reporting function of the Consumer Panel is oriented just as much, if not more, to the financial consumers whose interests it represents. It is clear from the language used at the Consumer Panel website that the CP sees itself as working for consumers and representing their interests. In contrast, the IAP mandate and Terms of Reference gives the impression of a body designed to work for, report to, and be accountable to the OSC.

ONE-WAY ACCOUNTABILITY

65. The accountability envisioned in the IAP/OSC relationship is one-sided and one-way. There is no indication that the Commission sees itself as being accountable to the IAP for what it does with its advice or recommendations. In the case of the UK Consumer Panel, there is a statutory provision establishing the accountability of the FSA to the Panel embedded in the Financial Services and Markets Act 2000. An equivalent provision was included in the Expert Panel's draft securities act:

"The Commission shall take into account the representations made by the advisory panels. If the Commission disagrees with a view expressed, or a proposal made, in the representation, it must give the panel a statement in writing of its reasons for disagreeing."

66. While the Canadian regulators do respond in writing (usually very cursory) to submissions in the formal notice and comment process, the mandate of the IAP extends beyond that process. There is a legitimate basis and precedent (as above) for expecting that the OSC will be accountable and responsive to the Panel for its input and advice beyond the formal comment process. It is notable that the Panel's Terms of Reference lack any provision for this accountability.

67. Another aspect of the role of the UK Consumer Panel, which is lacking with the IAP, is indicated in item 7 of its Terms of Reference: the Panel "can advise the Government on the scope of financial services regulation." It would be in the public interest if a suitably independent investor advisory panel (not the IAP as presently designed) could advise or report to the Ontario government (i.e., the Standing Committee on Finance and Economic Affairs) in appropriate circumstances.

REMUNERATION AND BUDGET: UNDER-RESOURCED PANEL

68. Consistent with the overall approach of the Commission in designing this Panel, there was no discussion or consultation about budgetary matters. Remuneration to Panel members is at a very low rate of $275/day or $34/hr, which is quite out of line with the remuneration of the members of the UK Consumer Panel. According to their most recent Annual Report, remuneration of Panel members averages approximately $650 CAD/day (as of January 2009 at the current £ exchange rate). This disparity (especially considering the ample salaries of senior Commission staff) is not inconsistent with past OSC practice. Despite the fact that the Commission studied the UK Consumer Panel prior to setting up the previous Investor Advisory Committee, we received no funding, not even a research budget.

69. On past occasions, I discussed the remuneration issue with former IAC member, the late Whipple Steinkrauss (a senior public servant and former Assistant Deputy Minister in the Ontario government).

Ms. Steinkrauss sat on various boards and committees and was familiar with the kind of per diem people would typically receive for such participation. Knowing her views on the matter, I am confident she would agree with the above assessment.

70. As it stands, it is unclear whether the annual budget of $50,000 (in addition to remuneration) is intended to include research costs. It does not appear so. Schedule A on the Terms of Reference states that this $50,000 is to facilitate the Panel's "ability to carry out its mandate through consultations with investors or the procurement of professional services to assist in drafting comment letters." This is one-fifth the amount allocated to the UK Consumer Panel for professional fees, including its research expenditure (approx. $200,000 CAD per annum averaged over two years). Moreover, the UK amount does not include the secretariat of staff provided by the FSA, whereas it appears that the OSC intends that the IAP should also use the allotted $50,000 for secretarial services.

71. I am not unaware that the population of the UK is several times greater than Ontario and that the UK Consumer Panel covers a broader range of financial issues. Nevertheless, Canada is by now twelve years behind the UK and Australia, which have had advisory panels since at least 1998. There is the need for a rigorous assessment of priorities at the beginning of such an enterprise. Moreover, there is the potential that an under-funded Panel will have an especially adverse effect on the retail investor component given that institutional investors already have a well-funded organization, the CCGG, with a dedicated research analyst.

72. Certain capabilities and facilities are required for an organization to undertake effective interest representation for a vulnerable and dispersed constituency. The UK Consumer Panel justifies its research budget as being necessary to understand the situation, perspective, and behaviour of consumers in order to properly identify its own priorities and influence the consumer priorities of the FSA. In contrast, it appears that the IAP will not be setting its own agenda and priorities, but will be a responder to OSC-initiated requests for comment. This, combined with the limited budget (if it even includes research costs), inevitably will limit the capacity of the Panel to discover and

understand the needs of those whose interests it represents. Institutional investors are in a much better position in this respect given the existence of the CCGG.

SUMMARY AND CONCLUSIONS

73. Professor Black's study emphasizes the importance of "involving consumers in the design and implementation of the regulatory regime." In her view, the effectiveness of regulation will be improved by the incorporation of information, perspectives, and solutions deriving from the consumer/retail investor side of the equation. The quality of regulatory decision-making will improve, the regime's democratic accountability will be enhanced, and trust in the regulator will be restored. (Black, p. 561)

74. The benefit of incorporating third parties representing the public interest into a regulatory regime was also noted by Professor Snider in her Expert Panel submission:

> "*Properly conceptualized and developed,* third parties reinforce regulatory power. They help regulators do the job they are obligated by statute to do." (emphasis mine)

75. The fundamental problem affecting the Commission's proposed Investor Advisory Panel is that it has not been properly conceptualized and developed. The Commission issued no white paper on the proposed Panel, nor did it solicit input from interested stakeholders. As it stands, the Panel is problematic in the following respects detailed above:

    1. Small number of members with a diluted focus on retail and institutional investor issues.
    2. In the Canadian context, the lack of engagement with SROs is a significant deficiency for retail investor participation in regulatory policy development.
    3. The IAP is demonstrably not an independent, arm's-length body relative to the Commission, given the nature and extent of the Commission's control over the Panel.

4. The accountability envisioned in the IAP/OSC relationship is one-sided.
5. The remuneration of Panel members is inadequate and the Panel is under-resourced. Inevitably this will have greater impact on the retail investor component given that institutional investors already have a well-funded body to represent their interests.
6. There was no consultation with interested stakeholders prior to the announcement of the IAP and the publication of its already adopted Terms of Reference.

76. Recommendation: in view of the significant problems with the design of the IAP, the Commission should put the application process on hold until the requisite consultations have been conducted. These consultations should be facilitated by an independent third party with appropriate expertise in stakeholder engagement.

    Thank you for giving this your attention. I will look forward to the Commission's response to these questions and concerns.

    Pamela J. Reeve, Ph.D.
    c. Hon. Dalton McGuinty, Premier
    c. Hon. Dwight Duncan, Minister of Finance
    c. Mr. Peter Wallace, Deputy Minister of Finance
    c. Mr. Ernie Hardeman, Chair,
       Standing Committee on Government Agencies
    c. Ms. Lisa MacLeod, Vice-Chair,
       Standing Committee on Government Agencies
    c. Mr. Norm Miller, PC Finance Critic
    c. Mr. Peter Tabuns, NDP Finance Critic

    For more information and copies of documents referenced in this letter, see:

    http://www.pjreeve.com/pjr/blog/Entries/ 2010/4/23_osc_investor_advisory_panel.html

## ACKNOWLEDGEMENTS

**MANY PEOPLE** assisted us in creating a finished work based on our forensic accounting cases and years of independent investment research. Bruce McDougall merits first mention for his rearrangement of draft chapters, considerable editing, and advice on which areas needed expansion and clarification for the benefit of everyday investors. It was our choice to deliberately repeat certain themes because it has been our experience that accounting and investment realities don't always sink in with investors the first time. There is a tendency to try to ignore the bad news and focus on only the good. Unfortunately, Canadians simply have not been kept abreast of how investor protection has deteriorated over the years. Neglect by lawmakers and self-regulatory agencies have caused billions of dollars of needless investor losses.

Throughout the writing and rewriting stages, Lisa Gallant-La Belle carefully typed and proofread the chapters. The vast majority of the case situations cited in the book were handled by specialists in our office, who must be thanked as a group.

Oliver Salzmann and Malcolm Lester placed their faith in the project from the outset and encouraged us to express the frustrations we have experienced over the years as investor advocates. Lawmakers have procrastinated far too long and have favoured the irrational lobbying of certain self-regulated groups. Canada's investor-protection system collapsed years ago, and the situation worsens with each passing year of legislative inaction. Thus, we definitely must thank the people and groups who work tirelessly, often with little credit, to try to stop the erosion and to encourage improvements. They have persevered despite encountering resistance from those parties who continue to benefit financially from the minimal oversight of investor needs in Canada.

Al Rosen and Mark Rosen

# INDEX

*References in the appendices are not included in the index.*

accounting
    assumptions and choices, 101–105, 182
        conventional practices, 100–101
        for transactions, change in method of, 39
        in Canada versus the US, 126
        one-size-fits-all, 93–99, 101, 180
        original purpose, 93
        principles-based approach, 36, 69, 94, 109, 127, 159, 184, 188, 197, 200
        systems, 106
    accounting and auditing rules, 15, 151, 199
        *See also* principles-based accounting and auditing rules
        development of, 31–32
        in Canada, 94–95, 97, 124
        in the UK, 69, 197
        in the US, 18, 33, 94, 136, 181, 184, 188
        manipulation of, 101–105, 107
        prescriptive, 188
        principles-based, 188
    accounting for transactions, change in method of, 39
    accounting standards, 188
        setting, 183, 189, 197–199
    Accounting Standards Board (AcSB), 198
    Accounting Standards Oversight Council (AcSOC), 198
    accounting techniques, creative, 64

accounts payable, 4, 49, 95, 115–116
accounts receivable, 4, 43, 49, 95, 133
accredited investors, 82–83
accrual accounting, 156
acquisition-related costs, 118–119
acquisitions, mergers and, 108, 116, 189
admissible assets versus non-admissible, 157–158
affiliated party.
    *See* related-party transactions
Air Canada, 113
Alberta, 4–5, 16
Alberta Teachers' Retirement Fund, 23
American Institute of Certified Public Accountants (AICPA), 197–198
amortization and depreciation, 150
Apotex, 176
Apple Computer, 68
Arthur Andersen, 32
asset impairment, 102–103
asset revaluation, 108, 127
asset valuation, 86, 126–127
assets.
    *See also* capitalized expenses
    expenses inappropriately reported as, 39, 115
    intangible, 73, 78, 127
    liquidation of, 100–101, 113
    loans as, 97
    long-term, 46
    non-current, 44
    of resource companies, 87–88, 91
    overstating, 38, 102, 106, 115, 126–127

self-constructed, 20–21
valuation under IFRS, 86, 108
*versus* expenses, 100–101
ATI Technologies, 67
auditing rules.
See accounting and auditing rules
auditors
and IFRS, 188–189
approval of misleading financial statements, xii–xiii
conflict of interest, xii–xiv, 128, 153–154
duty of care to investors, xii–xiii, 7–9, 13, 15, 19, 26, 146, 180, 199
junior, 6, 46
legal immunity of, 11–12, 13
legal responsibilities of, 189
liability of, 135, 181–182, 191
reaction to fraud, 4
relationship with corporate managers, 4, 6, 16, 17
role of, 14
support for IFRS, xiii–xiv, 188–189
tactics to limit responsibility, 71–72
audits
corporate versus investor interests, 31, 34
difference between US and Canada, 32
financial statement, 13–14, 17
inadequate, 19–21
income tax, 13
legislated, 17
procedures, 72
purpose of, 8–9, 11–12
quality of, 14
standards in the US, 33–34
state of in Canada, 32
under one-size-fits-all approach, 95–96

balance sheet, 164
banks.
See financial institutions
BDO Dunwoody, 142
Bellfield, Einar, 176–179
big bath, 104
biotech sector, 77
Black, Conrad, xii
board of directors, 14, 62, 71–72, 181, 191
bonds, 158–159, 174
bonuses.
See executive compensation

Bregman, Michael, 176
British Columbia Court of Appeal, 10, 194
British Columbia government, 145–146
British Columbia Securities Commission (BCSC), 65–66, 69, 144–146, 195
brokers, 81, 154
Brown, David, 63–66
Burgess, Frederick, 1–2
business income trusts (BITS), 3, 19, 51–52, 147–154, 172
effect of tax policy on, 29, 52, 153–154, 173

Canada Revenue Agency (CRA), 177–179
Canadian Airlines International, 113
Canadian Commercial Bank, 16, 27, 35, 128, 164
Canadian Institute of Chartered Accountants (CICA), 7, 32, 183, 198
Canadian securities legislation, 7–8, 17
capitalized expenses, 20–21, 102
cash, 54, 92
cash flow, 88–89, 101
cash-flow statement, 54, 110–116, 114, 127
cash value, 45
cash-based reporting, 127
Castor Holdings, 22–27
charitable donations, 178
CHOICE, 101–105
Chrysler Canada pension plan, 23
*CICA Handbook*, 7–8, 14
Civil Code in Quebec, 11
collusion, 44
commodities, 174–175
completed contract accounting, 47
Confederation Life, 35, 155–159, 164
Confederation Trust, 35, 164
cookie jar liabilities, 104
Coopers & Lybrand, 1–2, 23
Corel Corporation, 67
corporate activities, limits on reporting, 17
corporate lobbyists, xii, 196
corporate restructuring charges, 20
cost, 48, 110
cost of capital, 185
cost of goods sold, 115
cost-based accounting, 88
covenants, loan, 37, 107
Coventree, 164
Cowpland, Michael, 67

creative accounting, 64
Crocus Investment Fund, 57–62, 137
Cross Pacific Pearls, 141–146
cross-listing of stocks, 136
currencies, 174

debt, 113
Dell, 68
Deloitte & Touche, 2
depreciation and amortization, 150
derivative-based transactions, 99
distributable cash, 19, 67, 150, 153, 173
dividends
    distinction from income trust
        distributions, 148–149
    recording of, 47–48
donations, 178
Dow Jones Index, 174
Drabinsky, Garth, 26, 64
Duic, Daniel, 67
Dunn, Frank, 120–121

earn-outs, 108
earnings.
    *See* income
earnings from operations, 121
earnings quality, 181
EBITDA, 37
economic downturn
    of 1929, 11, 124–125, 127
    of the 1980s, 124, 128–129
    of the early 1990s, 156
    recent, xi, 163, 174
Enron, xii, 11, 29, 32, 33
Ernst & Young, 7
Estey, Willard, 16–17
estimated liabilities, 20
ethics of management, 48
European Union, 187
Exchange Traded Funds (ETFs)
    conventional, 174
    leveraged, 174–175
executive compensation, 116, 156
    at Nortel, 19, 119, 121
        manipulating numbers for, 6, 37, 104–105
        via executive-owned companies, 71, 73–75
        via loans, 70–71
        via profit-sharing, 105
expected revenue estimates, 40

expenses, 100–101, 189, 192
    versus assets, 101
fair market value, 72–74, 92
    in related-party transactions, 14, 191
    versus historical cost, 185–186
FBI, 64
film business, 132
finance companies, 78–79
Financial Accounting Standards Board
    (FASB), 65, 197–198
financial institutions, 163–167
    failures, 16–17, 128, 164, 190
financial ratios, 39
financial reporting
    guidance, 128
    in Canada, 125, 161
    in the US, 126
    one-size-fits-all, 91–92, 156, 158
financial restructuring, 37
financial statements, 42, 126
    audited, 62
    government, 88
    in a prospectus, 10
    manipulation of, 41–42
    misinterpretation of, 101–102, 190
    misleading, 182
    notes to, 39, 74, 103, 105, 107–109,
        111, 116, 143
    notes under IFRS, 185, 191
    purpose of, 7–8, 11–12, 14–15
financial trend lines, 39, 193
financial tricks, escalation of, 38–39
financing transactions, 54, 113, 116
*Forbes* magazine, 65
forensic accounting, 193–194
fraud
    by start-up companies, 78–79
    common scenarios for, 169–171
    conditions for, 2
    identifying, 20
    in Canada, xii, 4, 29, 55, 135, 171
    in scrap metal business, 133–135
    in the US, 27, 28
    tactics used in, 52–53

Galbraith, Arlan, 50
Generally Accepted Accounting
    Principles (GAAP), 16, 18, 64
    history, 124, 128–129

in Canada, 188, 198
in the US, 180, 187–188, 198
Generally Accepted Accounting Standards (GAAS), 18
Gottlieb, Myron, 26, 64
governance issues, 71
gross profit, 46

hedging, 89, 92
Hercules Managements, 7–12, 138, 199, 201
implications of, 10–12, 32, 123–125, 180
Ho, K.Y., 67
Hollinger International, 66
Hyndman, Doug, 69, 146, 195, 198

income, 100–101, 106, 111
reasons for deflating, 39, 42
reasons for inflating, 37–38
techniques for deflating, 39
techniques for inflating, 55
versus return of capital, 151
income statement, 103, 109
income tax legislation, 34, 184
income taxes, 42
income trusts, 148, 152–153
initial public offerings, 148, 170.
See also share issues
Institute of Chartered Accountants of Ontario, 63
institutional investors, 26
insurance companies, 107, 155–162
intangible assets, 127
International Accounting Standards Board (IASB), 187–188, 198
International Financial Reporting Standards (IFRS)
about, 16, 92, 95, 106, 127, 159, 181–183, 189, 198
accounting rules under, 55
adoption in Canada, xiii–xiv, 5–6, 18, 34, 68, 124, 125, 180–181
adoption outside of Canada, 186–190
analytical difficulties of, 190–193
asset recording under, 91
asset valuation under, 86
assumptions of supporters regarding, 183–188
attitude of the US to, 124, 187
auditor support of, xiii–xiv, 188–189
comparability under, 183–184, 192
fair market value under, 73, 76, 102
financial reporting of resource companies, 90
financial statement figures under, 17–18, 40, 44–47, 185–186, 189, 191–192
financial statements under, 98, 182, 185
in court cases, 193–194
in Europe, 187
off-balance sheet liabilities under, 103
related-party transactions under, 71–73
taxable income under, 108
valuation techniques under, 98
International Nesmont Industrial, 1–2
inventory, 116
Investment Counsel Association of Canada, 64
investment scams.
See fraud
investor lawsuits, 11, 18, 22–23, 193–194
class-action, 137–140
in Canada, 26–27, 28–29
jurisdictions, 137
investor losses, xiii, 3
investor protection in Canada, xi, xiv, 5, 29–30, 195
investor tips, 15–16, 27, 39, 42, 44, 49, 62, 74–75, 83–84, 88–89, 102–107, 112–113, 115–116, 153–154, 165–167, 171, 174–175
investors' rights in Canada, 62

John Labatt, 23
journalists. See media
judicial inquiries, 16, 199

*Kripps v. Touche Ross*, 10, 194

labour-sponsored venture capital funds, 57–58
Laidlaw International, 23
law firms, 30, 137–139, 154
lawmakers, 128, 199
attitude to investor actions in Canada, 11–12, 30
lack of protection of investors, 85
lawsuits, investor.
See investor lawsuits
legislation.
See income tax legislation; securities legislation

liabilities
    cookie jar, 104
    estimated, 20
    off–balance sheet, 103
limited partnership units, 178
Livent, xii, 26–27, 35, 64–66
loan covenants, 37

Madoff, Bernie, 27
maintenance capital expenditures, 150
majority control, 106
Management Discussion and Analysis (MD&A), 90, 105, 116
management ethics, 48
management numbers, 34
    auditor reliance on, 16, 17
    manipulation of, 35–39, 41–42, 181–182
    methods of manipulation of, 49, 106–109, 115, 189–190
    objectives behind, 109
    reasons for manipulation of, 36–38, 111
Manitoba, 3–4, 57–58, 58, 62
Manitoba Securities Commission, 58, 61–62
margin accounts, 170
mark-to-market transactions, 92, 159
media, 79–80, 149, 154
    treatment of auditors, 33
mergers and acquisitions, 108, 116, 189
metal recovery business.
    *See* scrap metal business
Minchella, Osy, 176–179
mines, 83
Mogilevich, Semion, 64
Montgomery, Elizabeth, 1–2
mortgages, 165, 168
mutual funds, 59, 169

NASDAQ, 1, 68, 174
National Business Systems (NBS), 41
*National Post,* 119
*National Post Business* magazine, 120
national securities commission, 11, 124, 146
national securities regulator
    formation of in Canada, 69, 195–197, 200
    in the US, 68–69, 195–197
    lack of in Canada, xii, 15, 62, 129
Nesmont.
    *See* International Nesmont Industrial

net earnings from operations, 118–119
net income, 118, 173
net realizable value (NRV), 45
netting financial statement figures, 96–98, 191–192
*New York Times,* 65
non-arm's-length transactions.
    *See* related-party transactions
non-bank asset-backed commercial paper (ABCP), 3, 29, 173–174
non-cash reporting, 164
non-cash reserves, 104
non-tangible assets, 73, 78, 127
Nortel Networks, 3, 19, 66–68, 105, 117–122, 123–124, 172–173
Northland Bank, 16, 27, 35, 128, 164
notes to financial statements.
    *See* financial statements

oil and gas sector, 148
Ontario, 11, 50
Ontario Securities Commission (OSC), 63–68
Overseas Credit and Guaranty (OCGC), 176–179
oversight committees, 30–32

parallel companies.
    *See* executive compensation
percentage-of-completion accounting, 47
Philip Services, 41
Pigeon King International, 50–51
Pineridge Capital, 142, 144
Ponzi schemes, 50–56, 87, 127, 139, 151, 183
Ponzi, Charles, 51
prescriptive accounting and auditing rules, 188
PricewaterhouseCoopers, 1–2, 23
primary market, 10
principles-based financial reporting.
    *See* accounting
private companies, 60–61
private placements, 81–83, 85
pro-forma reporting, 19, 67, 106
profitability ratios, 37
profits, 1, 27, 46, 101, 127
    in financial sector, 156–157
provincial securities commissions, 69, 76, 86, 99, 124, 161, 196
provincial securities regulators.
    *See* national securities regulator

public offerings, 37
pyramid schemes, 127

Quebec, 11, 23–25, 131–132, 137–138

Rankin, Andrew, 67
RBC Dominion Securities, 67
real estate sector, 148
recession.
    *See* economic downturn
registered retirement accounts, 57
regulators.
    *See* national securities regulator
related-party transactions, 14, 20, 71–76, 86, 90, 96
    under IFRS, 189, 191
reporting corporate activities, limits on, 17
Research in Motion (RIM), 68
resource companies, 84, 86–92, 151
resource sector, 77, 80, 148
restructuring charges, 20, 109
retail investors, 77–78
return on investment.
    *See* yield
revenue
    increasing, 40–41, 48–49
    inflated, 103–104
    techniques for inflating, 42–43
revenue recognition, 39, 103–104, 184, 189
    early, 44–47
    policies, 42
revenue, estimate of expected, 40
reverse mortgages, 165, 168
risk, 169
Roth, John, 119–120

sales, 49
techniques for manipulating, 43–48
sales practices, 154
sampling, 15–16, 18, 72
scams.
    *See* fraud
scrap metal business, 133–135
Second Cup, 176
secondary market, 10
Securities and Exchange Commission (SEC), 33, 65–66, 68, 122, 129, 136, 195.
    *See also* national securities regulator
securities commission.

    *See* national securities commission
securities enforcement, 28, 121–122, 136–137, 196–197, 199–201
    in Canada, 129, 161
securities legislation, 128, 183
    in Canada, 7–8, 30, 34, 82, 91, 105, 128
    in Ontario, 11
securities market in Canada, 29–30, 79–80, 125
securities regulation, 165
    in Canada, 79, 125–126, 145–146, 150
    in the 1960s, 158
    in the US, 64, 66–57
securities regulators.
    *See* national securities regulator
segment reporting, 109
self-dealing transactions.
    *See* related-party transactions
self-regulating organizations (SROs), xii, 30–32, 91, 199, 201
Senate Banking Committee, in Canada, 32
share issues, 55
share prices, 1
Sherman, Barry, 176
short selling, 171
Singleton, Jon W., 58–59
standard setting, 183, 189, 197–199
Standard Trust, 164
start-up companies, 77–79, 85, 142–143
stock market crash.
    *See* economic downturn
stock options, 38, 68, 119–120
Stolzenberg, Wolfgang, 24–25
subsidiary companies, 74–76
Supreme Court of Canada, 7–9, 15, 31, 123, 183, 201
swindles.
    *See* fraud

tax shelters, 176–179
taxes, 108
Teachers Investment and Housing Co-operative, 164
tech market bubble, 40, 117, 170
technology sector, 77
*Time* magazine, 120
tips for investing. *See* investor tips
Toronto Stock Exchange (TSX), 11, 41, 68, 80, 174
transactions, changes in method of accounting for, 39
trend lines, 39, 193

US Steel, 126

valuation, 40, 185, 192–193
techniques, 98, 102
Vancouver Stock Exchange (VSE), 1, 65, 69, 141, 144–146, 195
venture funds, 77.
　See also labour-sponsored venture capital funds
Victoria Mortgage, 164
VisuaLabs, 132

*Wall Street Journal*, 118
Watson, Michael, 66, 68
Wellington West Capital, 58

Wersebe, Karsten von, 24
Widdrington, Peter N., 22–23
Wightman, Elliot C., 22–23
WorldCom, xii, 11, 29

YBM Magnex, 64–66
yield, 149, 156, 173
York-Hannover Developments, 24

Zelitt, Sheldon, 132

Printed in Canada